DEAD KINGS ™

VOLUME 1

HARD ROAD HOME

STEVE ORLANDO
MATTHEW DOW SMITH
LAUREN AFFE
THOMAS MAUER

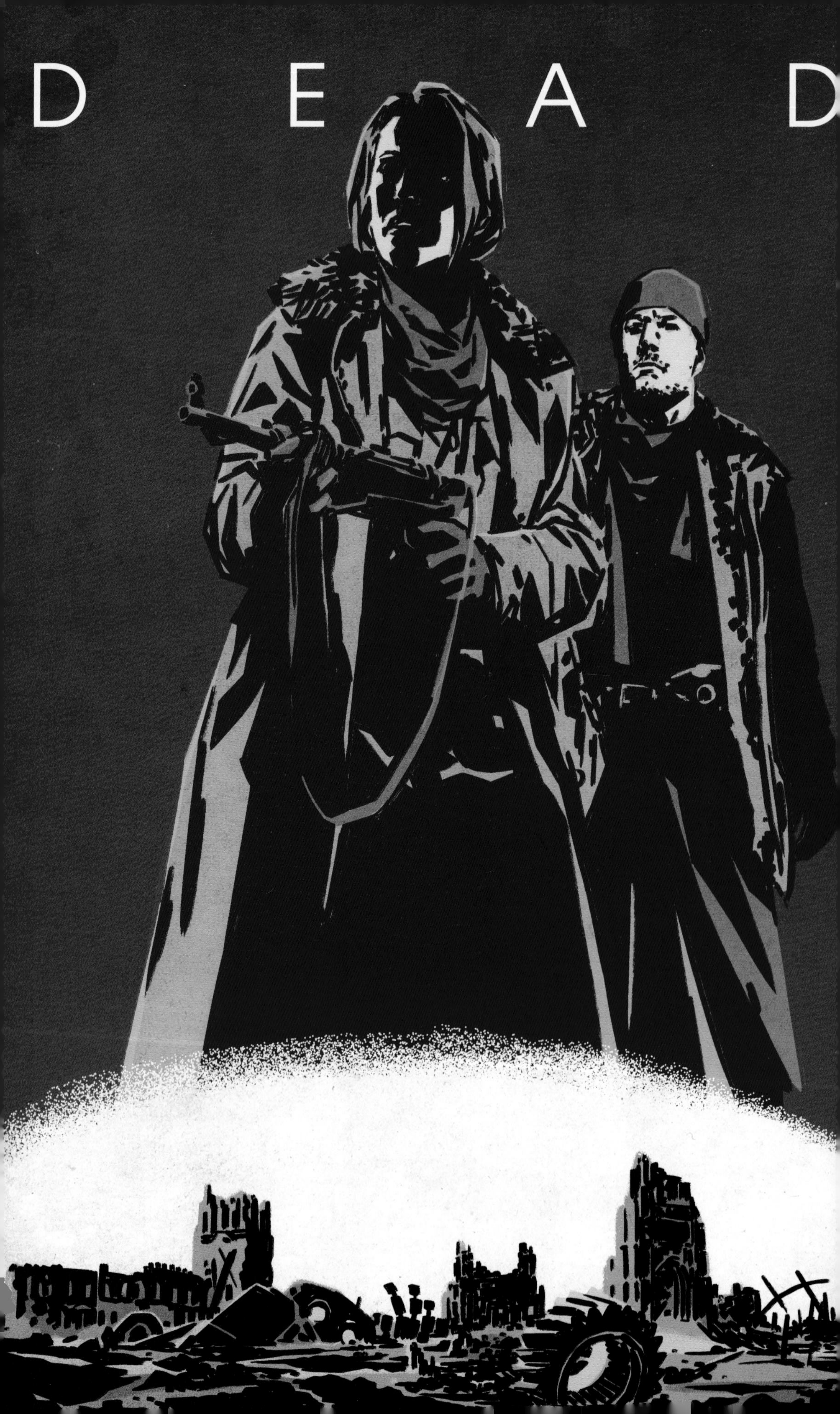
D E A D

KINGS
VOLUME 1
HARD ROAD HOME

STEVE ORLANDO writer & co-creator

MATTHEW DOW SMITH artist & co-creator

LAUREN AFFE colorist

THOMAS MAUER letterer

MATTHEW DOW SMITH front cover & original covers

RUSS BRAUN w/ **JOSE VILLARRUBIA** & **MICHAEL GAYDOS** variant covers

CHARLES PRITCHETT logo designer

COREY BREEN book designer

MIKE MARTS editor

AFTERSHOCK™

MIKE MARTS - Editor-in-Chief • **JOE PRUETT** - Publisher/CCO • **LEE KRAMER** - President • **JON KRAMER** - Chief Executive Officer
STEVE ROTTERDAM - SVP, Sales & Marketing • **DAN SHIRES** - VP, Film & Television UK • **CHRISTINA HARRINGTON** - Managing Editor
MARC HAMMOND - Sr. Retail Sales Development Manager • **RUTHANN THOMPSON** - Sr. Retailer Relations Manager • **BLAKE STOCKER** - Chief Financial Officer
AARON MARION - Publicist • **LISA MOODY** - Finance • **RYAN CARROLL** - Development Coordinator • **CHARLES PRITCHETT** - Comics Production
COREY BREEN - Collections Production • **TEDDY LEO** - Editorial Assistant • **STEPHANIE CASEBIER** & **SARAH PRUETT** - Publishing Assistants

AfterShock Logo Design by **COMICRAFT**
Publicity: contact **AARON MARION** (aaron@publichausagency.com) & **RYAN CROY** (ryan@publichausagency.com) at **PUBLICHAUS**
Special thanks to: **IRA KURGAN, MARINE KSADZHIKYAN, ANTONIA LIANOS, STEPHAN NILSON** & **JULIE PIFHER**

AFTERSHOCKCOMICS.COM Follow us on social media 🐦 📷 f

I N T R O D U C T I O N

COMMUNITY EFFORT

Let's get this out of the way up front: this a good book, made by good friends. If you're reading this foreword in the store, trying to decide whether to buy it, I can assure you, buy it.

DEAD KINGS is a post-apocalyptic hellscape by way of Russian folklore, and for me, some of the best work that Steve Orlando and Matthew Dow Smith have done (aided and abetted by colorist Lauren Affe and letterer Thomas Mauer). Steve moves between epic world building and small human moments with grace. Matt does the same, from widescreen scope to intimate sequences. None of which is a surprise to me, of course, as they're not only accomplished creators, but two of my best friends.

I've known Matt for two decades. Long enough for him to be Uncle Matt to my kids. Long enough for the drawing table in my son's room to be the drawing table that Matt once used. I first met Steve...well, according to Steve, I first met him at a Wizard World Chicago convention, when I signed some *Mystic* comics for him at the CrossGen Comics booth. Cut to years later, and we're both living in the Albany, NY area, as Steve is breaking into comics.

Steve's the new guy, but he's welcomed into the local comics community, which consists of guys like me, Matt Smith, sculptor Paul Harding, painter Richard Clark and more, as well as our retailer friends who own the local comics shops. We'd meet for breakfast, for dinner, for drinks, for barbecues at each other's houses, even some golf. This book you're holding is a result of seeds first planted in that community. And that's really what I'm writing about here: community, and what it means to creative endeavors.

What creators do, especially comics creators, is a solitary pursuit. So social interaction, which inevitably becomes creative interaction, is vital. It gets us out of our own heads, and into a place where we can inspire and be inspired by others. It's all fodder, all grist for the mill. A creative community supports and nourishes everybody in it.

I was brought into the comics community in New York State's Hudson Valley early in my career. In fact, that's how I have a career, having been ushered into comics by Jim Starlin. The rest of the community included people like Bernie Wrightson, Terry Austin, Fred Hembeck and Joe Staton. I learned from them, and I hope I've paid that forward.

Would DEAD KINGS exist without Matt and Steve having been part of that Albany comics community? Maybe. But probably not in the form you hold in your hands. This is, in so many ways, a community effort. I'm glad to have been part of their community, and I'm glad to have this story. You'll be glad, too.

— RON MARZ
May 2019

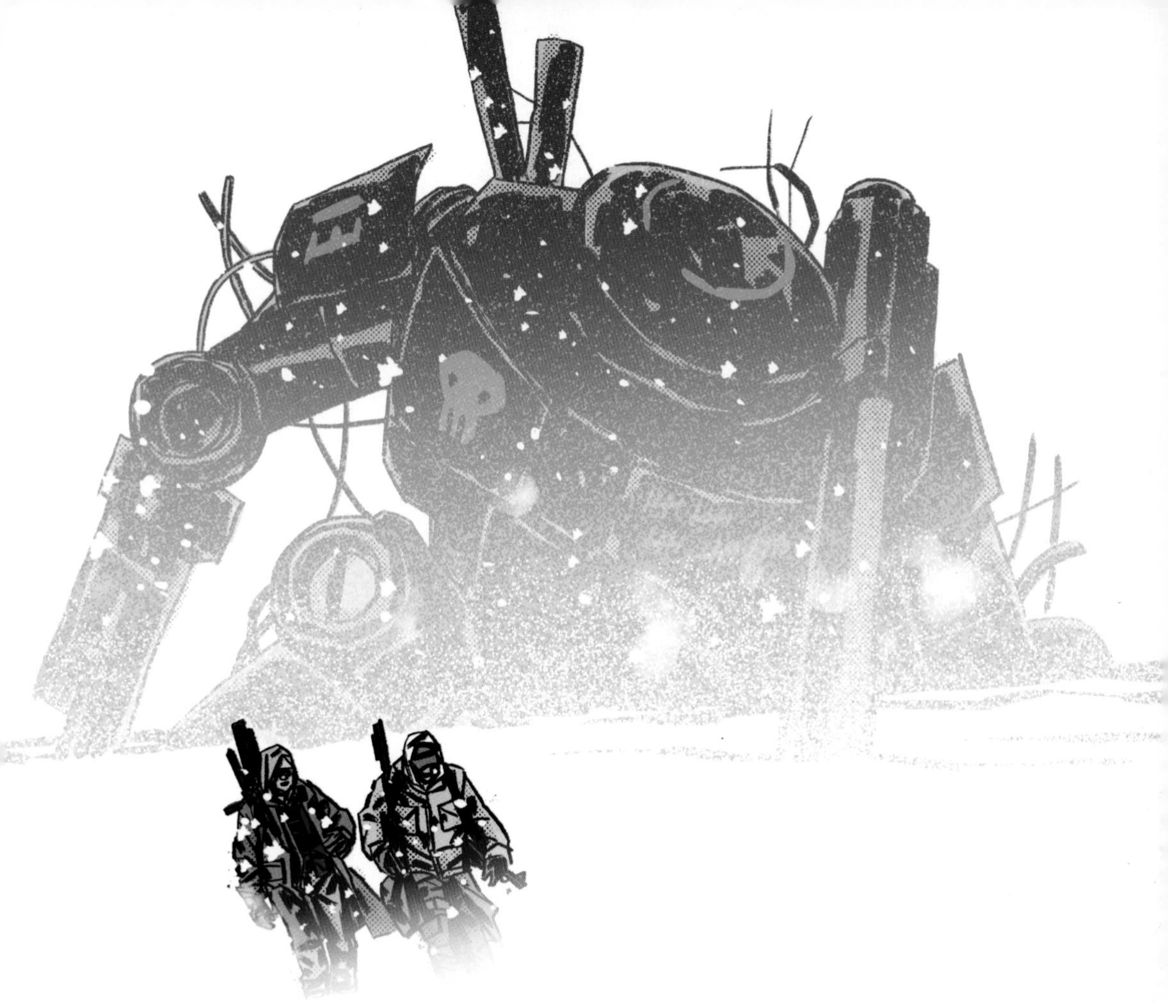

1

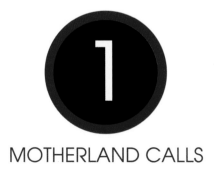

MOTHERLAND CALLS

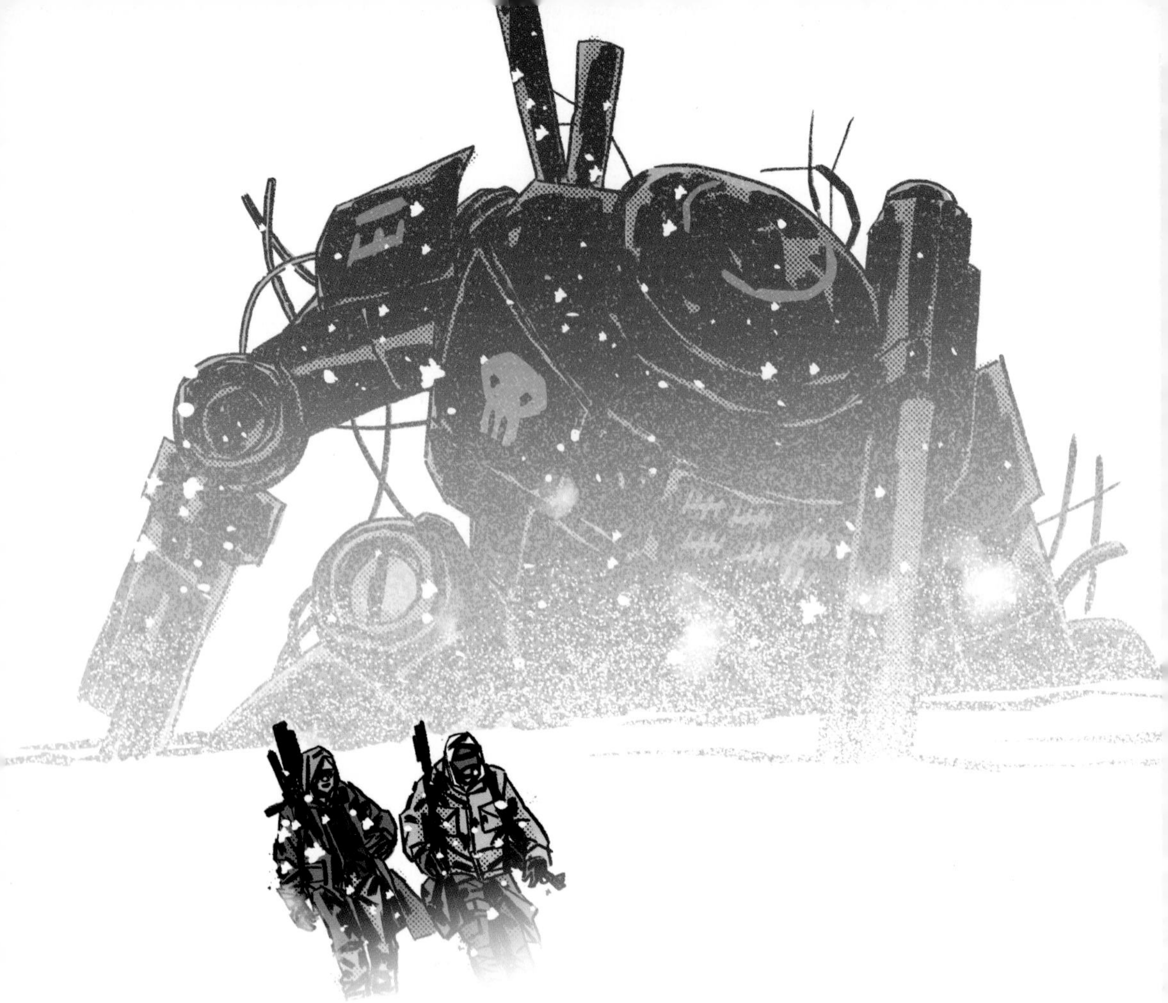

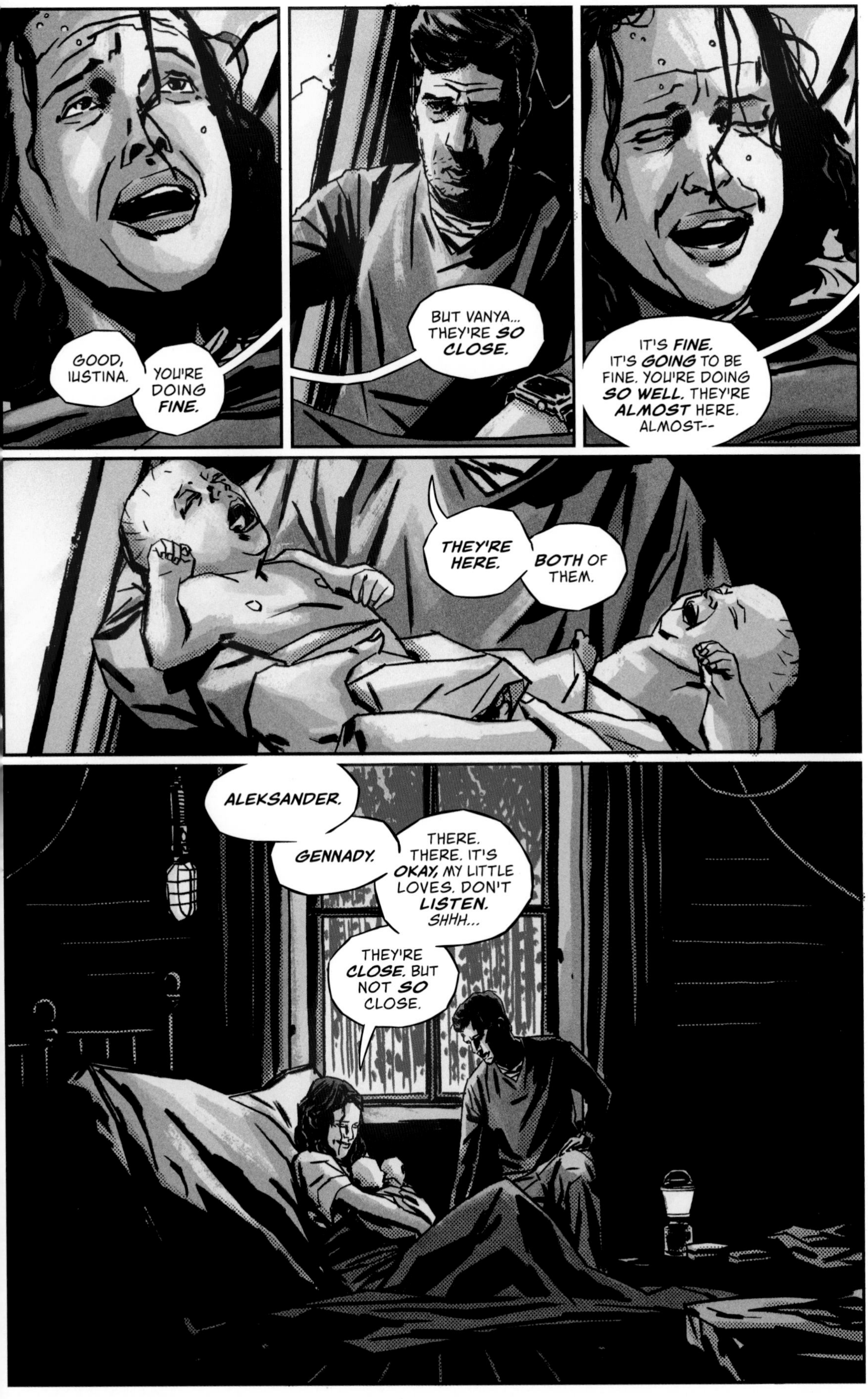

GOOD, IUSTINA.
YOU'RE DOING **FINE.**
BUT VANYA... THEY'RE **SO CLOSE.**
IT'S **FINE.** IT'S **GOING** TO BE FINE. YOU'RE DOING **SO WELL.** THEY'RE **ALMOST** HERE. ALMOST--
THEY'RE HERE.
BOTH OF THEM.
ALEKSANDER.
GENNADY.
THERE. THERE. IT'S **OKAY,** MY LITTLE LOVES. DON'T **LISTEN.** *SHHH...*
THEY'RE **CLOSE.** BUT NOT **SO** CLOSE.

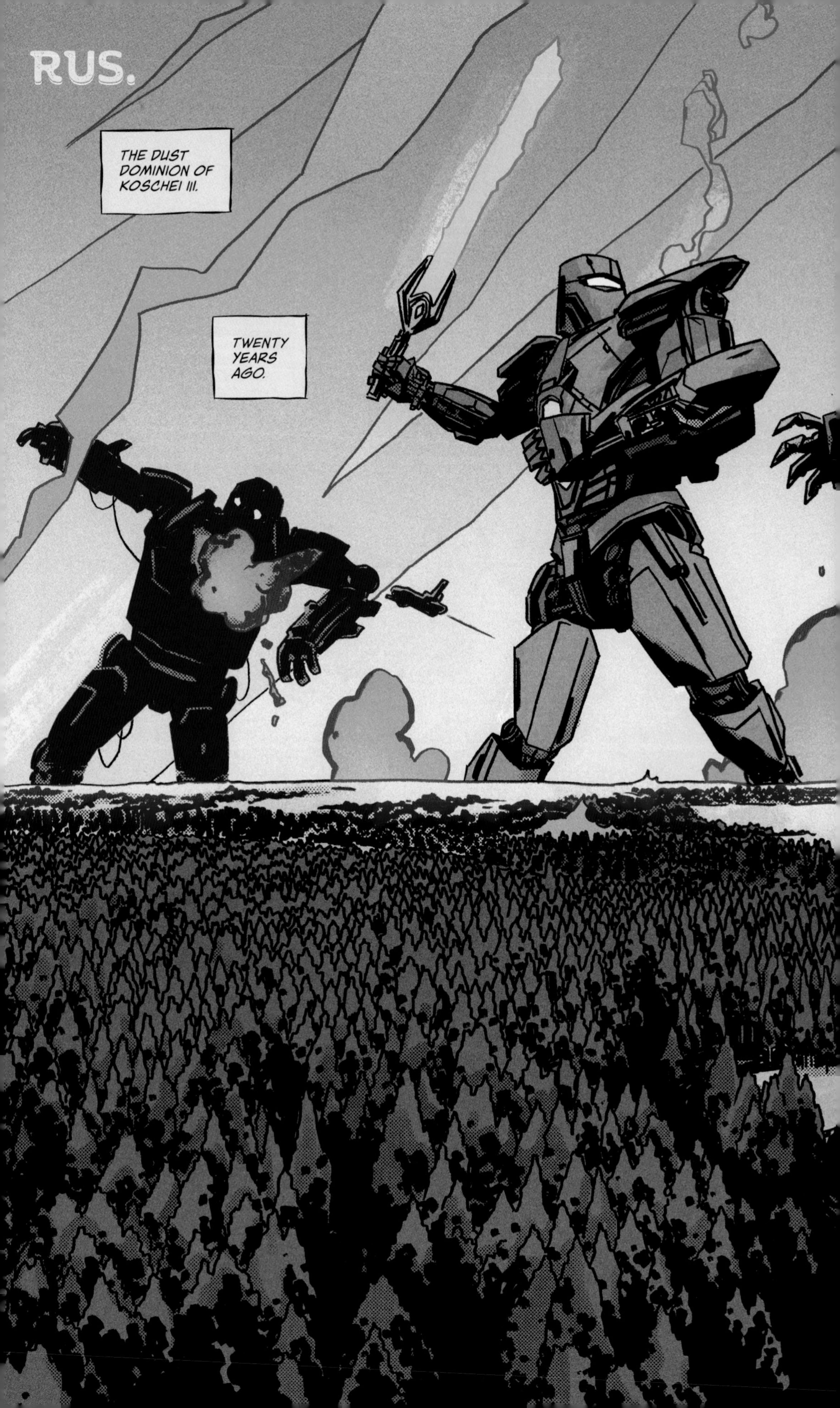
RUS.
THE DUST DOMINION OF KOSCHEI III.
TWENTY YEARS AGO.

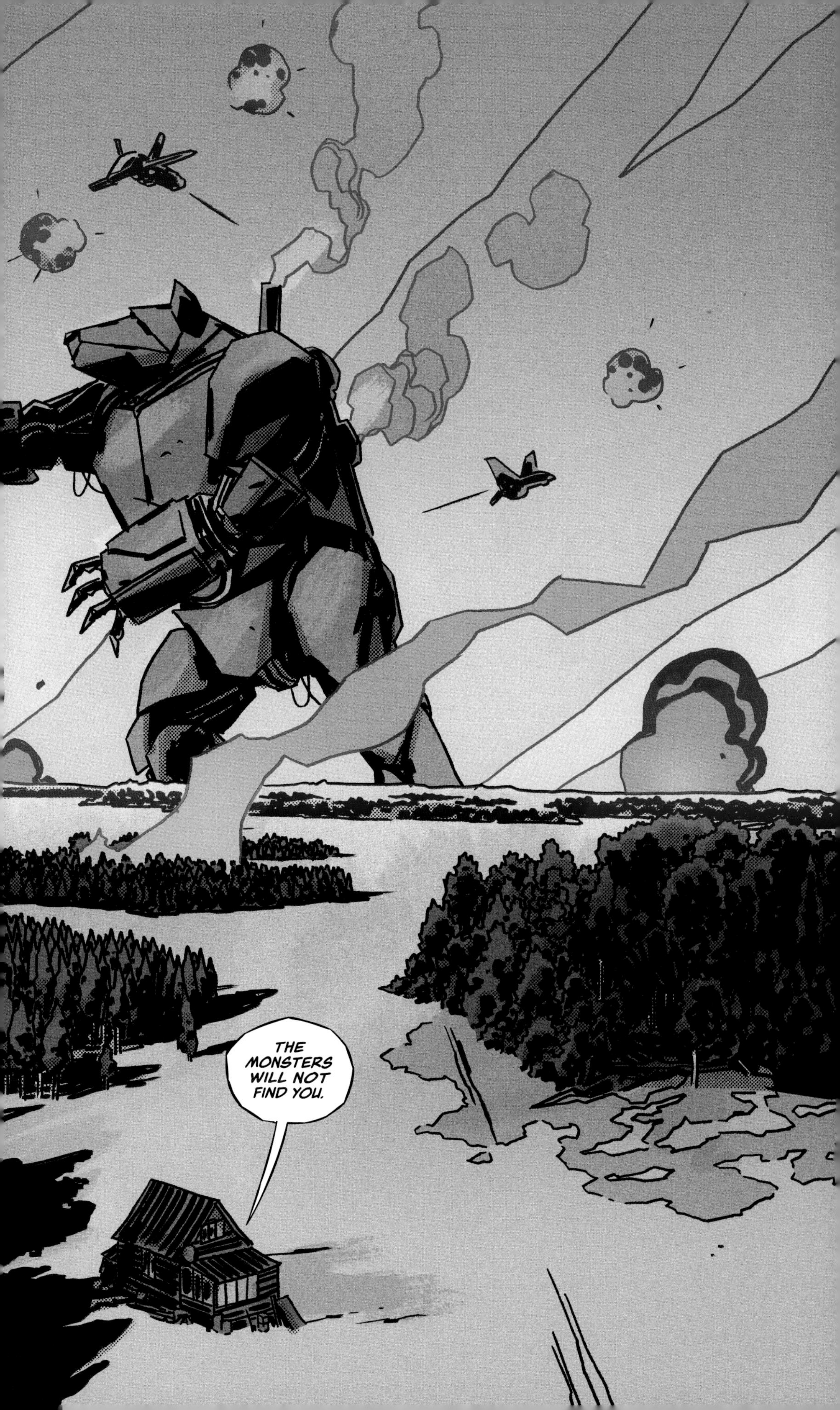
THE MONSTERS WILL NOT FIND YOU.

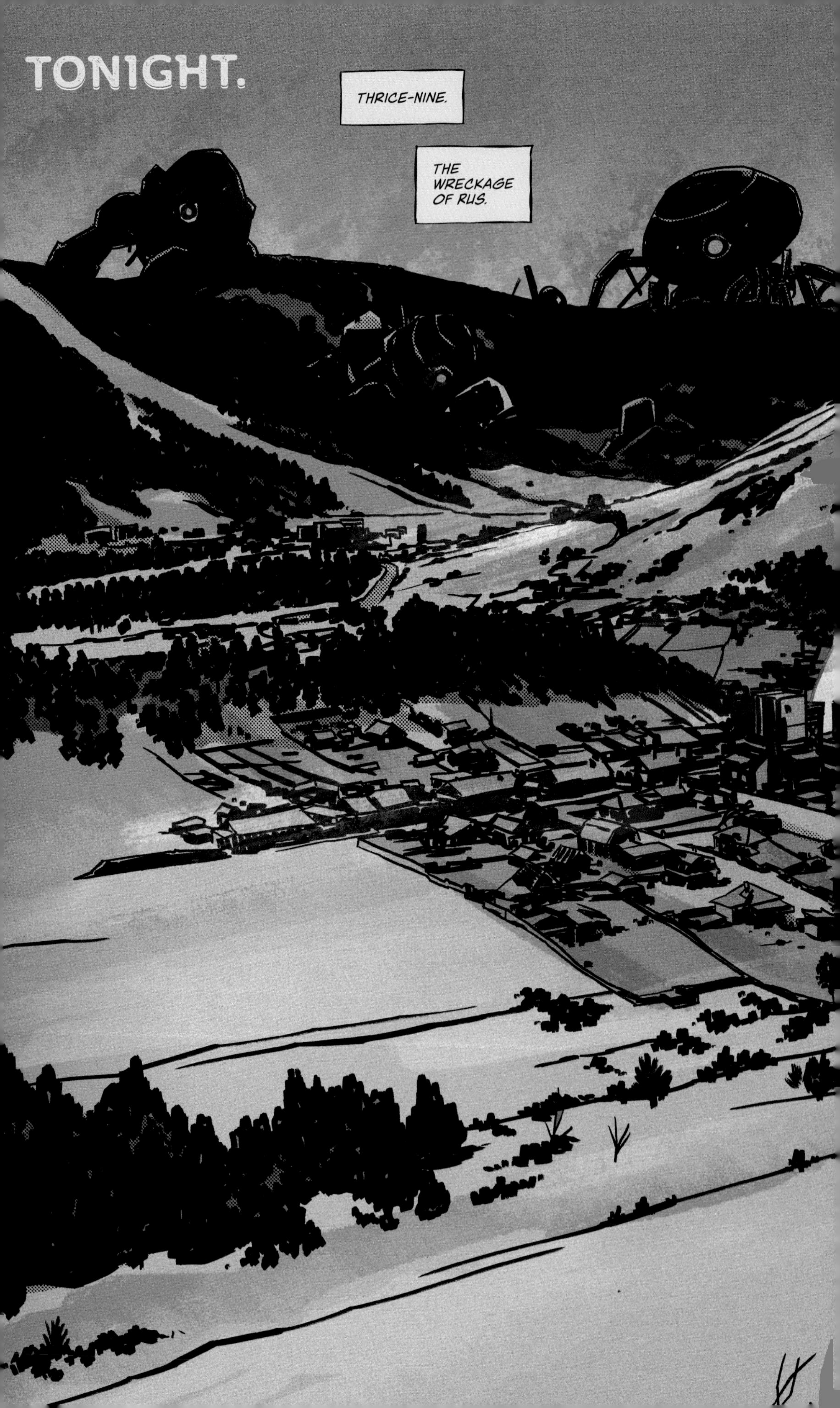
TONIGHT.
THRICE-NINE.
THE WRECKAGE OF RUS.

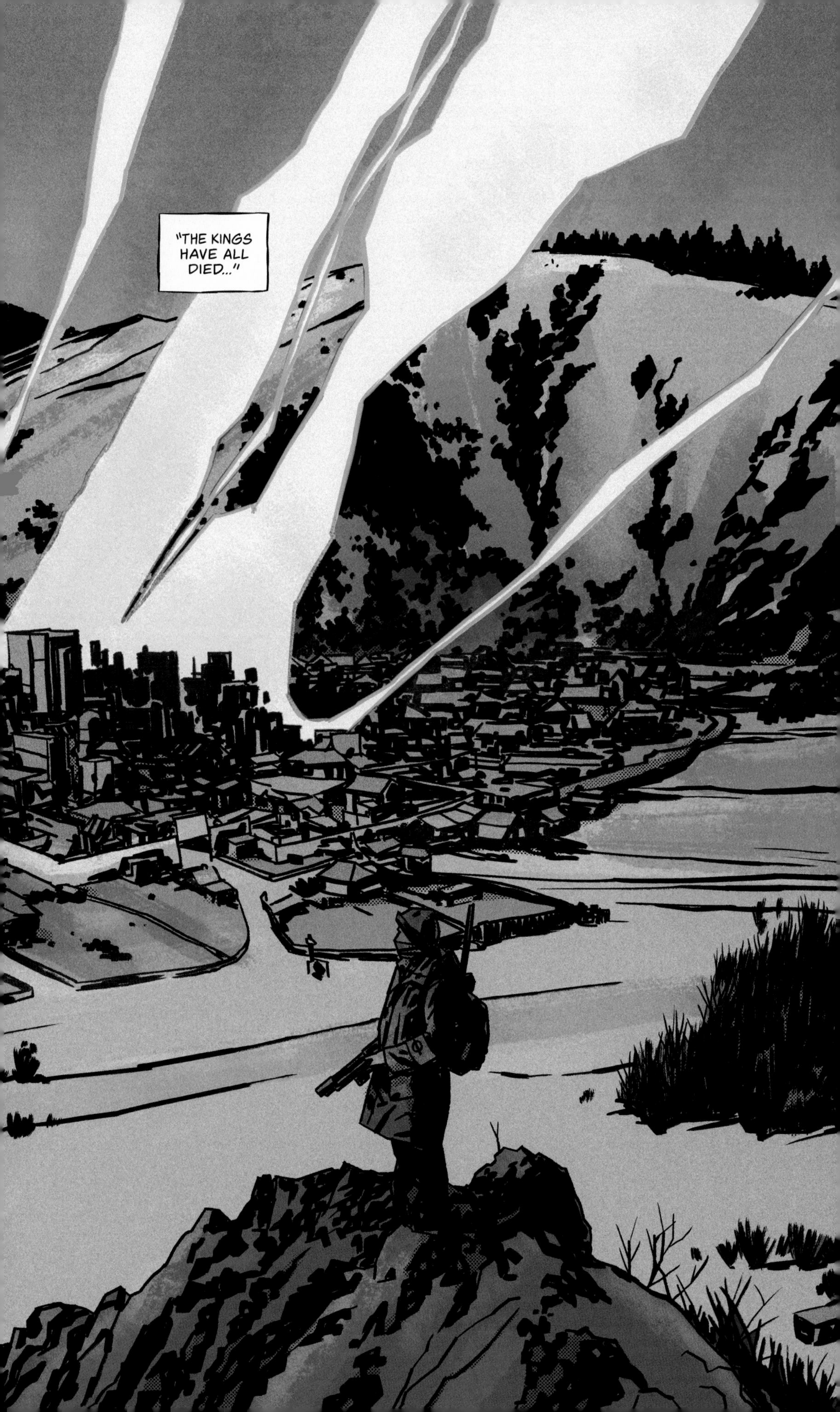
"THE KINGS HAVE ALL DIED..."

AEMSTELREDAMME.

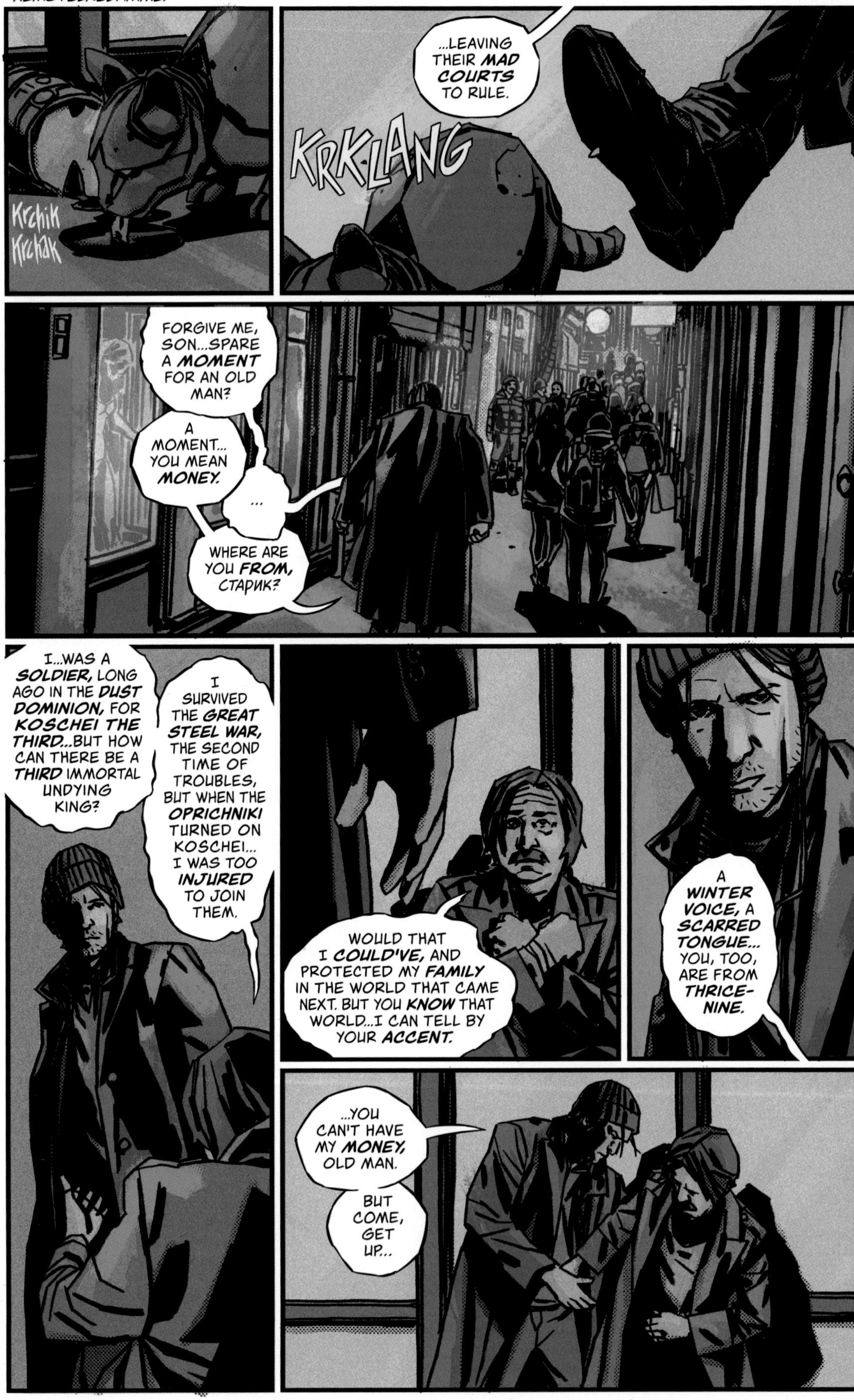

Krchik Krchak
...LEAVING THEIR MAD COURTS TO RULE.
KRKLANG
FORGIVE ME, SON...SPARE A MOMENT FOR AN OLD MAN?
A MOMENT... YOU MEAN MONEY.
...
WHERE ARE YOU FROM, СТАРИК?
I...WAS A SOLDIER, LONG AGO IN THE DUST DOMINION, FOR KOSCHEI THE THIRD...BUT HOW CAN THERE BE A THIRD IMMORTAL UNDYING KING?
I SURVIVED THE GREAT STEEL WAR, THE SECOND TIME OF TROUBLES, BUT WHEN THE OPRICHNIKI TURNED ON KOSCHEI... I WAS TOO INJURED TO JOIN THEM.
WOULD THAT I COULD'VE, AND PROTECTED MY FAMILY IN THE WORLD THAT CAME NEXT. BUT YOU KNOW THAT WORLD...I CAN TELL BY YOUR ACCENT.
A WINTER VOICE, A SCARRED TONGUE... YOU, TOO, ARE FROM THRICE-NINE.
...YOU CAN'T HAVE MY MONEY, OLD MAN.
BUT COME, GET UP...

"AND WE CAN SHARE A *MEAL*."

THANK YOU, SON. I AM *LEV*.

I'M *SASHA*. SASHA VIKTOROVICH VASNETSOV. ORDER WHAT YOU WANT, ON *ME*.

PELMENI! WITH *BUTTER* AND *SOUR CREAM!* THE NIGHTS ARE *COLD* AND MY BONES THIN.

HOW...*NICE* TO HAVE *RUS* AT OUR INN. WE'LL SET YOUR FOOD BOILING... WHILE YOU *NINERS* TELL ME WHAT THE *HELL* YOU'RE DOING HERE?

WE *APPRECIATE* YOUR OPEN-MINDEDNESS.

WHEN...I WAS *YOUNG*, I HAD THE APTITUDES OF A *STEEL BOGATYR*. RUS REFURBISHED MY BRAIN WITH LOVE OF COUNTRY AND MY BODY WITH MURDER ARMOR. RUS WAS MY *MOTHER*, MY FATHER... MY *LOVER*.

WHEN THE WAR ENDED *ALL THREE* ABANDONED ME. MY BODY WAS RUS, AND RUS WAS ASH.

SO I LIMPED ACROSS THE BORDER...TO *MOURN* MY ANEMIC HEROISM--

STOP. I KNOW PEOPLE WHO CARRY THOSE TALES... *YOU'RE* NOT ONE OF THEM. *YOU* ARE FULL OF SHIT.

DAMN RIGHT...IT'S *NOT MY* STORY.

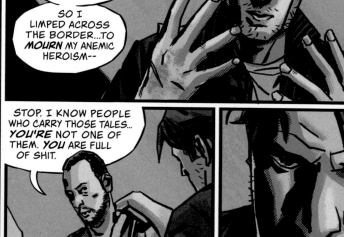

THE *STORY* BELONGS TO SOMEONE I'VE BEEN TRYING TO FIND FOR MONTHS, ONE OF THE *STEEL POLIANITSI*, SISTERS TO THE STEEL BOGATYRI, A *LEGEND* AMONG THEM...

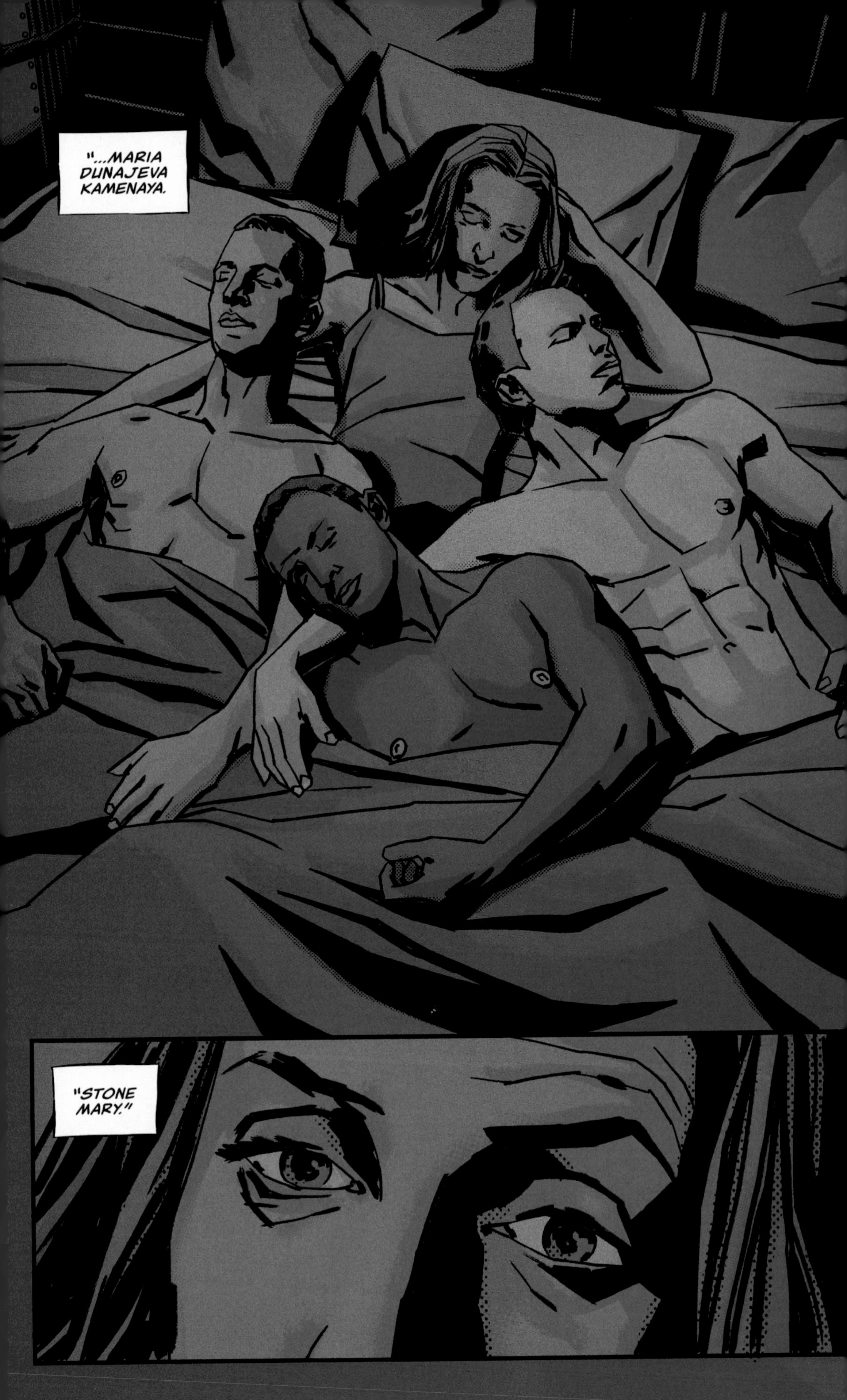
"...MARIA DUNAJEVA KAMENAYA.
"STONE MARY."

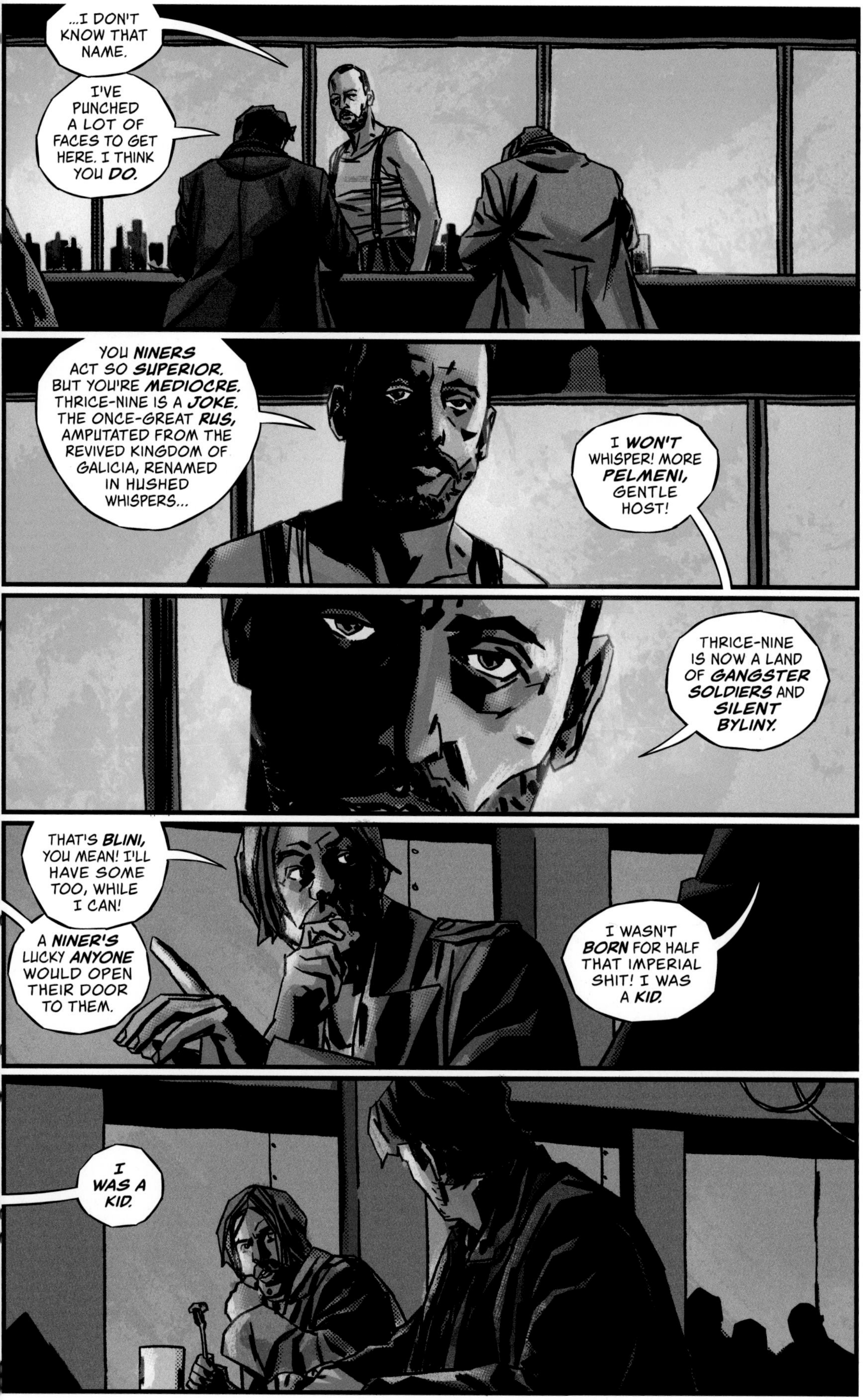

...I DON'T KNOW THAT NAME.
I'VE PUNCHED A LOT OF FACES TO GET HERE. I THINK YOU **DO.**
YOU **NINERS** ACT SO **SUPERIOR.** BUT YOU'RE **MEDIOCRE.** THRICE-NINE IS A **JOKE.** THE ONCE-GREAT **RUS,** AMPUTATED FROM THE REVIVED KINGDOM OF GALICIA, RENAMED IN HUSHED WHISPERS...
I **WON'T** WHISPER! MORE **PELMENI,** GENTLE HOST!
THRICE-NINE IS NOW A LAND OF **GANGSTER SOLDIERS** AND **SILENT BYLINY.**
THAT'S **BLINI,** YOU MEAN! I'LL HAVE SOME TOO, WHILE I CAN!
A **NINER'S** LUCKY **ANYONE** WOULD OPEN THEIR DOOR TO THEM.
I WASN'T **BORN** FOR HALF THAT IMPERIAL SHIT! I WAS A **KID.**
I WAS A KID.

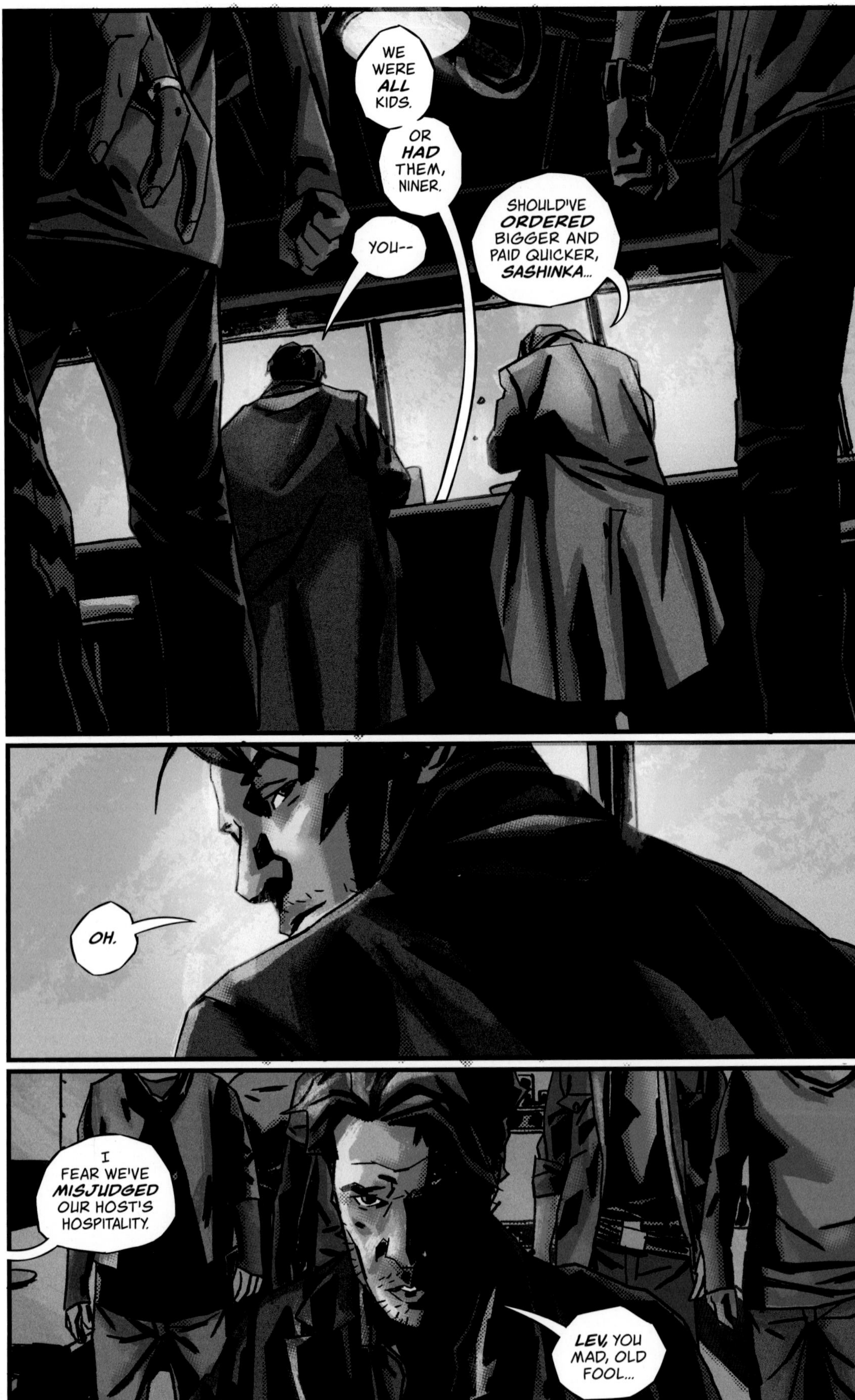

WE WERE ALL KIDS.
OR HAD THEM, NINER.
YOU--
SHOULD'VE ORDERED BIGGER AND PAID QUICKER, SASHINKA...
OH.
I FEAR WE'VE MISJUDGED OUR HOST'S HOSPITALITY.
LEV, YOU MAD, OLD FOOL...

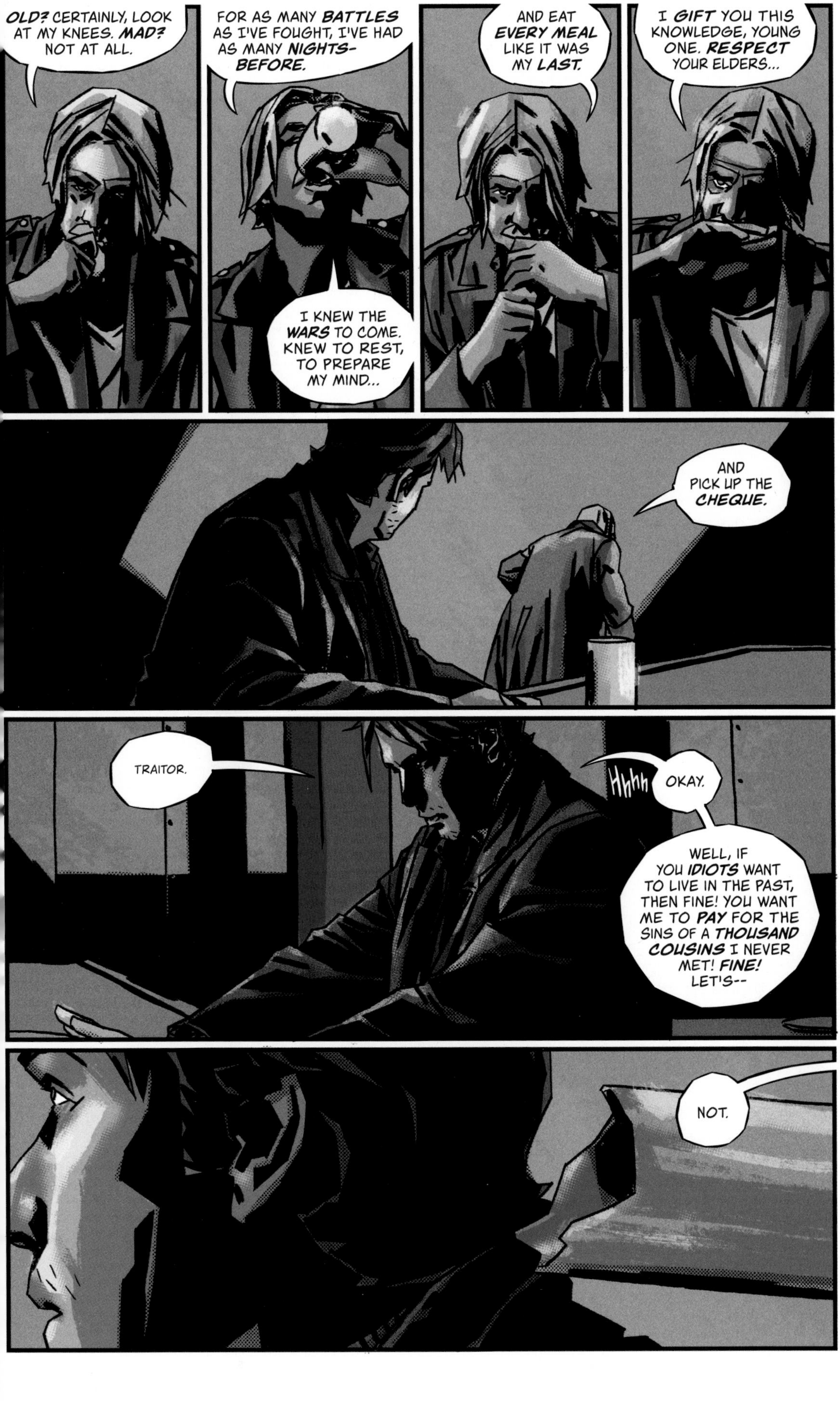

OLD? CERTAINLY, LOOK AT MY KNEES. MAD? NOT AT ALL.
FOR AS MANY BATTLES AS I'VE FOUGHT, I'VE HAD AS MANY NIGHTS-BEFORE.
I KNEW THE WARS TO COME. KNEW TO REST, TO PREPARE MY MIND...
AND EAT EVERY MEAL LIKE IT WAS MY LAST.
I GIFT YOU THIS KNOWLEDGE, YOUNG ONE. RESPECT YOUR ELDERS...
AND PICK UP THE CHEQUE.
TRAITOR.
Hhhh
OKAY.
WELL, IF YOU IDIOTS WANT TO LIVE IN THE PAST, THEN FINE! YOU WANT ME TO PAY FOR THE SINS OF A THOUSAND COUSINS I NEVER MET! FINE! LET'S--
NOT.

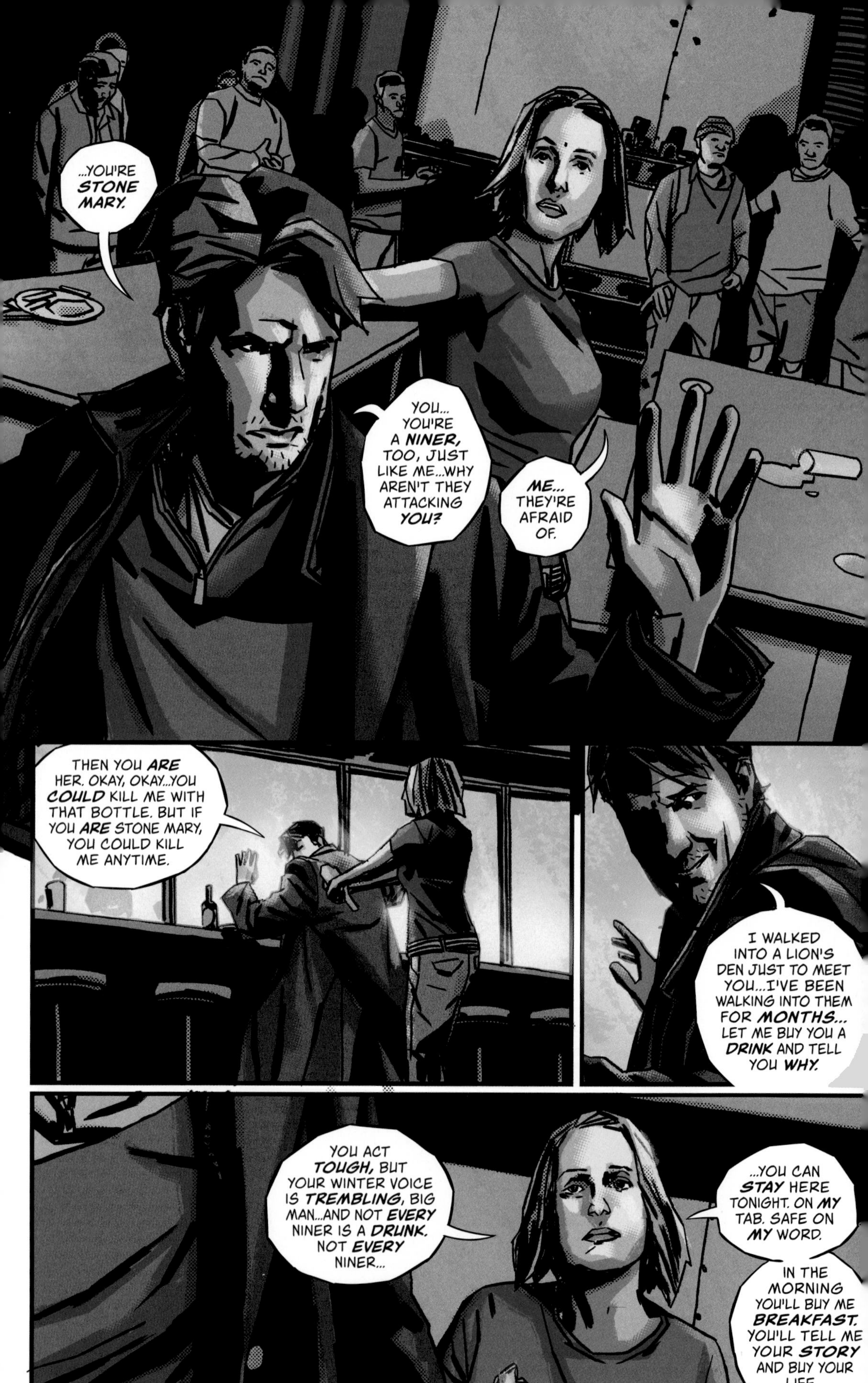
...YOU'RE STONE MARY.
YOU... YOU'RE A NINER, TOO, JUST LIKE ME...WHY AREN'T THEY ATTACKING YOU?
ME... THEY'RE AFRAID OF.
THEN YOU ARE HER. OKAY, OKAY...YOU COULD KILL ME WITH THAT BOTTLE. BUT IF YOU ARE STONE MARY, YOU COULD KILL ME ANYTIME.
I WALKED INTO A LION'S DEN JUST TO MEET YOU...I'VE BEEN WALKING INTO THEM FOR MONTHS... LET ME BUY YOU A DRINK AND TELL YOU WHY.
YOU ACT TOUGH, BUT YOUR WINTER VOICE IS TREMBLING, BIG MAN...AND NOT EVERY NINER IS A DRUNK. NOT EVERY NINER...
...YOU CAN STAY HERE TONIGHT. ON MY TAB. SAFE ON MY WORD.
IN THE MORNING YOU'LL BUY ME BREAKFAST. YOU'LL TELL ME YOUR STORY AND BUY YOUR LIFE...

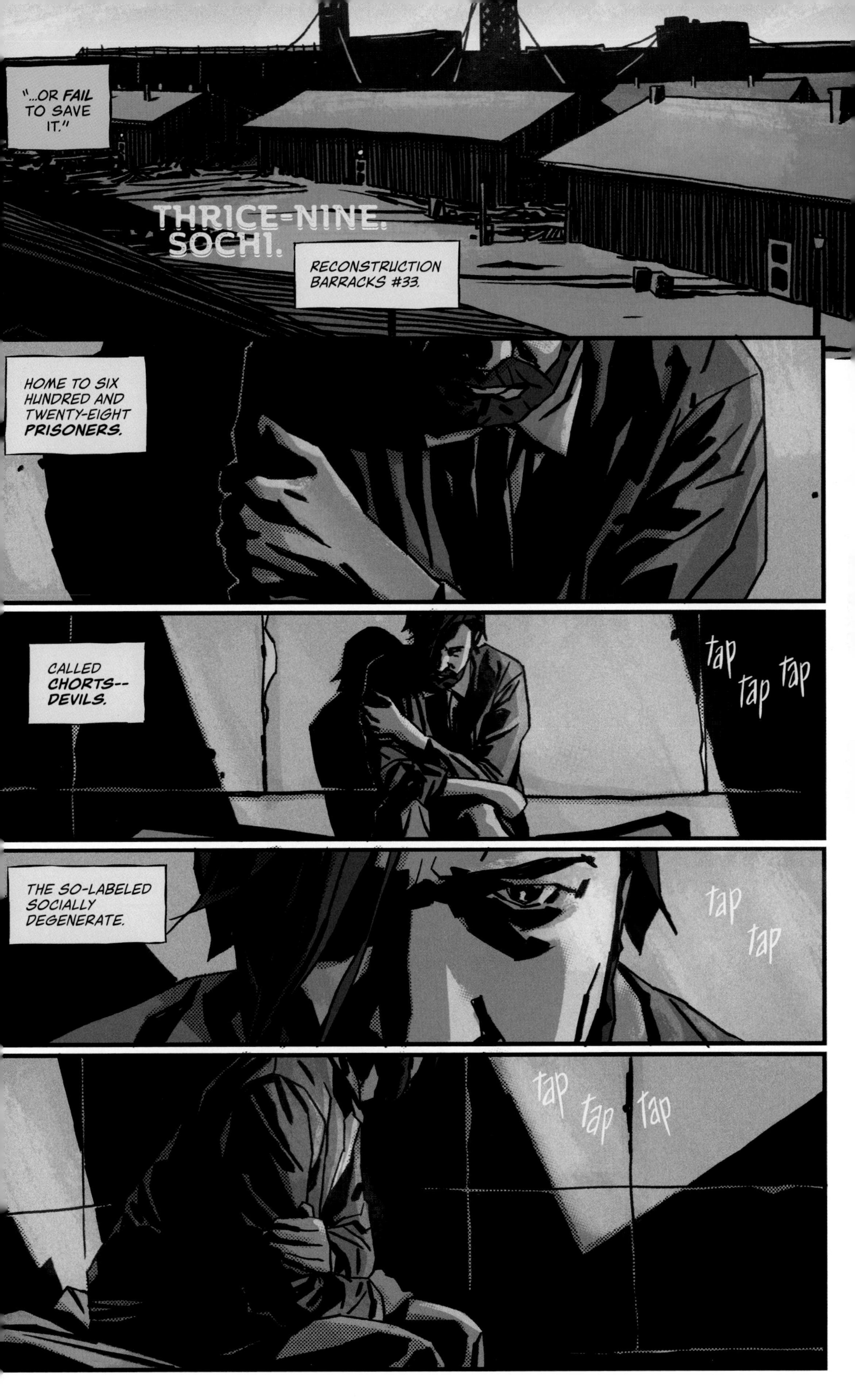
"...OR FAIL TO SAVE IT."
THRICE-NINE. SOCHI.
RECONSTRUCTION BARRACKS #33.
HOME TO SIX HUNDRED AND TWENTY-EIGHT PRISONERS.
CALLED CHORTS-- DEVILS.
tap tap tap
THE SO-LABELED SOCIALLY DEGENERATE.
tap tap
tap tap tap

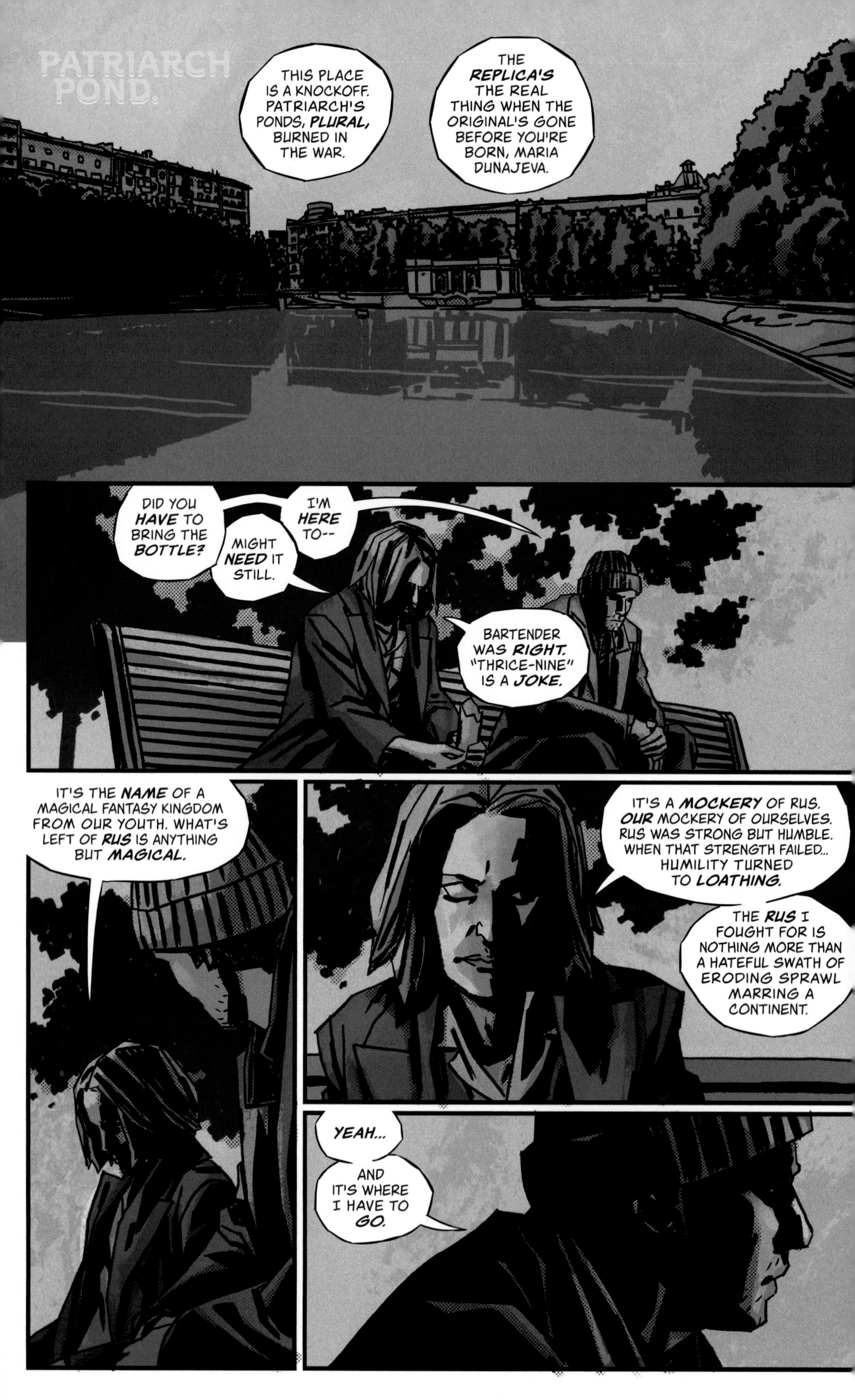
PATRIARCH POND.
THIS PLACE IS A KNOCKOFF. PATRIARCH'S PONDS, PLURAL, BURNED IN THE WAR.
THE REPLICA'S THE REAL THING WHEN THE ORIGINAL'S GONE BEFORE YOU'RE BORN, MARIA DUNAJEVA.
DID YOU HAVE TO BRING THE BOTTLE?
I'M HERE TO--
MIGHT NEED IT STILL.
BARTENDER WAS RIGHT. "THRICE-NINE" IS A JOKE.
IT'S THE NAME OF A MAGICAL FANTASY KINGDOM FROM OUR YOUTH. WHAT'S LEFT OF RUS IS ANYTHING BUT MAGICAL.
IT'S A MOCKERY OF RUS. OUR MOCKERY OF OURSELVES. RUS WAS STRONG BUT HUMBLE. WHEN THAT STRENGTH FAILED... HUMILITY TURNED TO LOATHING.
THE RUS I FOUGHT FOR IS NOTHING MORE THAN A HATEFUL SWATH OF ERODING SPRAWL MARRING A CONTINENT.
YEAH...
AND IT'S WHERE I HAVE TO GO.

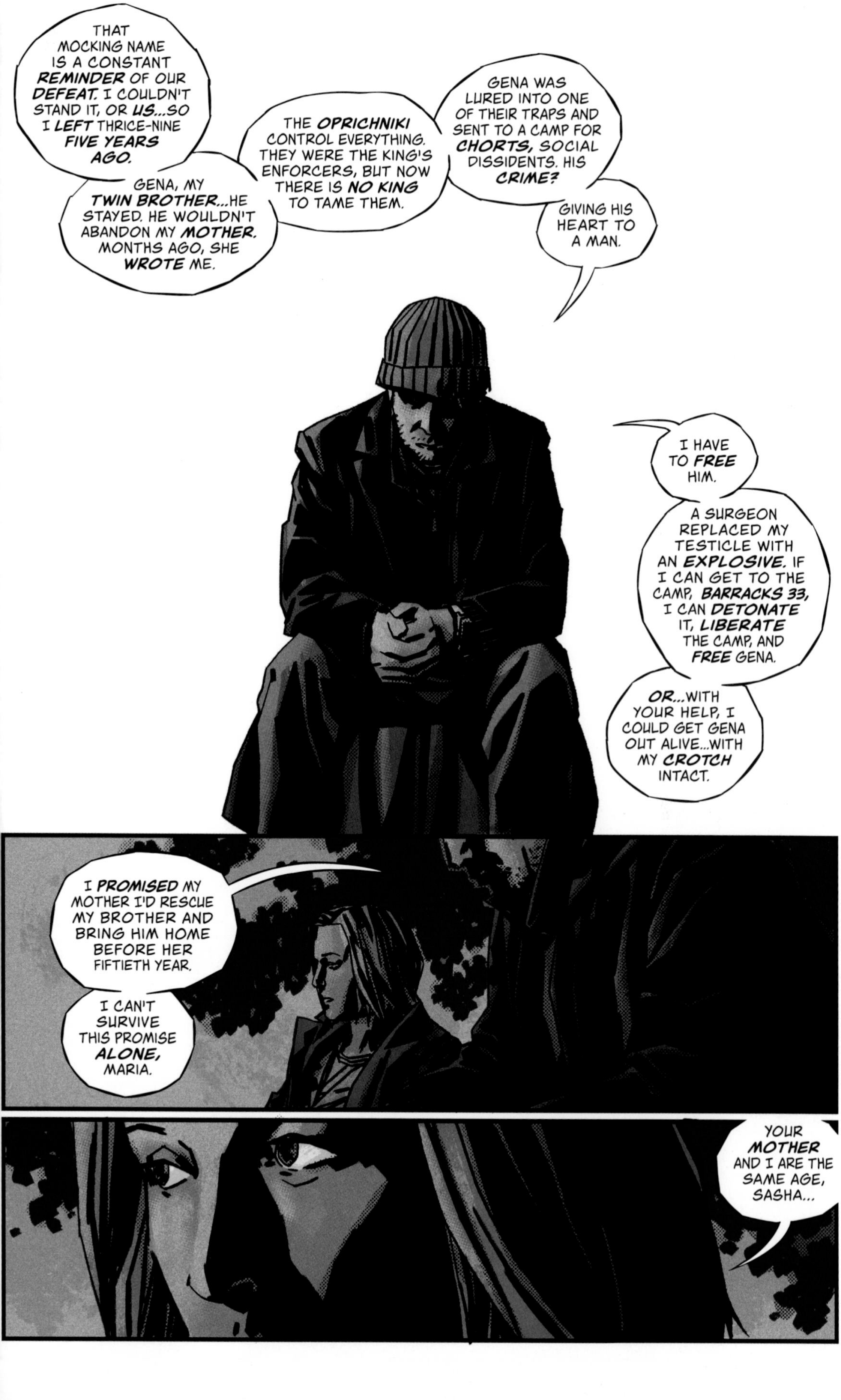
THAT MOCKING NAME IS A CONSTANT REMINDER OF OUR DEFEAT. I COULDN'T STAND IT, OR US...SO I LEFT THRICE-NINE FIVE YEARS AGO.
GENA, MY TWIN BROTHER...HE STAYED. HE WOULDN'T ABANDON MY MOTHER. MONTHS AGO, SHE WROTE ME.
THE OPRICHNIKI CONTROL EVERYTHING. THEY WERE THE KING'S ENFORCERS, BUT NOW THERE IS NO KING TO TAME THEM.
GENA WAS LURED INTO ONE OF THEIR TRAPS AND SENT TO A CAMP FOR CHORTS, SOCIAL DISSIDENTS. HIS CRIME?
GIVING HIS HEART TO A MAN.
I HAVE TO FREE HIM.
A SURGEON REPLACED MY TESTICLE WITH AN EXPLOSIVE. IF I CAN GET TO THE CAMP, BARRACKS 33, I CAN DETONATE IT, LIBERATE THE CAMP, AND FREE GENA.
OR...WITH YOUR HELP, I COULD GET GENA OUT ALIVE...WITH MY CROTCH INTACT.
I PROMISED MY MOTHER I'D RESCUE MY BROTHER AND BRING HIM HOME BEFORE HER FIFTIETH YEAR.
I CAN'T SURVIVE THIS PROMISE ALONE, MARIA.
YOUR MOTHER AND I ARE THE SAME AGE, SASHA...

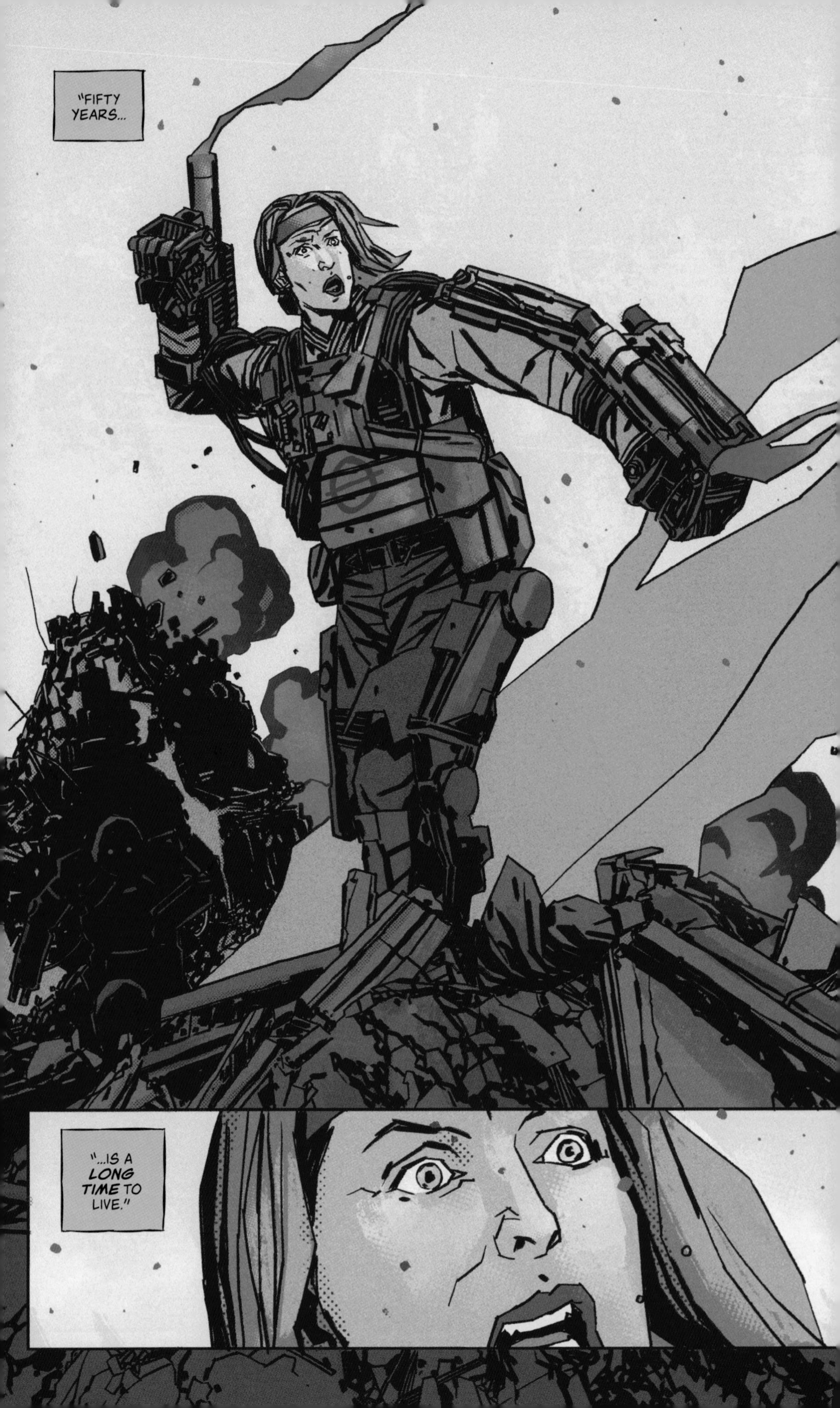
"FIFTY YEARS...
"...IS A *LONG TIME* TO LIVE."

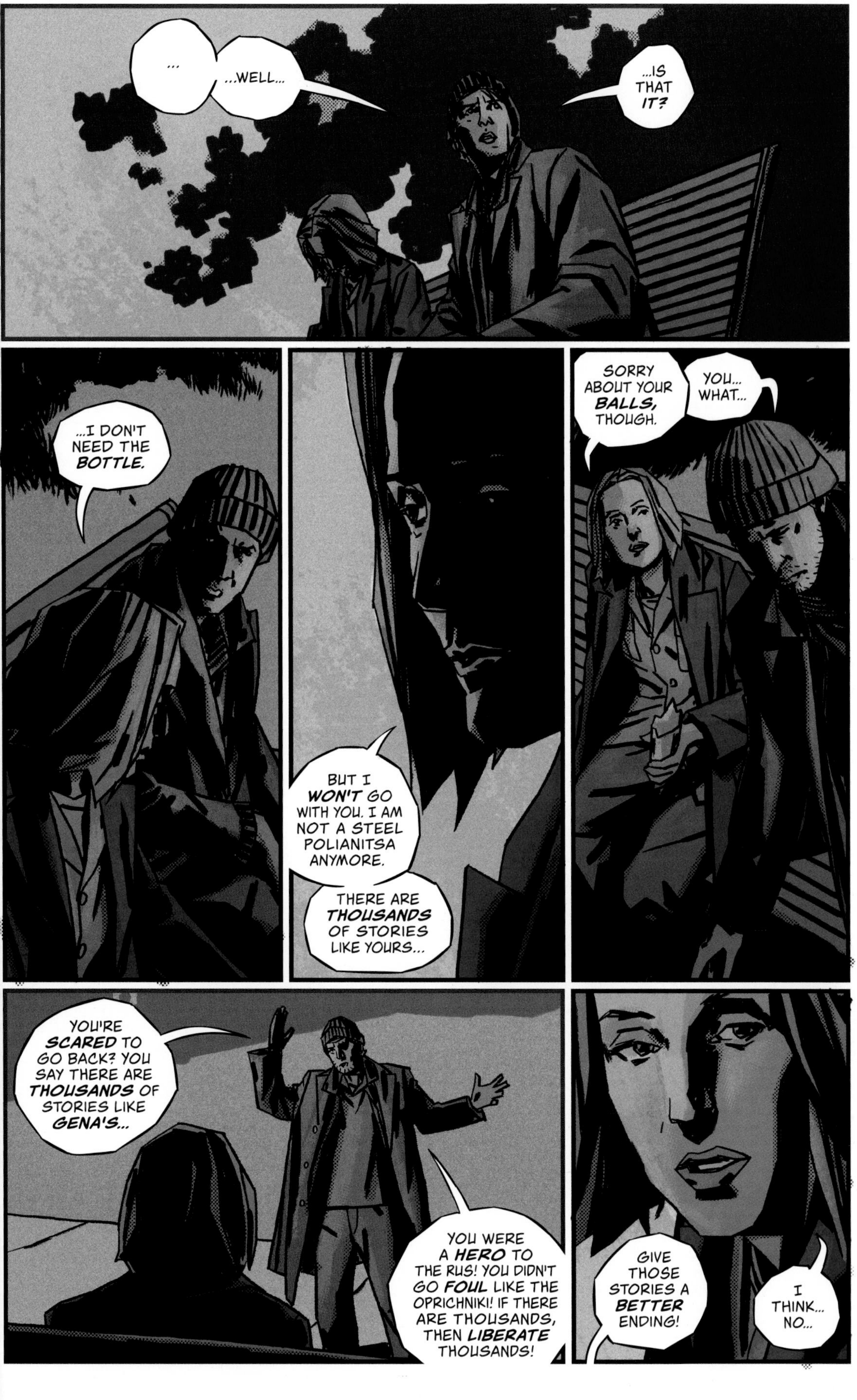
...
...WELL...
...IS THAT IT?
...I DON'T NEED THE BOTTLE.
BUT I WON'T GO WITH YOU. I AM NOT A STEEL POLIANITSA ANYMORE.
THERE ARE THOUSANDS OF STORIES LIKE YOURS...
SORRY ABOUT YOUR BALLS, THOUGH.
YOU... WHAT...
YOU'RE SCARED TO GO BACK? YOU SAY THERE ARE THOUSANDS OF STORIES LIKE GENA'S...
YOU WERE A HERO TO THE RUS! YOU DIDN'T GO FOUL LIKE THE OPRICHNIKI! IF THERE ARE THOUSANDS, THEN LIBERATE THOUSANDS!
GIVE THOSE STORIES A BETTER ENDING!
I THINK... NO...

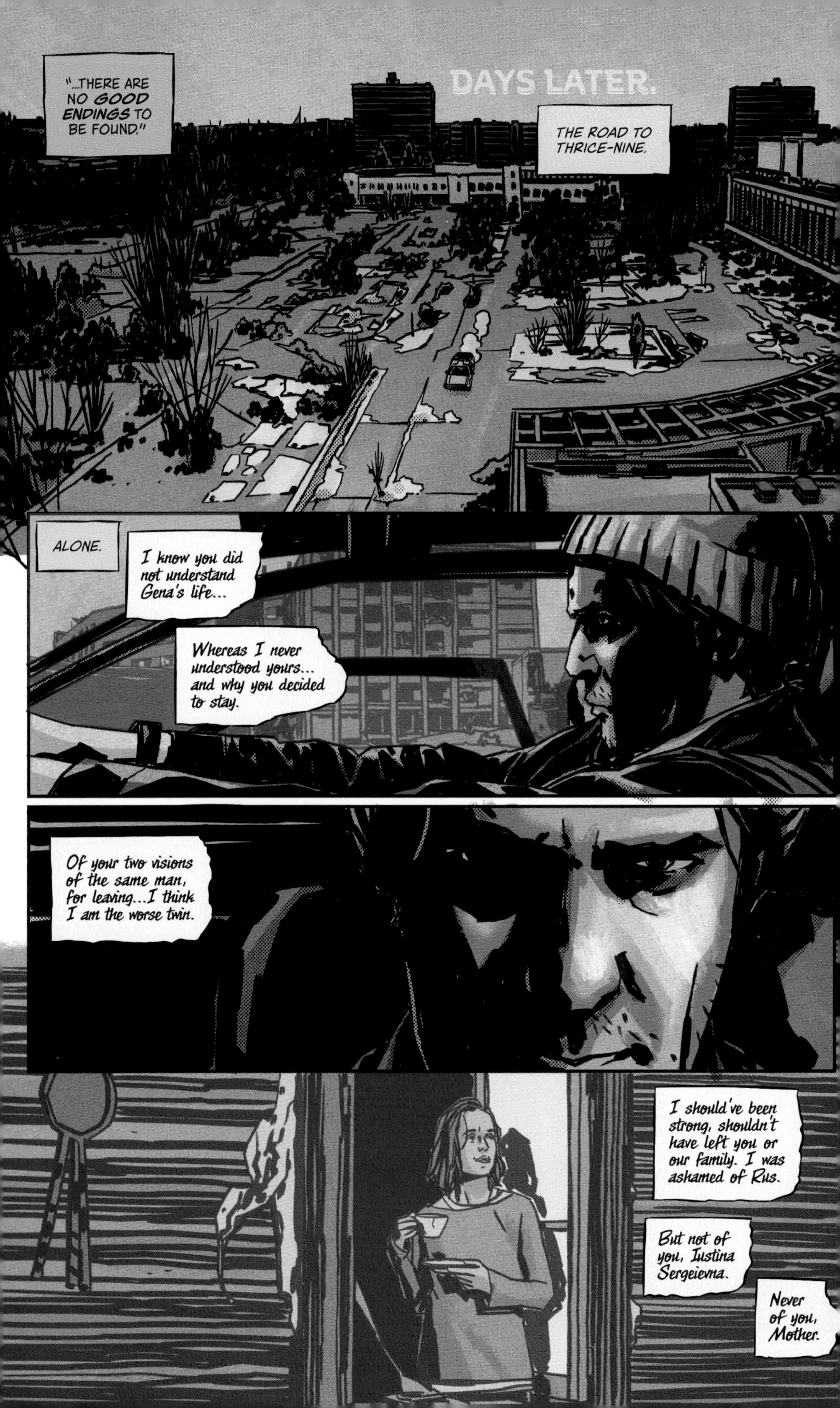
"...THERE ARE NO GOOD ENDINGS TO BE FOUND."
DAYS LATER.
THE ROAD TO THRICE-NINE.
ALONE.
I know you did not understand Gena's life...
Whereas I never understood yours... and why you decided to stay.
Of your two visions of the same man, for leaving...I think I am the worse twin.
I should've been strong, shouldn't have left you or our family. I was ashamed of Rus.
But not of you, Iustina Sergeievna.
Never of you, Mother.

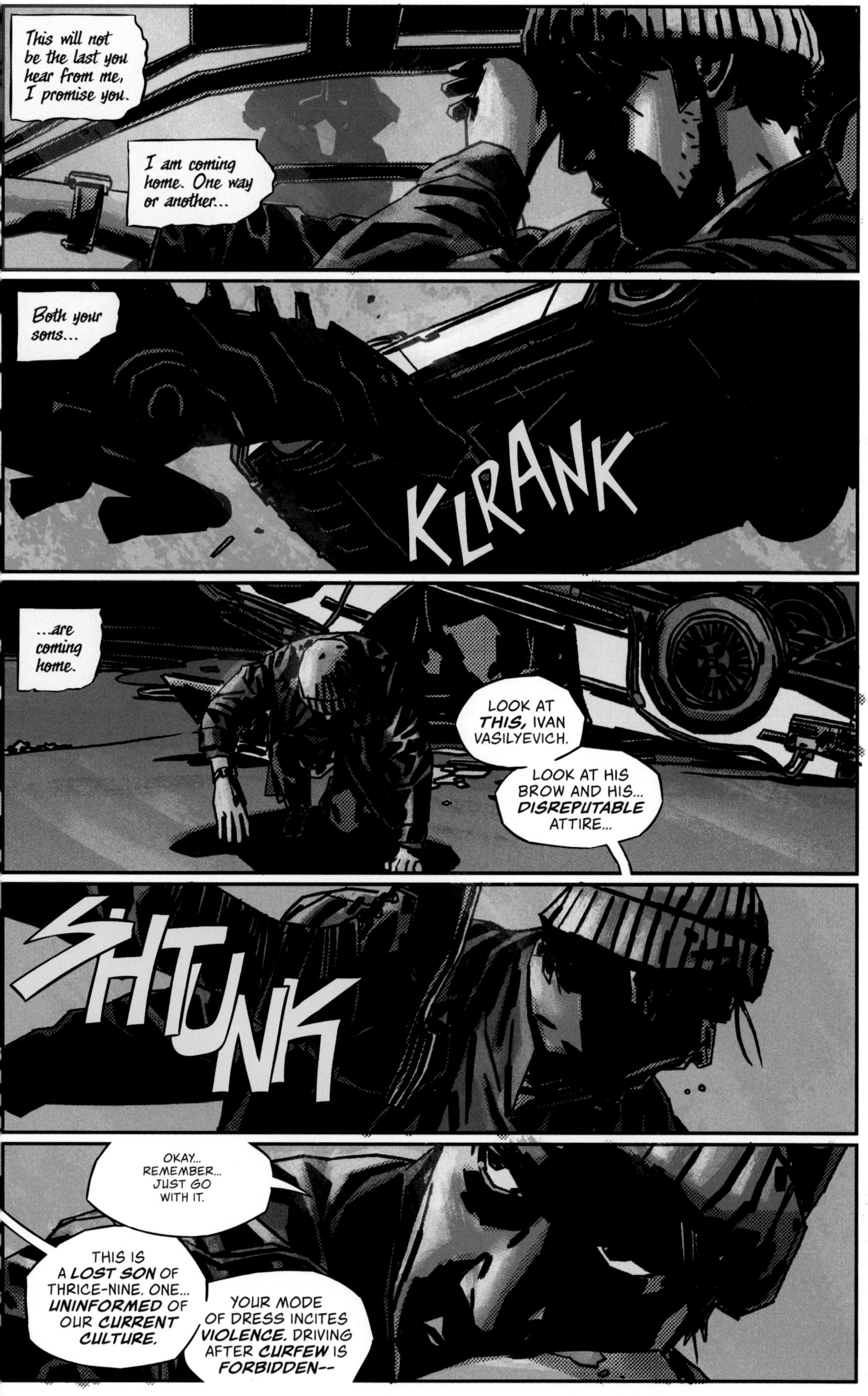
This will not be the last you hear from me, I promise you.
I am coming home. One way or another...
Both your sons...
KLRANK
...are coming home.
LOOK AT THIS, IVAN VASILYEVICH.
LOOK AT HIS BROW AND HIS... DISREPUTABLE ATTIRE...
SHTUNK
OKAY... REMEMBER... JUST GO WITH IT.
THIS IS A LOST SON OF THRICE-NINE. ONE... UNINFORMED OF OUR CURRENT CULTURE.
YOUR MODE OF DRESS INCITES VIOLENCE. DRIVING AFTER CURFEW IS FORBIDDEN--

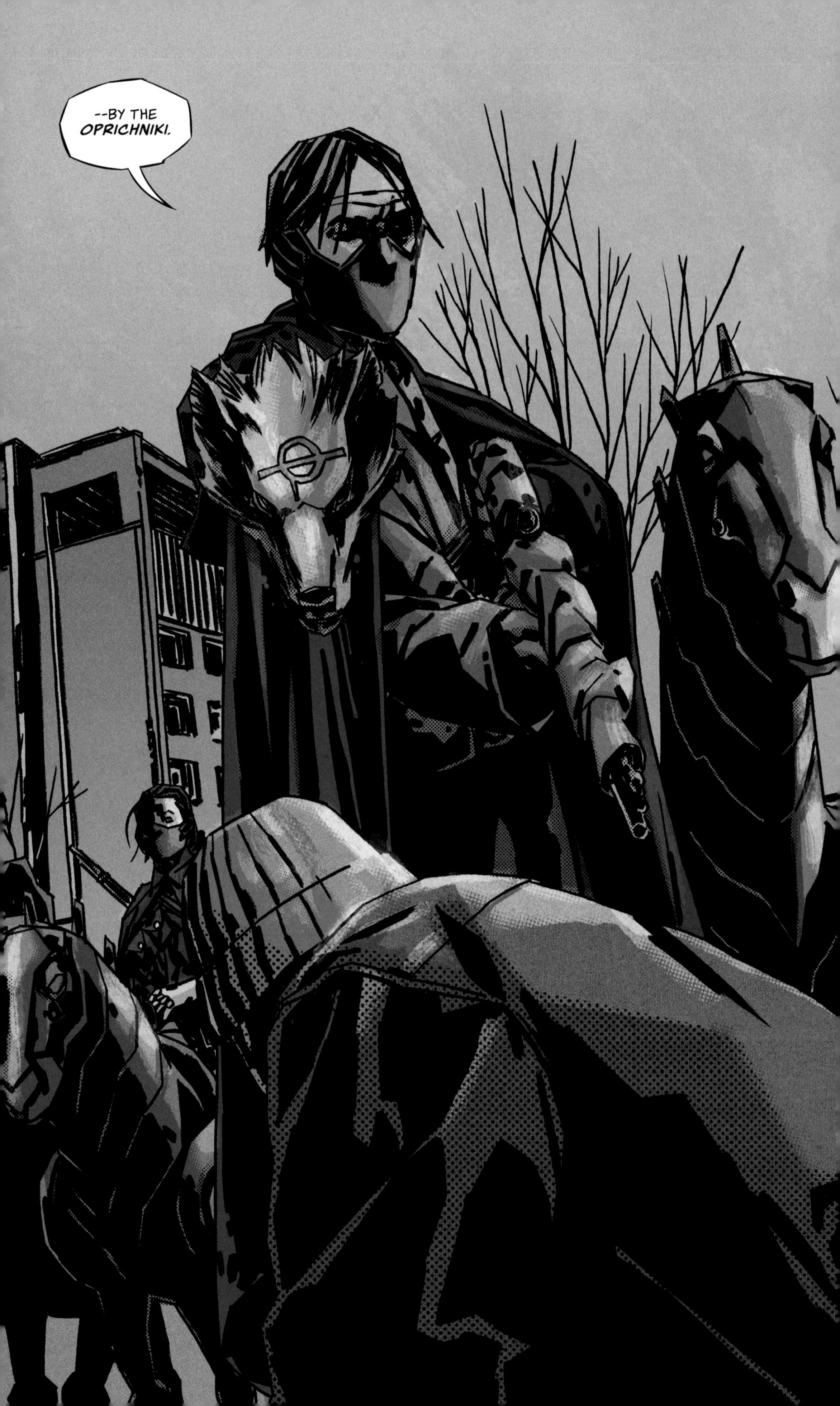
--BY THE OPRICHNIKI.

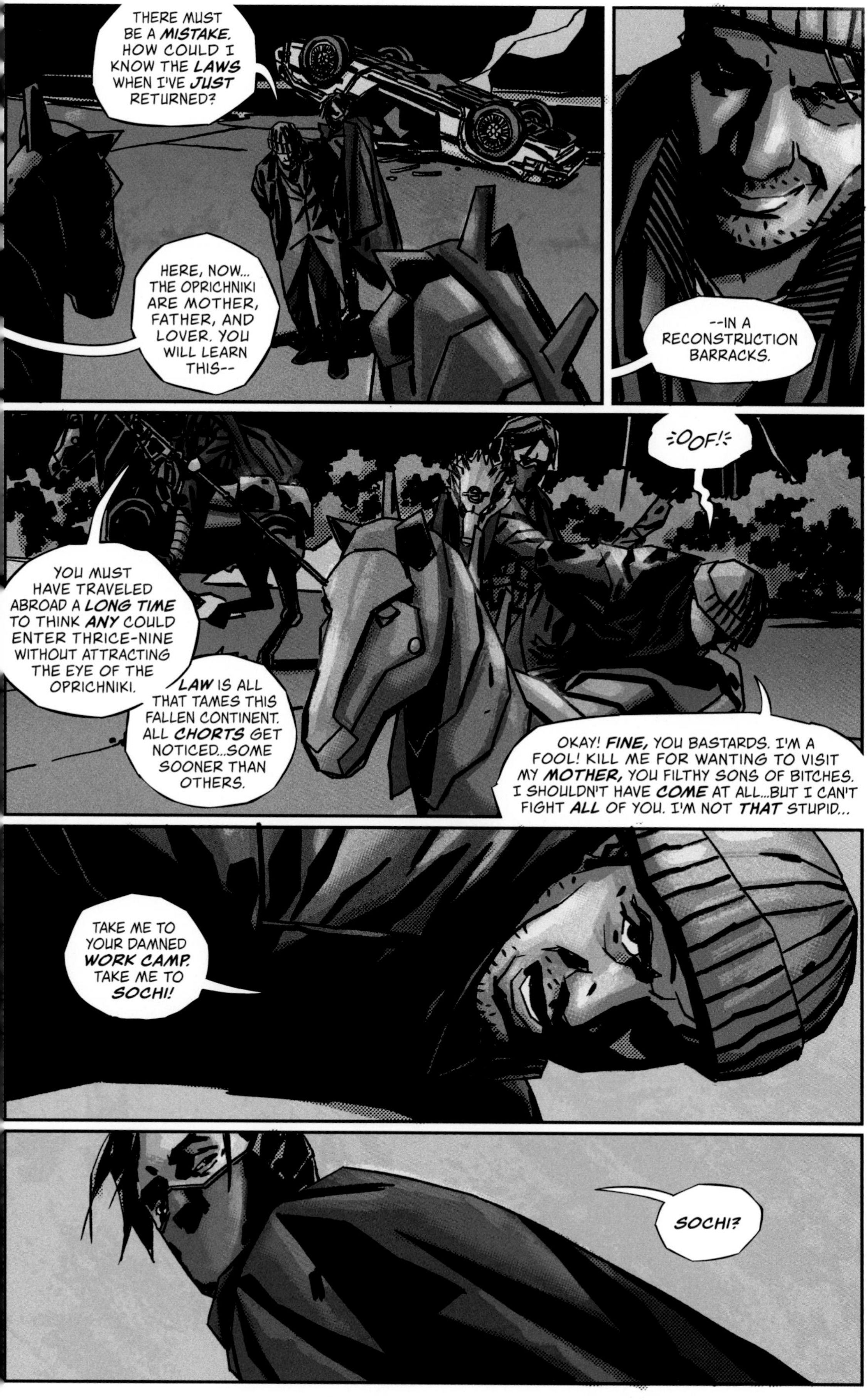
THERE MUST BE A ***MISTAKE.*** HOW COULD I KNOW THE ***LAWS*** WHEN I'VE ***JUST*** RETURNED?
HERE, NOW... THE OPRICHNIKI ARE MOTHER, FATHER, AND LOVER. YOU WILL LEARN THIS--
--IN A RECONSTRUCTION BARRACKS.
OOF!
YOU MUST HAVE TRAVELED ABROAD A ***LONG TIME*** TO THINK ***ANY*** COULD ENTER THRICE-NINE WITHOUT ATTRACTING THE EYE OF THE OPRICHNIKI.
LAW IS ALL THAT TAMES THIS FALLEN CONTINENT. ALL ***CHORTS*** GET NOTICED...SOME SOONER THAN OTHERS.
OKAY! ***FINE,*** YOU BASTARDS. I'M A FOOL! KILL ME FOR WANTING TO VISIT MY ***MOTHER,*** YOU FILTHY SONS OF BITCHES. I SHOULDN'T HAVE ***COME*** AT ALL...BUT I CAN'T FIGHT ***ALL*** OF YOU. I'M NOT ***THAT*** STUPID...
TAKE ME TO YOUR DAMNED ***WORK CAMP.*** TAKE ME TO ***SOCHI!***
SOCHI?

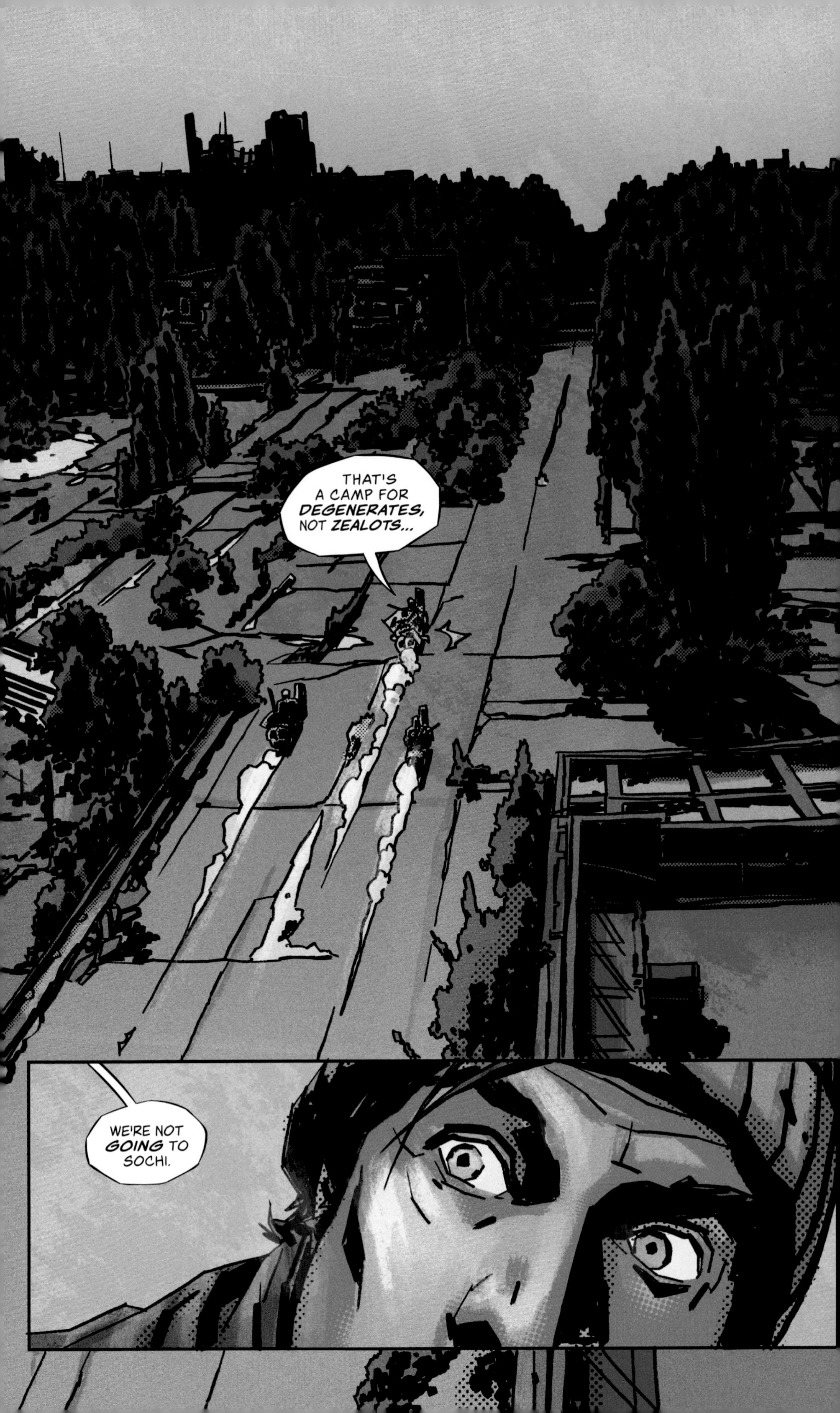
THAT'S A CAMP FOR DEGENERATES, NOT ZEALOTS...
WE'RE NOT GOING TO SOCHI.

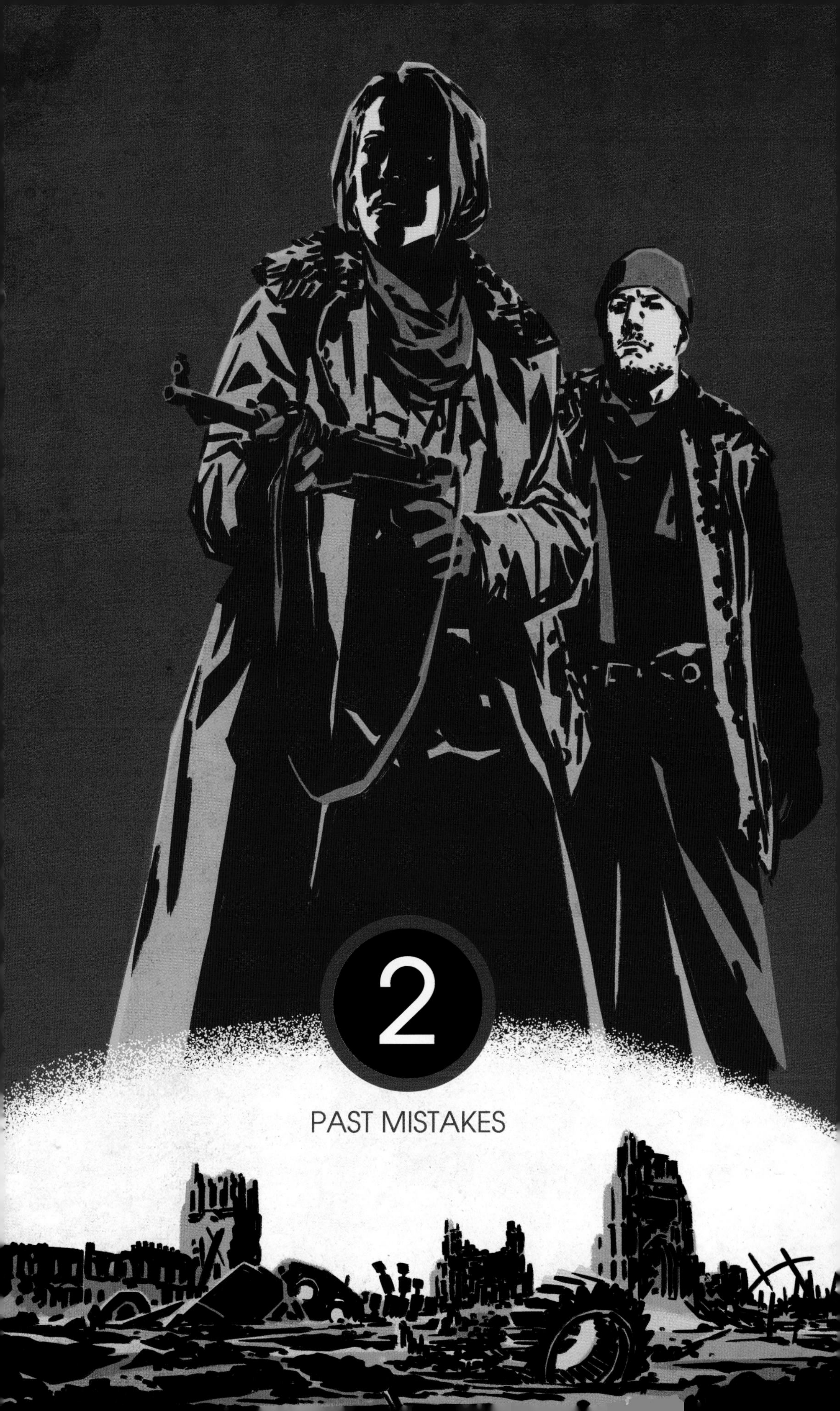

2

PAST MISTAKES

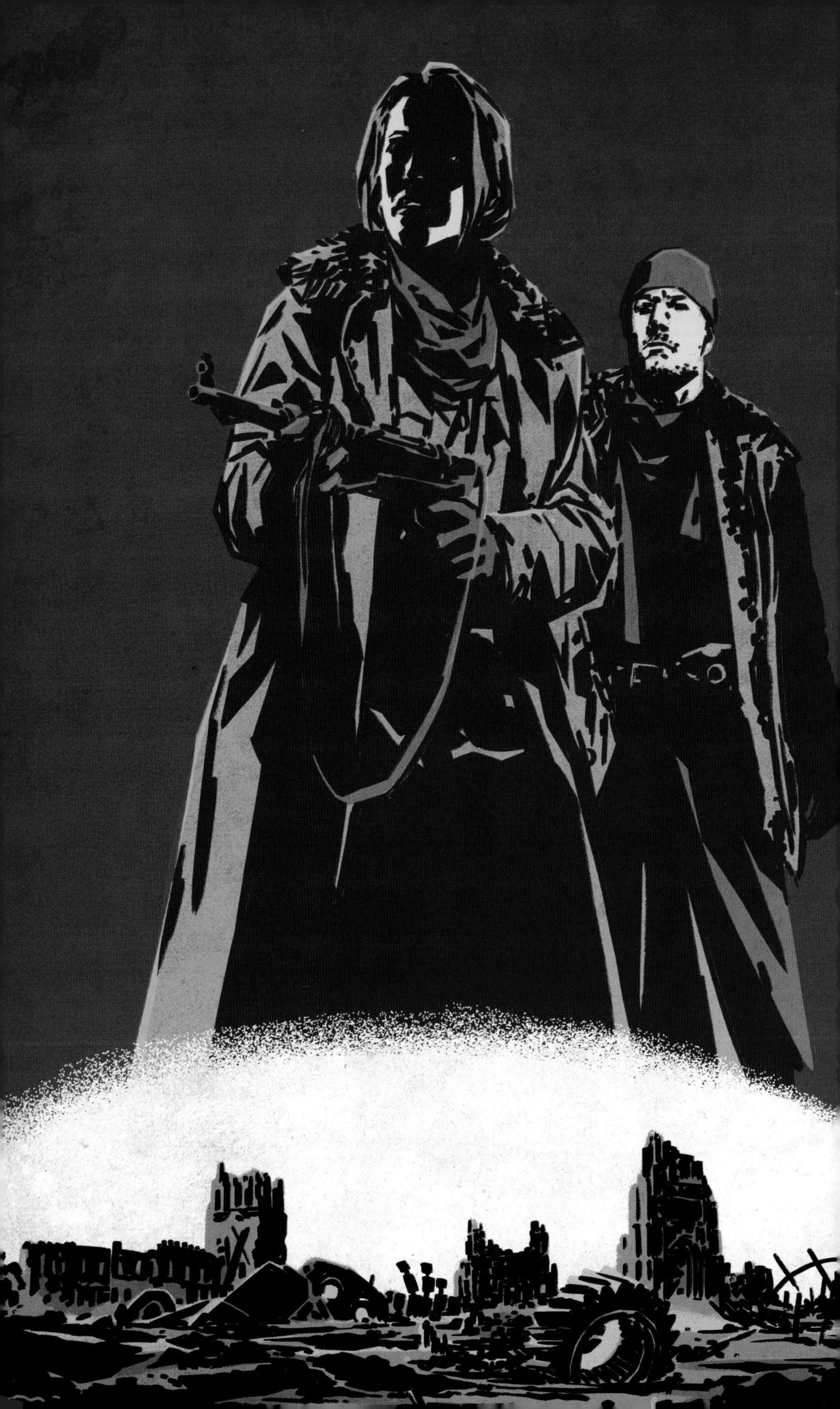

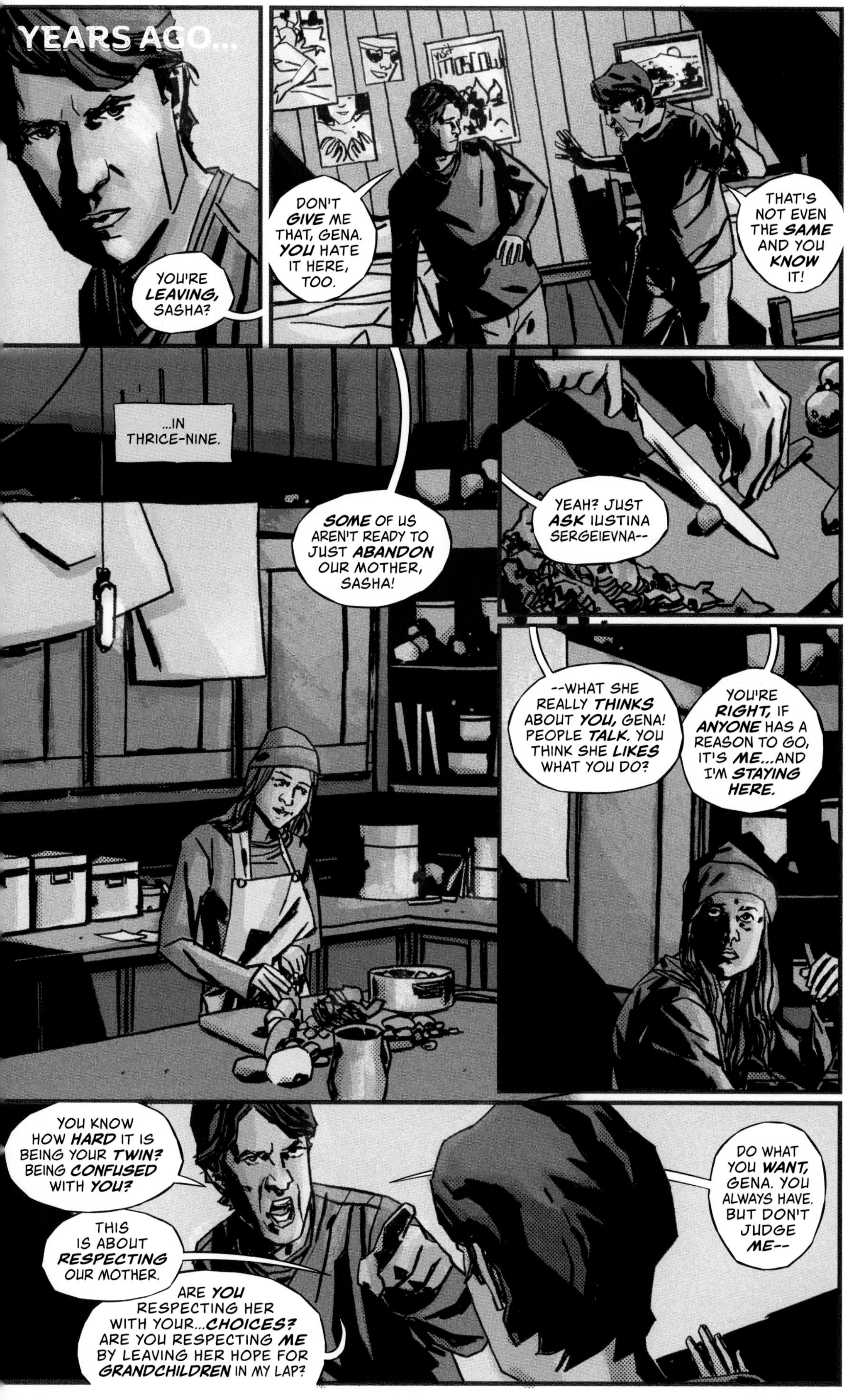

YEARS AGO...
YOU'RE LEAVING, SASHA?
DON'T GIVE ME THAT, GENA. YOU HATE IT HERE, TOO.
THAT'S NOT EVEN THE SAME AND YOU KNOW IT!
...IN THRICE-NINE.
SOME OF US AREN'T READY TO JUST ABANDON OUR MOTHER, SASHA!
YEAH? JUST ASK IUSTINA SERGEIEVNA--
--WHAT SHE REALLY THINKS ABOUT YOU, GENA! PEOPLE TALK. YOU THINK SHE LIKES WHAT YOU DO?
YOU'RE RIGHT, IF ANYONE HAS A REASON TO GO, IT'S ME...AND I'M STAYING HERE.
YOU KNOW HOW HARD IT IS BEING YOUR TWIN? BEING CONFUSED WITH YOU?
THIS IS ABOUT RESPECTING OUR MOTHER.
ARE YOU RESPECTING HER WITH YOUR...CHOICES? ARE YOU RESPECTING ME BY LEAVING HER HOPE FOR GRANDCHILDREN IN MY LAP?
DO WHAT YOU WANT, GENA. YOU ALWAYS HAVE. BUT DON'T JUDGE ME--

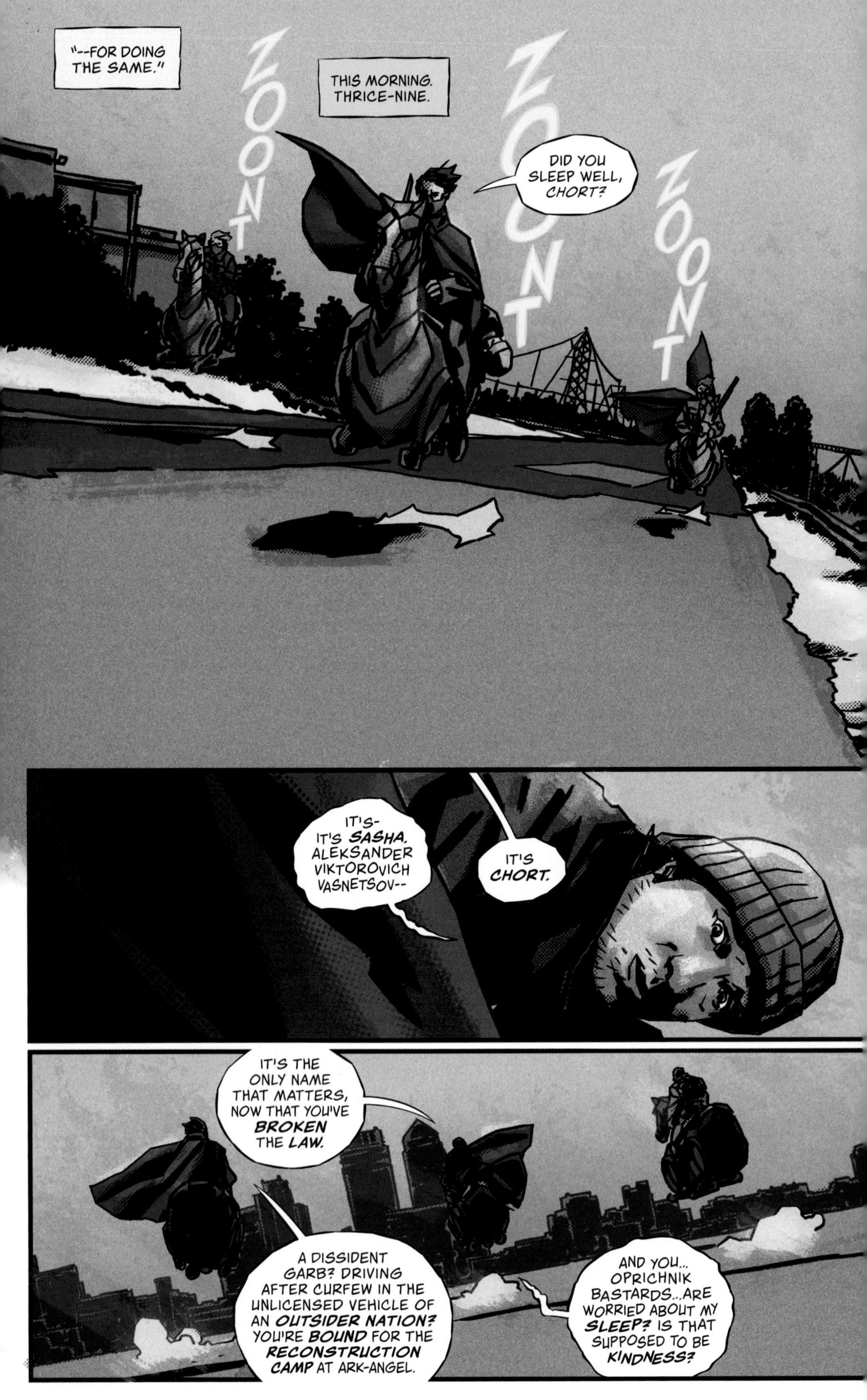
"--FOR DOING THE SAME."
THIS MORNING. THRICE-NINE.
ZOONT
ZOONT
ZOONT
DID YOU SLEEP WELL, CHORT?
IT'S- IT'S SASHA. ALEKSANDER VIKTOROVICH VASNETSOV--
IT'S CHORT.
IT'S THE ONLY NAME THAT MATTERS, NOW THAT YOU'VE BROKEN THE LAW.
A DISSIDENT GARB? DRIVING AFTER CURFEW IN THE UNLICENSED VEHICLE OF AN OUTSIDER NATION? YOU'RE BOUND FOR THE RECONSTRUCTION CAMP AT ARK-ANGEL.
AND YOU... OPRICHNIK BASTARDS...ARE WORRIED ABOUT MY SLEEP? IS THAT SUPPOSED TO BE KINDNESS?

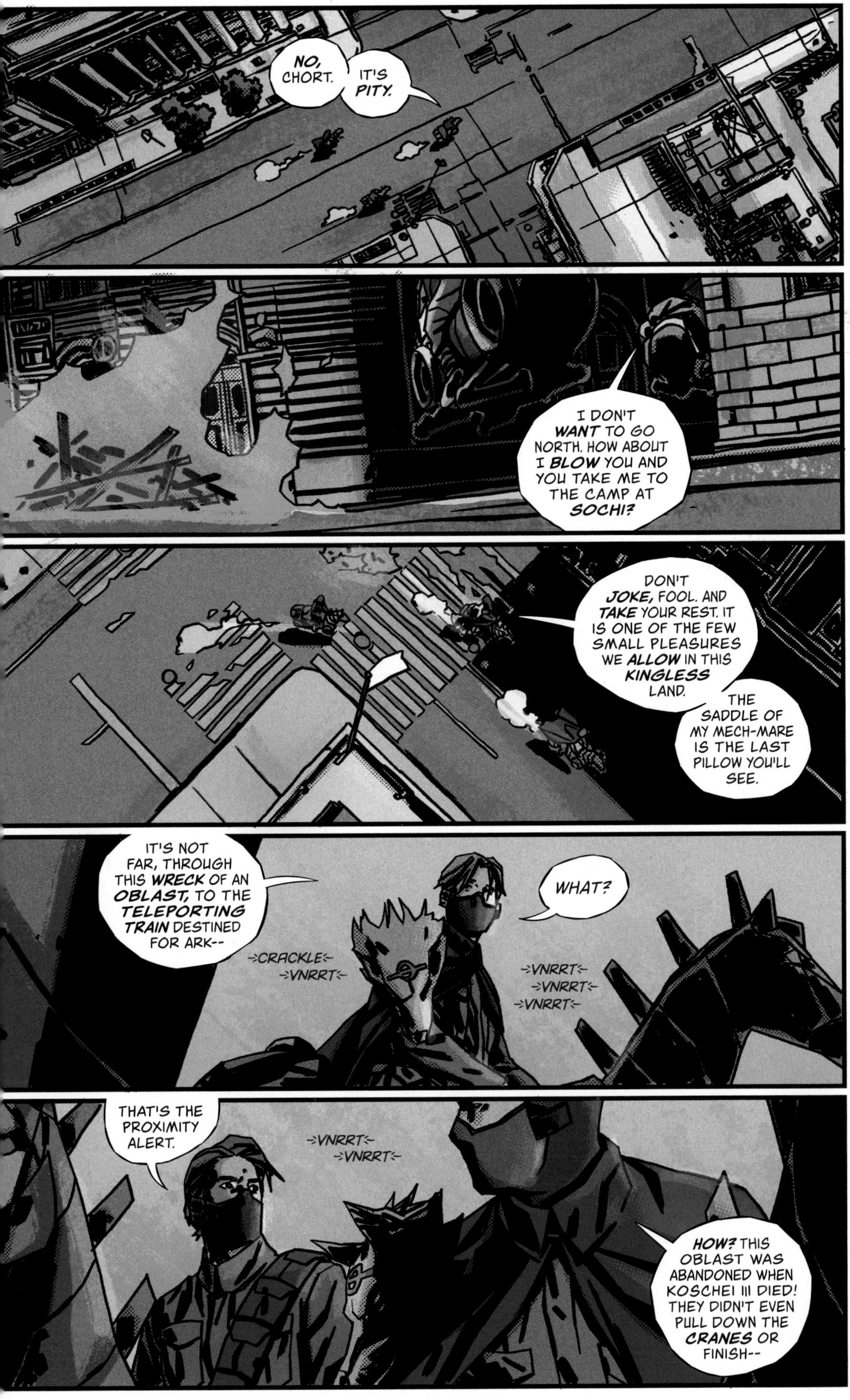
NO, CHORT.
IT'S PITY.
I DON'T WANT TO GO NORTH. HOW ABOUT I BLOW YOU AND YOU TAKE ME TO THE CAMP AT SOCHI?
DON'T JOKE, FOOL. AND TAKE YOUR REST. IT IS ONE OF THE FEW SMALL PLEASURES WE ALLOW IN THIS KINGLESS LAND.
THE SADDLE OF MY MECH-MARE IS THE LAST PILLOW YOU'LL SEE.
IT'S NOT FAR, THROUGH THIS WRECK OF AN OBLAST, TO THE TELEPORTING TRAIN DESTINED FOR ARK--
WHAT?
CRACKLE
VNRRT
VNRRT
VNRRT
VNRRT
THAT'S THE PROXIMITY ALERT.
VNRRT
VNRRT
HOW? THIS OBLAST WAS ABANDONED WHEN KOSCHEI III DIED! THEY DIDN'T EVEN PULL DOWN THE CRANES OR FINISH--

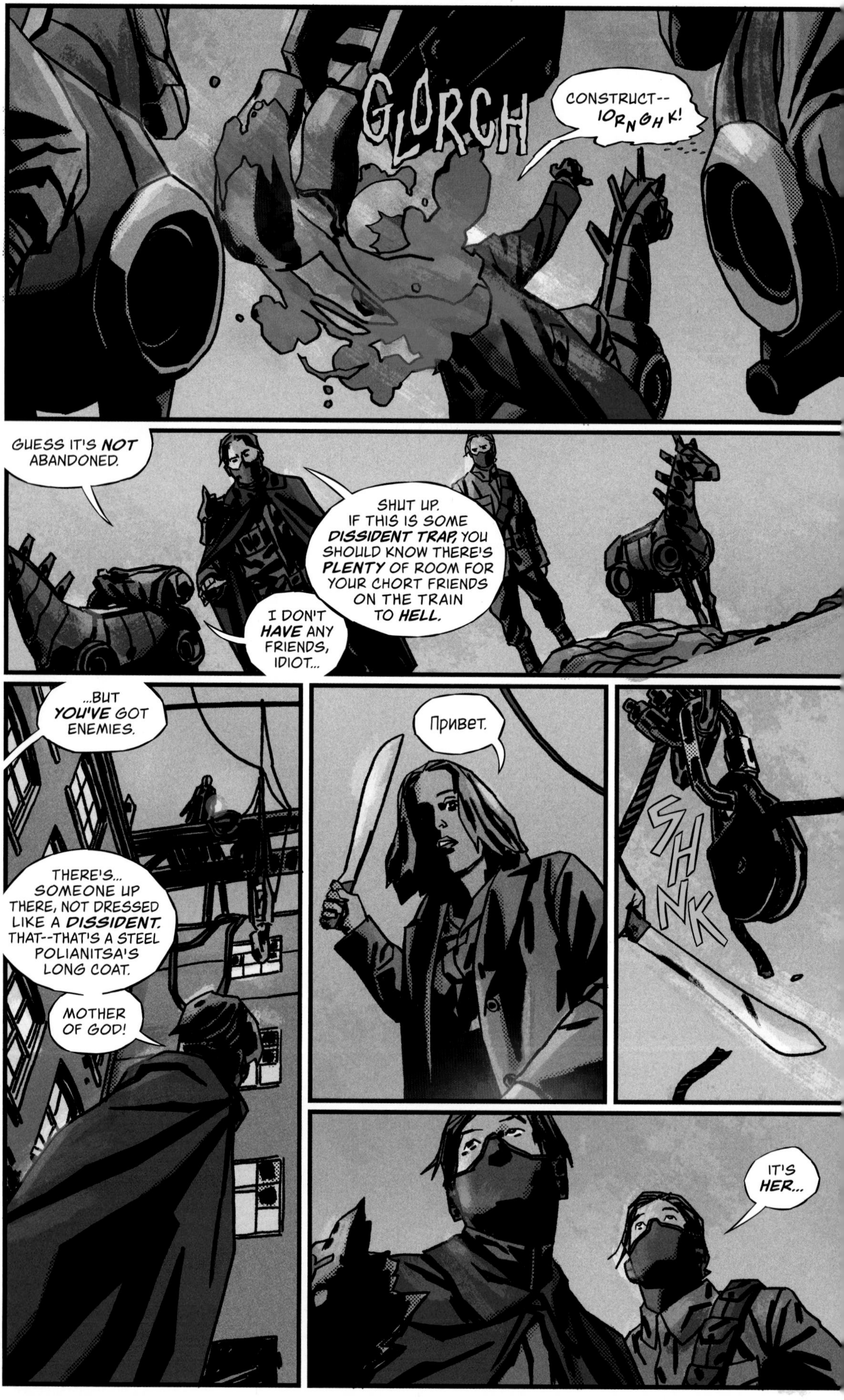
GLORCH
CONSTRUCT-- IORNGHK!
GUESS IT'S **NOT** ABANDONED.
SHUT UP. IF THIS IS SOME ***DISSIDENT TRAP,*** YOU SHOULD KNOW THERE'S **PLENTY** OF ROOM FOR YOUR CHORT FRIENDS ON THE TRAIN TO **HELL.**
I DON'T **HAVE** ANY FRIENDS, IDIOT...
...BUT ***YOU'VE*** GOT ENEMIES.
THERE'S... SOMEONE UP THERE, NOT DRESSED LIKE A ***DISSIDENT.*** THAT--THAT'S A STEEL POLIANITSA'S LONG COAT.
MOTHER OF GOD!
Привет.
SHNK
IT'S ***HER...***

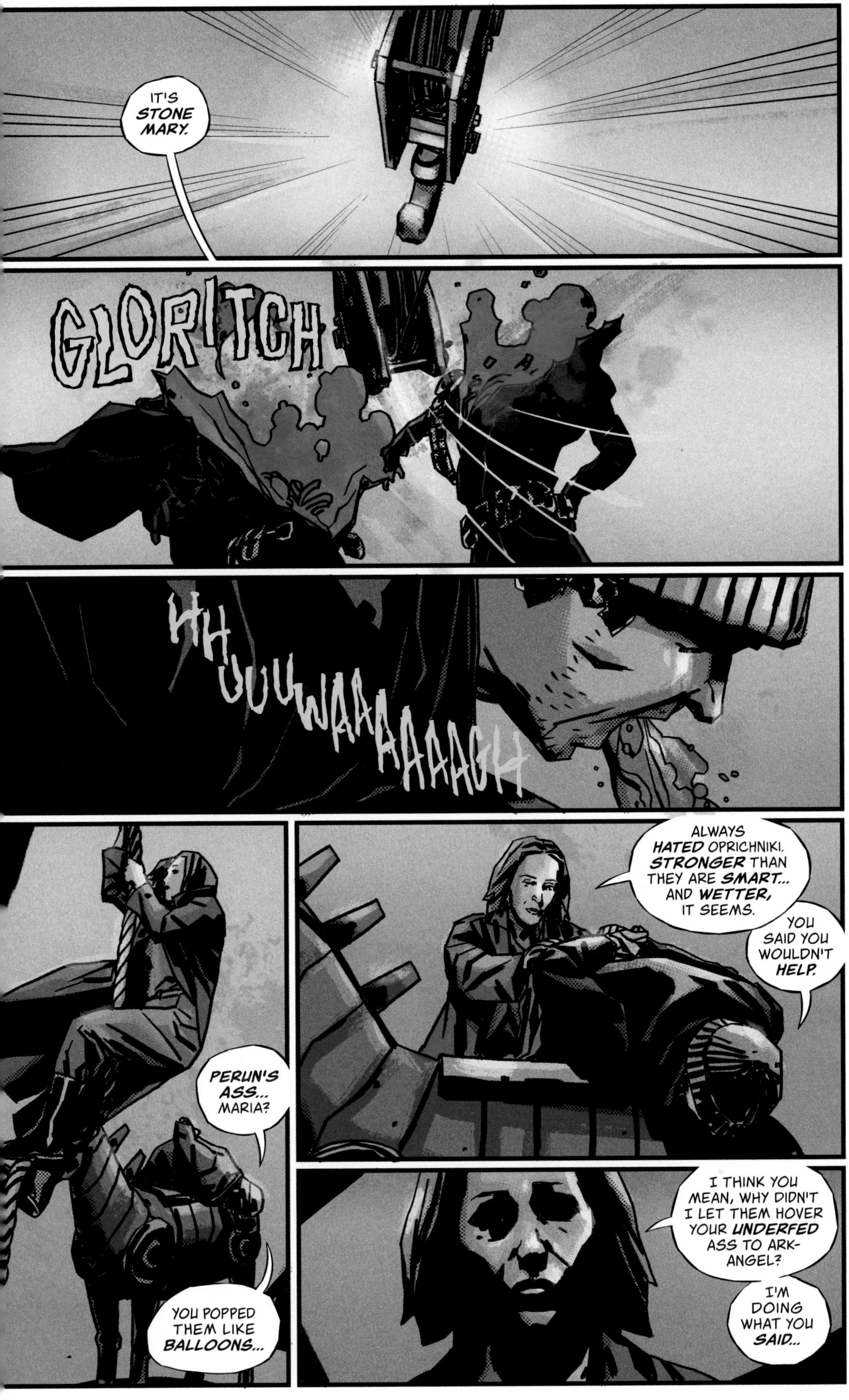
IT'S STONE MARY.
GLORITCH
HHUUUWAAAAAAAGH
ALWAYS HATED OPRICHNIKI. STRONGER THAN THEY ARE SMART... AND WETTER, IT SEEMS.
PERUN'S ASS... MARIA?
YOU POPPED THEM LIKE BALLOONS...
YOU SAID YOU WOULDN'T HELP.
I THINK YOU MEAN, WHY DIDN'T I LET THEM HOVER YOUR UNDERFED ASS TO ARK-ANGEL?
I'M DOING WHAT YOU SAID...

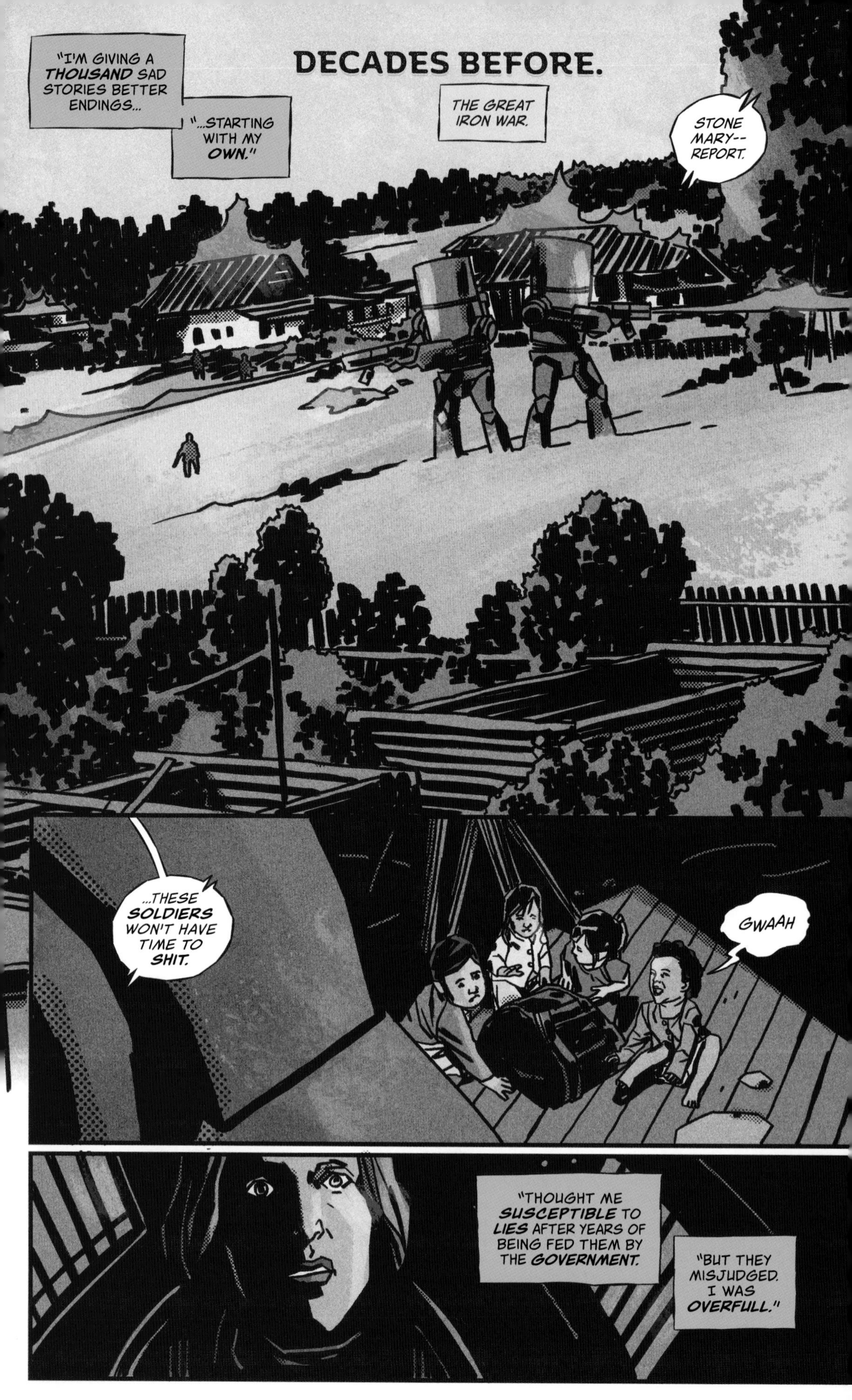
DECADES BEFORE.
"I'M GIVING A THOUSAND SAD STORIES BETTER ENDINGS...
"...STARTING WITH MY OWN."
THE GREAT IRON WAR.
STONE MARY-- REPORT.
...THESE SOLDIERS WON'T HAVE TIME TO SHIT.
GWAAH
"THOUGHT ME SUSCEPTIBLE TO LIES AFTER YEARS OF BEING FED THEM BY THE GOVERNMENT.
"BUT THEY MISJUDGED. I WAS OVERFULL."

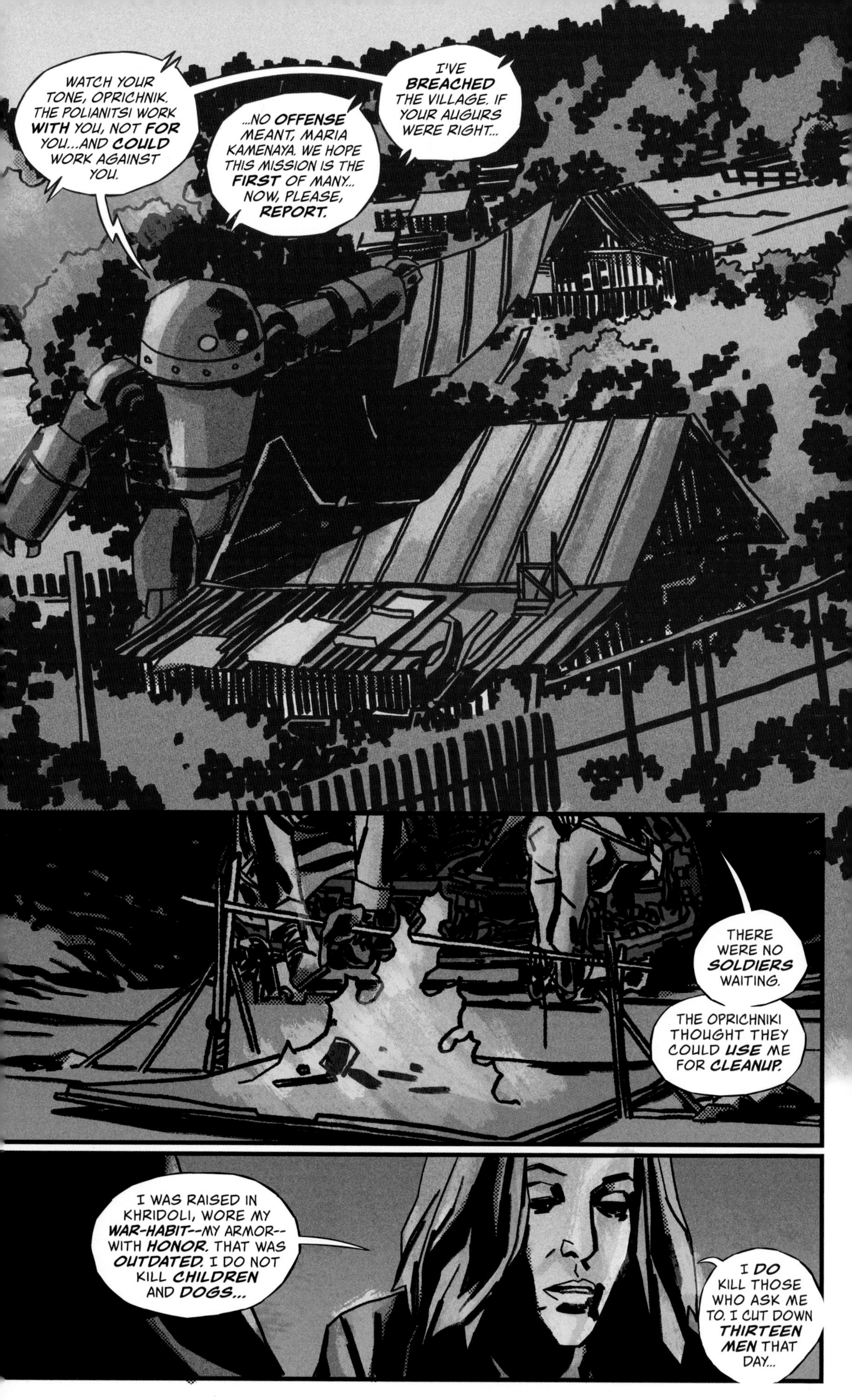
WATCH YOUR TONE, OPRICHNIK. THE POLIANITSI WORK WITH YOU, NOT FOR YOU...AND COULD WORK AGAINST YOU.
...NO OFFENSE MEANT, MARIA KAMENAYA. WE HOPE THIS MISSION IS THE FIRST OF MANY... NOW, PLEASE, REPORT.
I'VE BREACHED THE VILLAGE. IF YOUR AUGURS WERE RIGHT...
THERE WERE NO SOLDIERS WAITING.
THE OPRICHNIKI THOUGHT THEY COULD USE ME FOR CLEANUP.
I WAS RAISED IN KHRIDOLI, WORE MY WAR-HABIT--MY ARMOR--WITH HONOR. THAT WAS OUTDATED. I DO NOT KILL CHILDREN AND DOGS...
I DO KILL THOSE WHO ASK ME TO. I CUT DOWN THIRTEEN MEN THAT DAY...

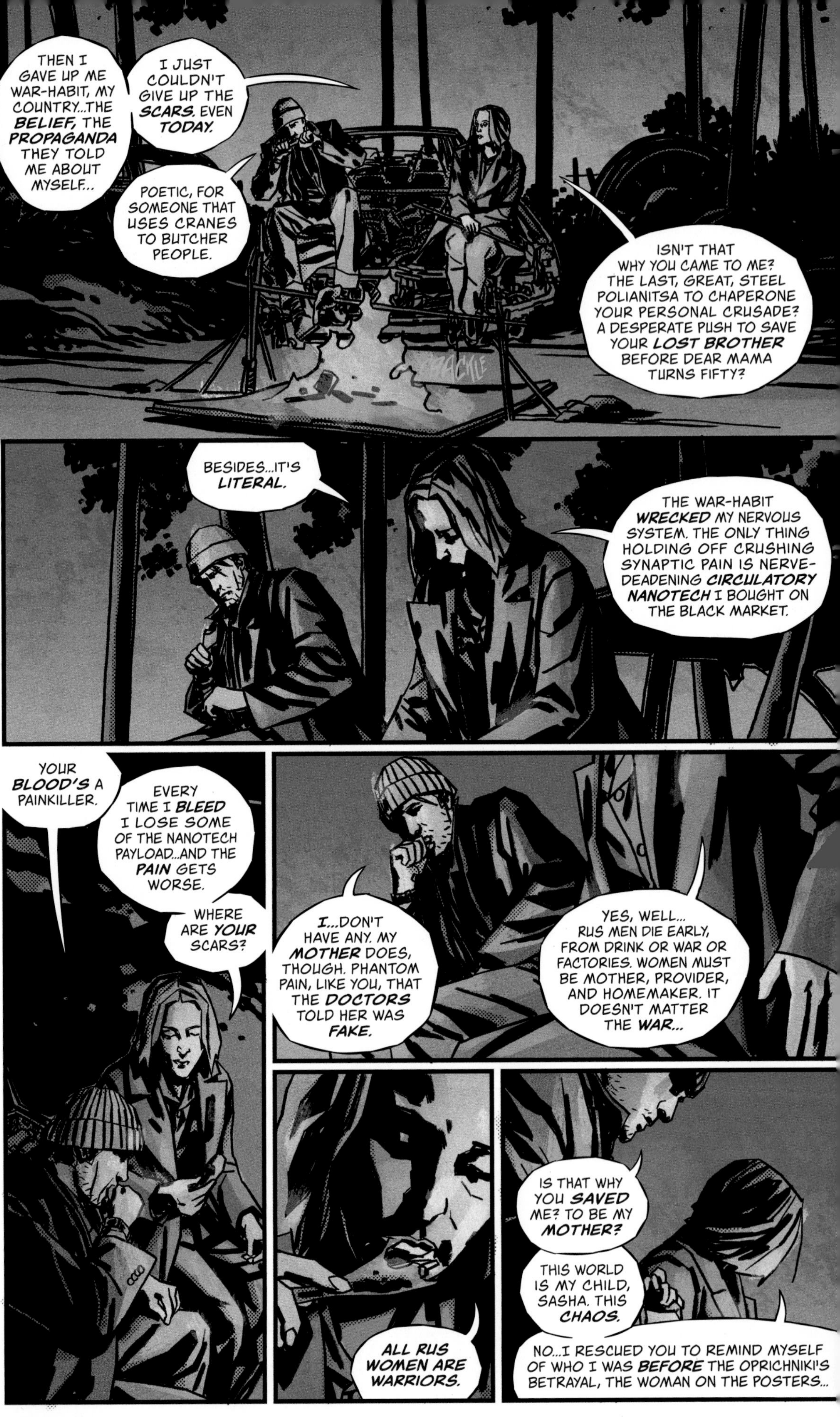
THEN I GAVE UP ME WAR-HABIT, MY COUNTRY...THE BELIEF, THE PROPAGANDA THEY TOLD ME ABOUT MYSELF...
I JUST COULDN'T GIVE UP THE SCARS. EVEN TODAY.
POETIC, FOR SOMEONE THAT USES CRANES TO BUTCHER PEOPLE.
ISN'T THAT WHY YOU CAME TO ME? THE LAST, GREAT, STEEL POLIANITSA TO CHAPERONE YOUR PERSONAL CRUSADE? A DESPERATE PUSH TO SAVE YOUR LOST BROTHER BEFORE DEAR MAMA TURNS FIFTY?
CRACKLE
BESIDES...IT'S LITERAL.
THE WAR-HABIT WRECKED MY NERVOUS SYSTEM. THE ONLY THING HOLDING OFF CRUSHING SYNAPTIC PAIN IS NERVE-DEADENING CIRCULATORY NANOTECH I BOUGHT ON THE BLACK MARKET.
YOUR BLOOD'S A PAINKILLER.
EVERY TIME I BLEED I LOSE SOME OF THE NANOTECH PAYLOAD...AND THE PAIN GETS WORSE.
WHERE ARE YOUR SCARS?
I...DON'T HAVE ANY. MY MOTHER DOES, THOUGH. PHANTOM PAIN, LIKE YOU, THAT THE DOCTORS TOLD HER WAS FAKE.
YES, WELL... RUS MEN DIE EARLY, FROM DRINK OR WAR OR FACTORIES. WOMEN MUST BE MOTHER, PROVIDER, AND HOMEMAKER. IT DOESN'T MATTER THE WAR...
ALL RUS WOMEN ARE WARRIORS.
IS THAT WHY YOU SAVED ME? TO BE MY MOTHER?
THIS WORLD IS MY CHILD, SASHA. THIS CHAOS.
NO...I RESCUED YOU TO REMIND MYSELF OF WHO I WAS BEFORE THE OPRICHNIKI'S BETRAYAL, THE WOMAN ON THE POSTERS...

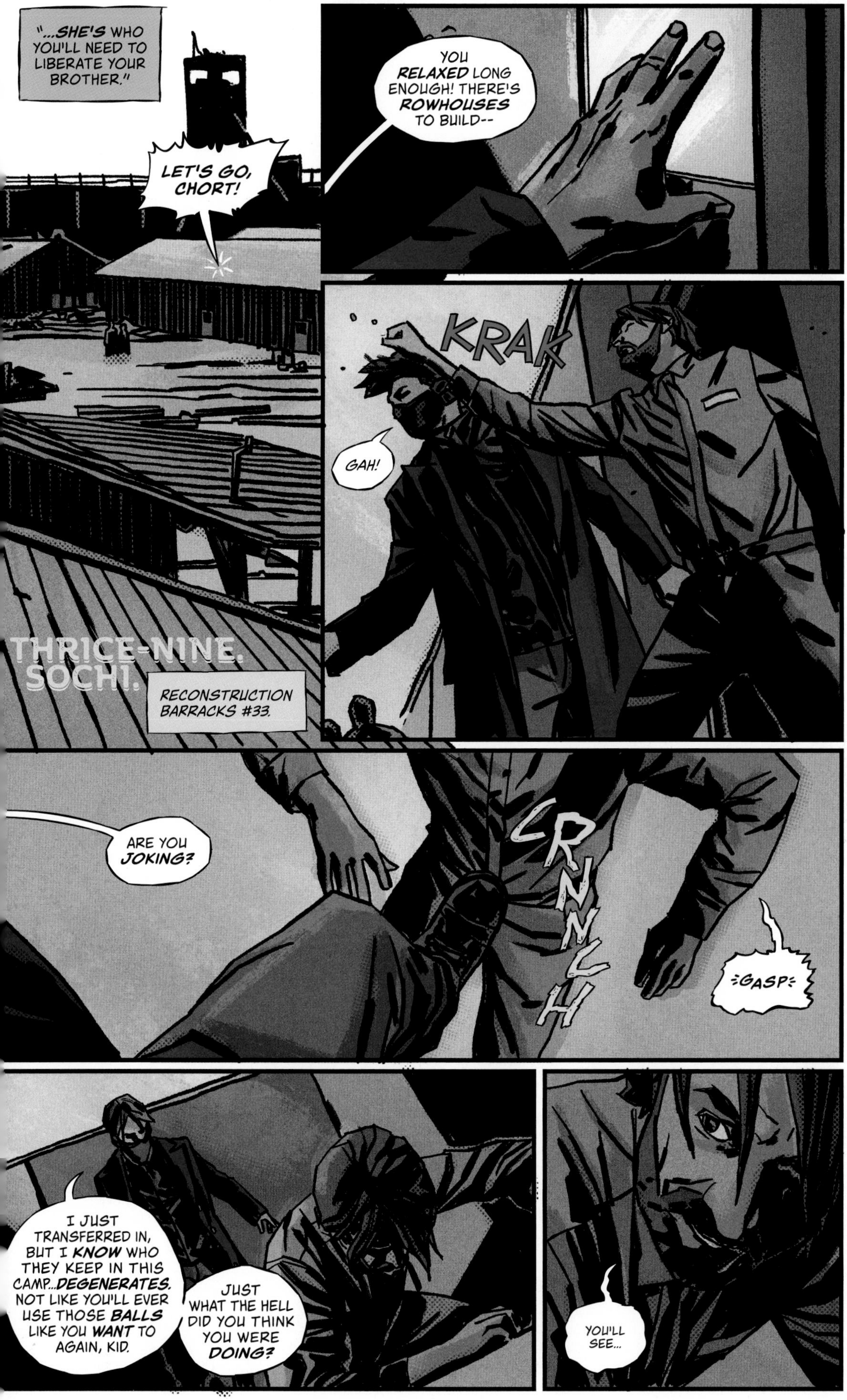
"...SHE'S WHO YOU'LL NEED TO LIBERATE YOUR BROTHER."
LET'S GO, CHORT!
THRICE-NINE. SOCHI.
RECONSTRUCTION BARRACKS #33.
YOU RELAXED LONG ENOUGH! THERE'S ROWHOUSES TO BUILD--
KRAK
GAH!
ARE YOU JOKING?
CRNNUH
GASP
I JUST TRANSFERRED IN, BUT I KNOW WHO THEY KEEP IN THIS CAMP...DEGENERATES. NOT LIKE YOU'LL EVER USE THOSE BALLS LIKE YOU WANT TO AGAIN, KID.
JUST WHAT THE HELL DID YOU THINK YOU WERE DOING?
YOU'LL SEE...

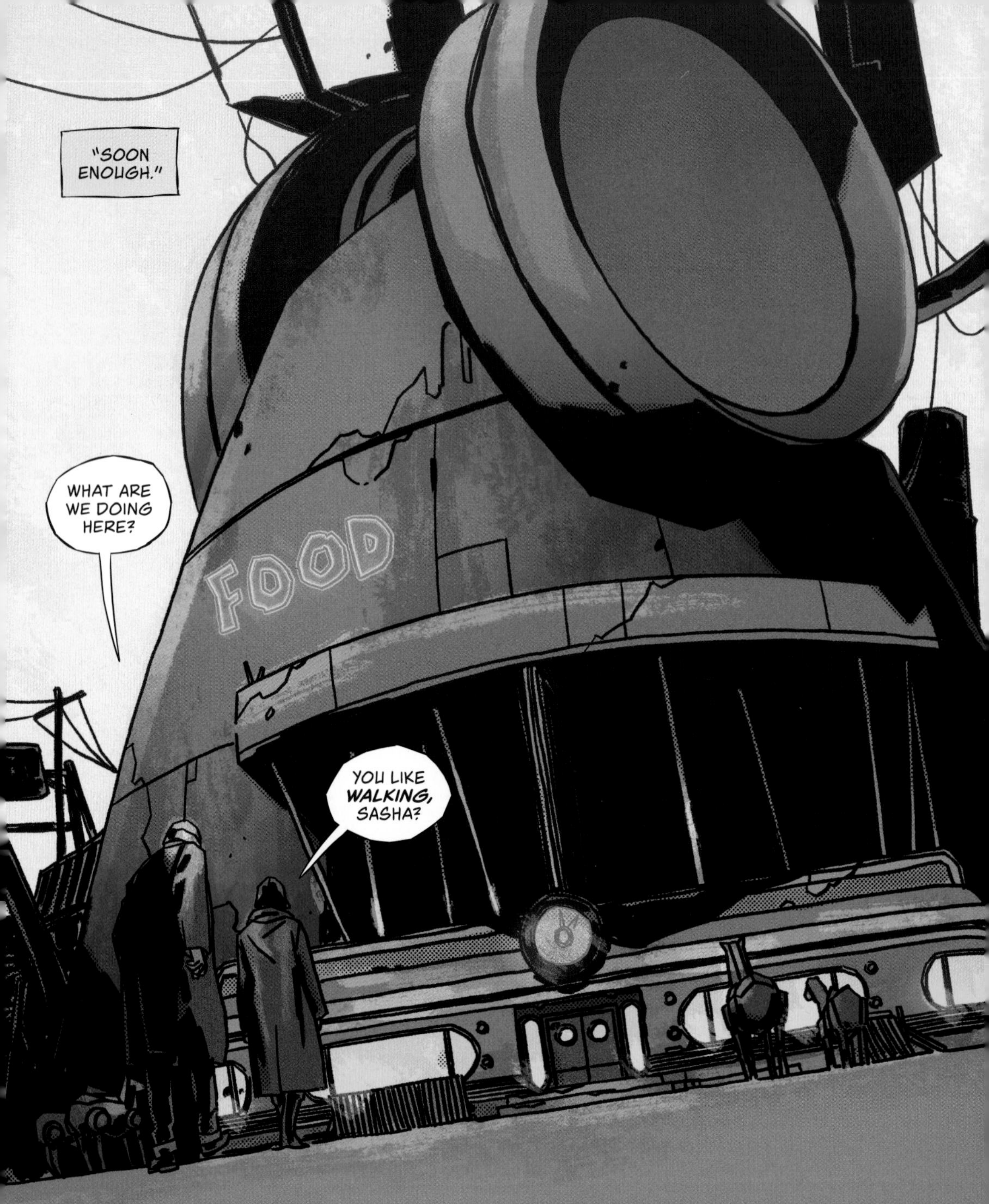
"SOON ENOUGH."
WHAT ARE WE DOING HERE?
FOOD
YOU LIKE **WALKING,** SASHA?

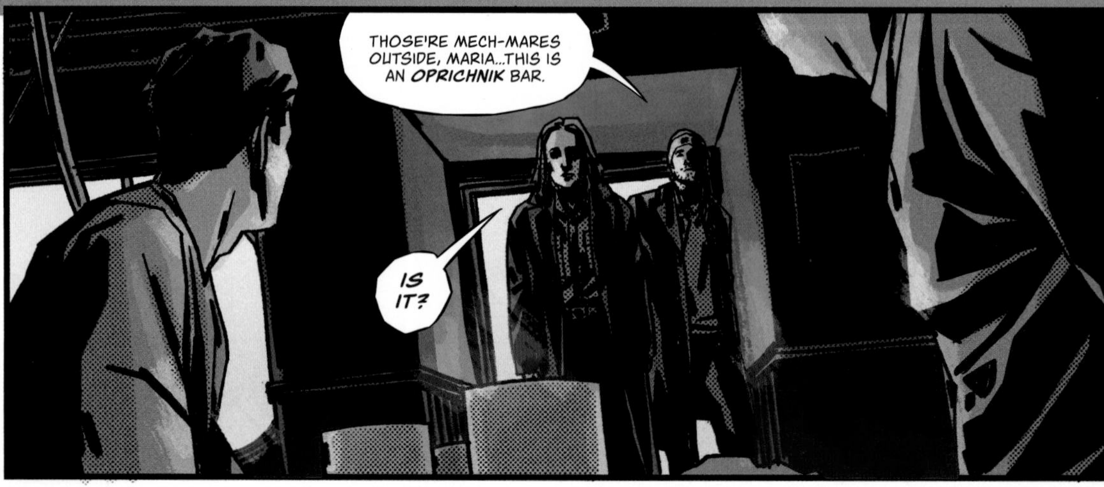
THOSE'RE MECH-MARES OUTSIDE, MARIA...THIS IS AN ***OPRICHNIK*** BAR.
IS IT?

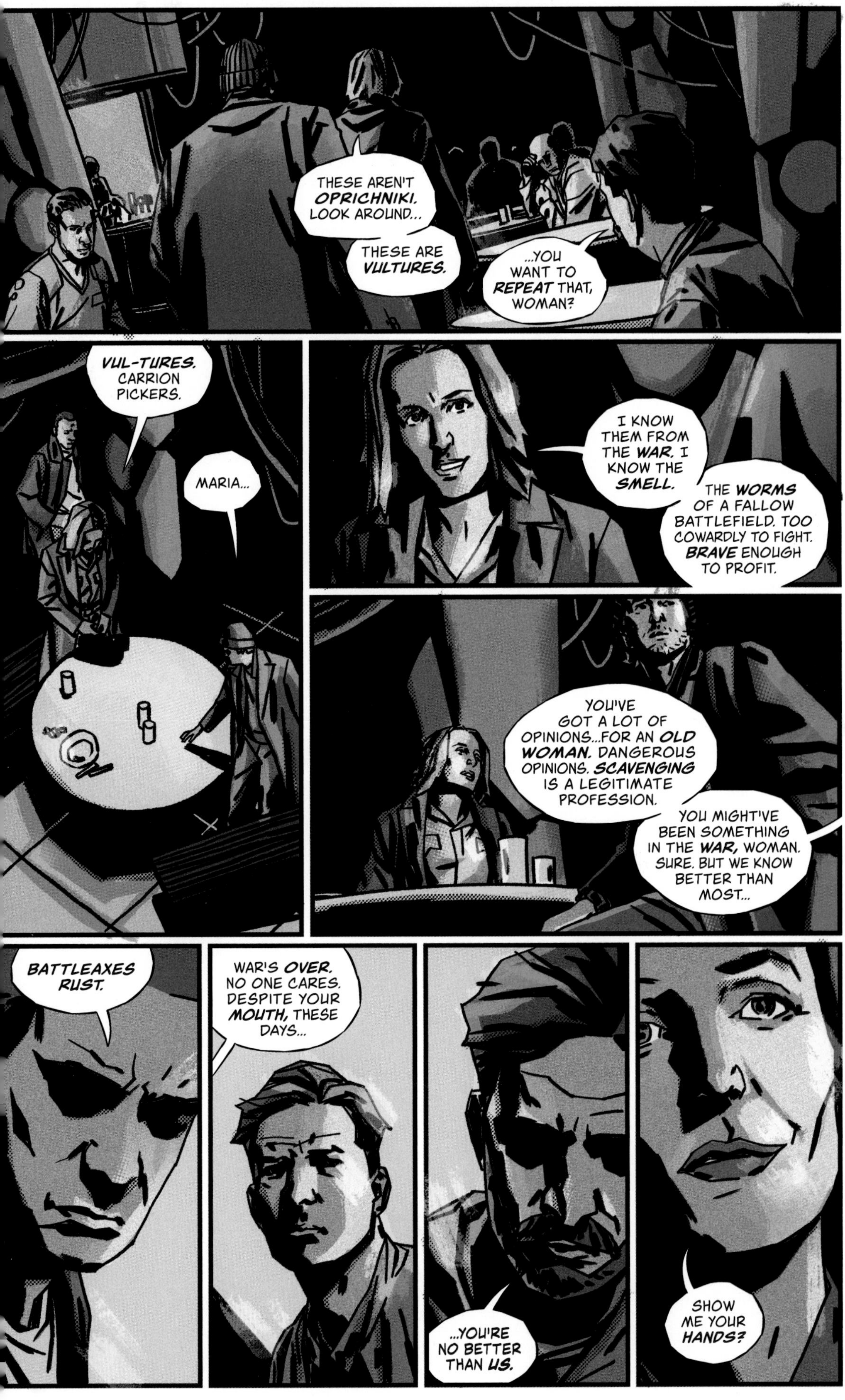

THESE AREN'T OPRICHNIKI. LOOK AROUND...
THESE ARE VULTURES.
...YOU WANT TO REPEAT THAT, WOMAN?
VUL-TURES. CARRION PICKERS.
MARIA...
I KNOW THEM FROM THE WAR. I KNOW THE SMELL.
THE WORMS OF A FALLOW BATTLEFIELD. TOO COWARDLY TO FIGHT. BRAVE ENOUGH TO PROFIT.
YOU'VE GOT A LOT OF OPINIONS...FOR AN OLD WOMAN. DANGEROUS OPINIONS. SCAVENGING IS A LEGITIMATE PROFESSION.
YOU MIGHT'VE BEEN SOMETHING IN THE WAR, WOMAN. SURE. BUT WE KNOW BETTER THAN MOST...
BATTLEAXES RUST.
WAR'S OVER. NO ONE CARES. DESPITE YOUR MOUTH, THESE DAYS...
...YOU'RE NO BETTER THAN US.
SHOW ME YOUR HANDS?

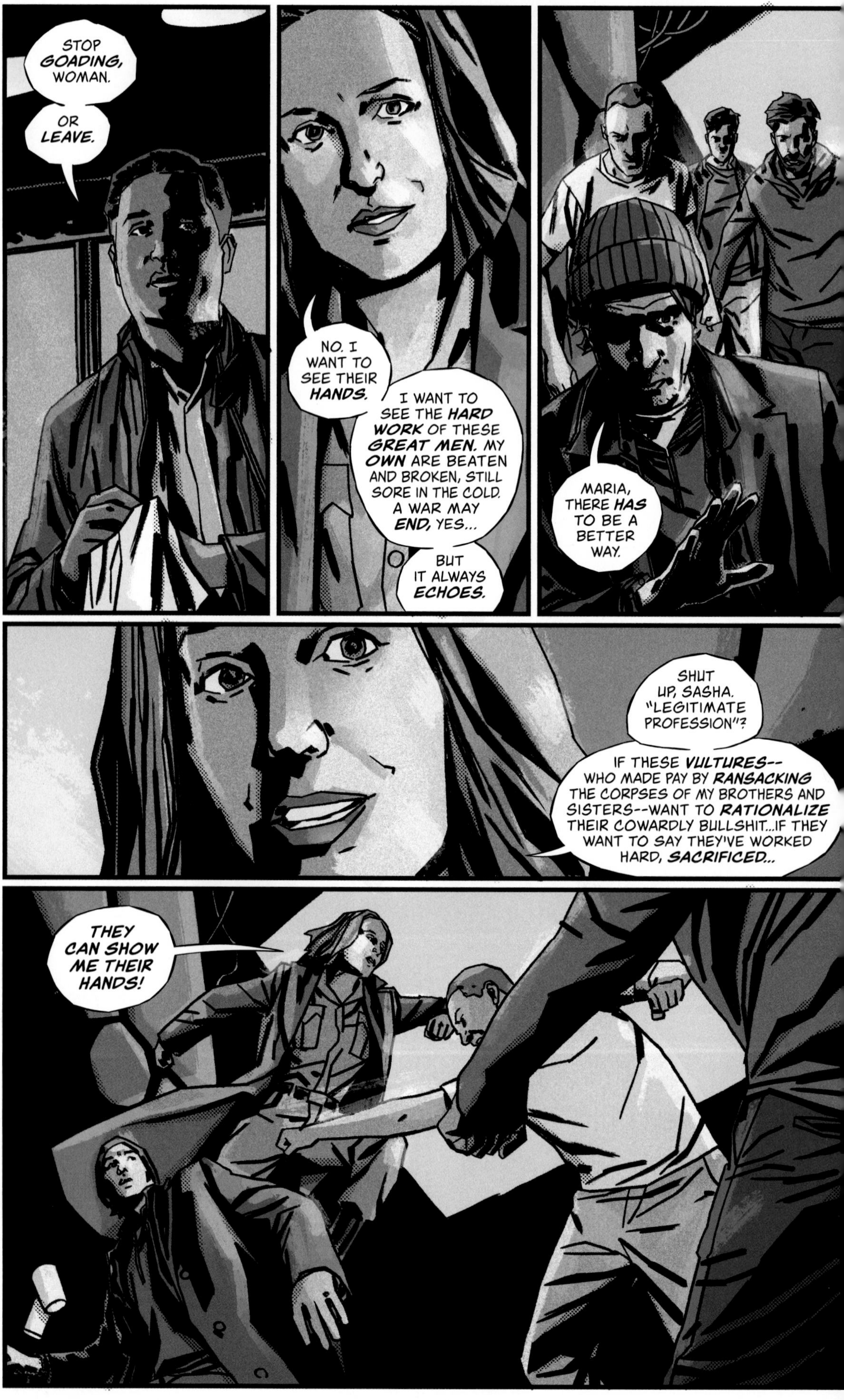

STOP GOADING, WOMAN.
OR LEAVE.
NO. I WANT TO SEE THEIR HANDS.
I WANT TO SEE THE HARD WORK OF THESE GREAT MEN. MY OWN ARE BEATEN AND BROKEN, STILL SORE IN THE COLD. A WAR MAY END, YES...
BUT IT ALWAYS ECHOES.
MARIA, THERE HAS TO BE A BETTER WAY.
SHUT UP, SASHA. "LEGITIMATE PROFESSION"?
IF THESE VULTURES-- WHO MADE PAY BY RANSACKING THE CORPSES OF MY BROTHERS AND SISTERS--WANT TO RATIONALIZE THEIR COWARDLY BULLSHIT...IF THEY WANT TO SAY THEY'VE WORKED HARD, SACRIFICED...
THEY CAN SHOW ME THEIR HANDS!

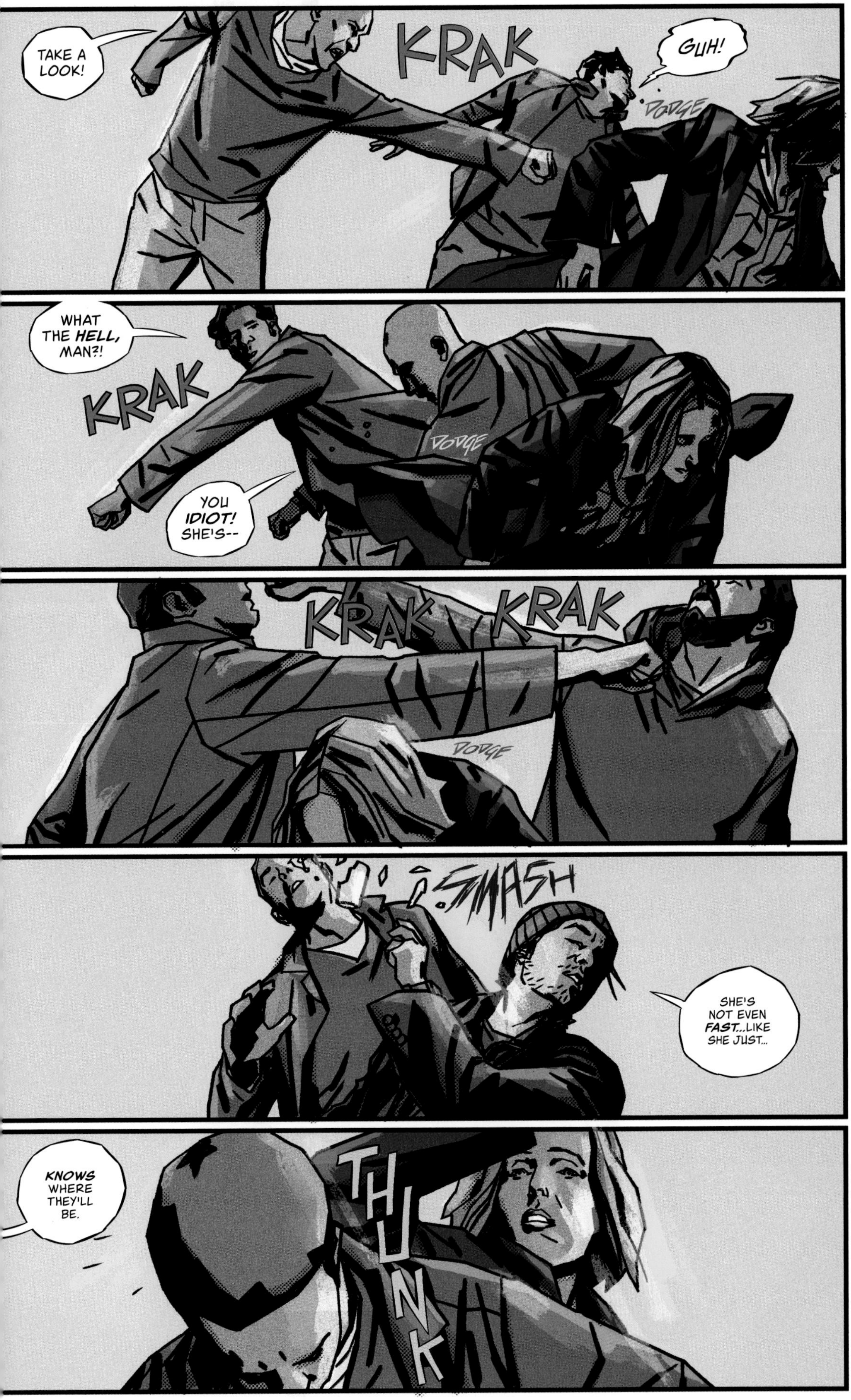
TAKE A LOOK!
KRAK
GUH!
DODGE
WHAT THE HELL, MAN?!
KRAK
DODGE
YOU IDIOT! SHE'S--
KRAK
KRAK
DODGE
SMASH
SHE'S NOT EVEN FAST...LIKE SHE JUST...
KNOWS WHERE THEY'LL BE.
THUNK

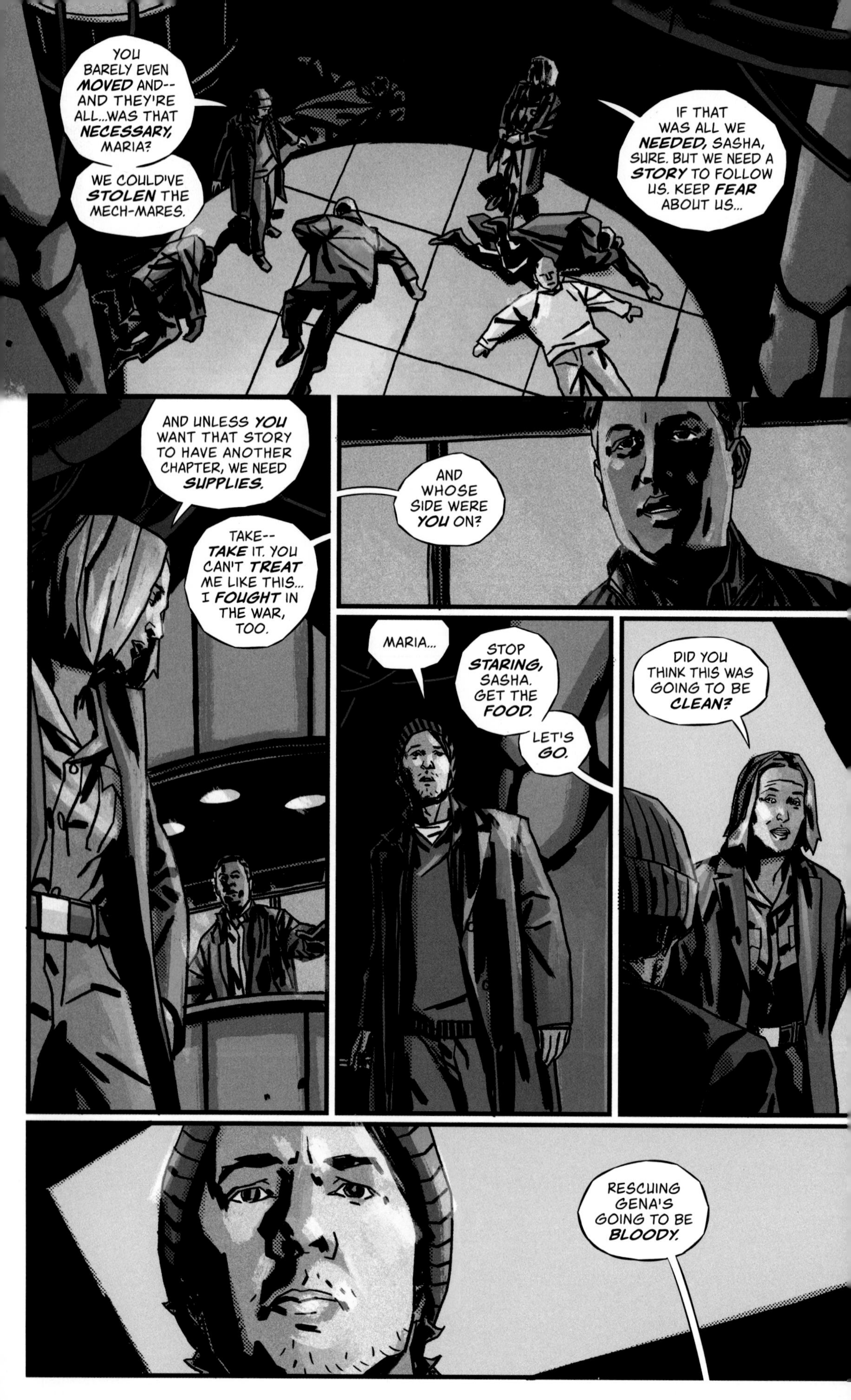
YOU BARELY EVEN MOVED AND-- AND THEY'RE ALL...WAS THAT NECESSARY, MARIA?
WE COULD'VE STOLEN THE MECH-MARES.
IF THAT WAS ALL WE NEEDED, SASHA, SURE. BUT WE NEED A STORY TO FOLLOW US. KEEP FEAR ABOUT US...
AND UNLESS YOU WANT THAT STORY TO HAVE ANOTHER CHAPTER, WE NEED SUPPLIES.
TAKE-- TAKE IT. YOU CAN'T TREAT ME LIKE THIS... I FOUGHT IN THE WAR, TOO.
AND WHOSE SIDE WERE YOU ON?
MARIA...
STOP STARING, SASHA. GET THE FOOD.
LET'S GO.
DID YOU THINK THIS WAS GOING TO BE CLEAN?
RESCUING GENA'S GOING TO BE BLOODY.

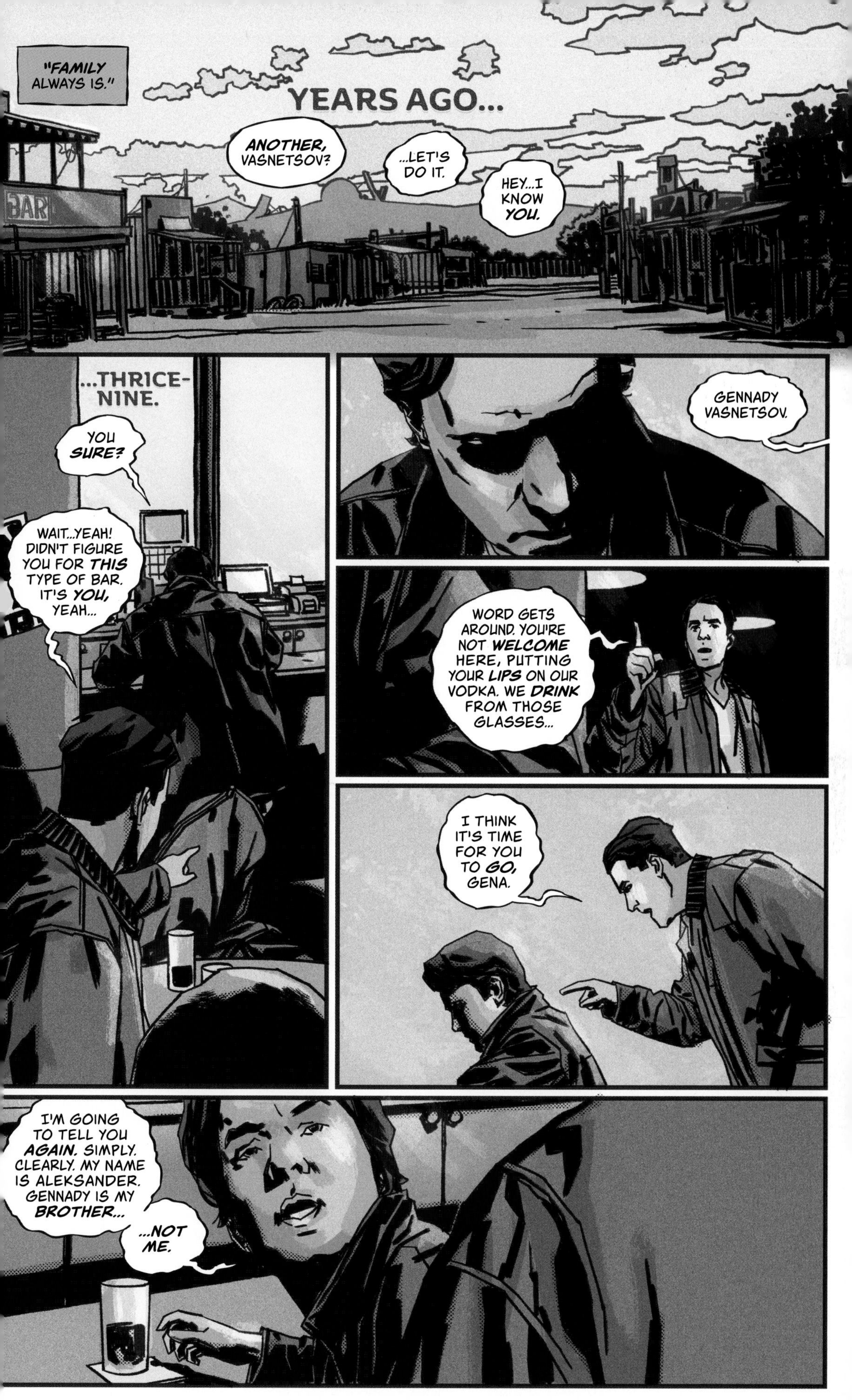
"FAMILY ALWAYS IS."
YEARS AGO...
BAR
ANOTHER, VASNETSOV?
...LET'S DO IT.
HEY...I KNOW YOU.
...THRICE-NINE.
YOU SURE?
WAIT...YEAH! DIDN'T FIGURE YOU FOR THIS TYPE OF BAR. IT'S YOU, YEAH...
GENNADY VASNETSOV.
WORD GETS AROUND. YOU'RE NOT WELCOME HERE, PUTTING YOUR LIPS ON OUR VODKA. WE DRINK FROM THOSE GLASSES...
I THINK IT'S TIME FOR YOU TO GO, GENA.
I'M GOING TO TELL YOU AGAIN. SIMPLY. CLEARLY. MY NAME IS ALEKSANDER. GENNADY IS MY BROTHER...
...NOT ME.

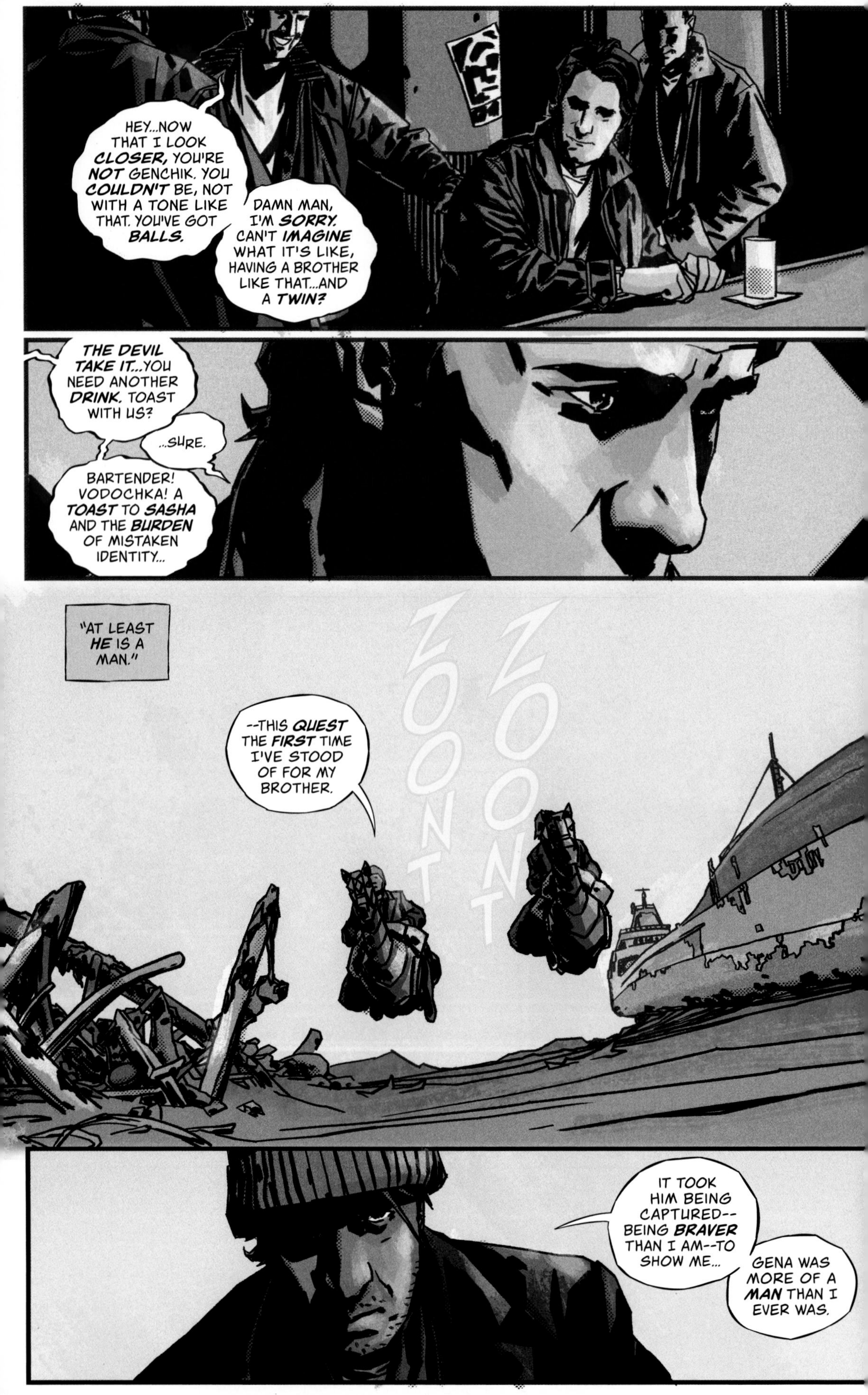
HEY...NOW THAT I LOOK CLOSER, YOU'RE NOT GENCHIK. YOU COULDN'T BE, NOT WITH A TONE LIKE THAT. YOU'VE GOT BALLS.
DAMN MAN, I'M SORRY. CAN'T IMAGINE WHAT IT'S LIKE, HAVING A BROTHER LIKE THAT...AND A TWIN?
THE DEVIL TAKE IT...YOU NEED ANOTHER DRINK. TOAST WITH US?
...SURE.
BARTENDER! VODOCHKA! A TOAST TO SASHA AND THE BURDEN OF MISTAKEN IDENTITY...
"AT LEAST HE IS A MAN."
ZOONT
ZOONT
--THIS QUEST THE FIRST TIME I'VE STOOD OF FOR MY BROTHER.
IT TOOK HIM BEING CAPTURED-- BEING BRAVER THAN I AM--TO SHOW ME...
GENA WAS MORE OF A MAN THAN I EVER WAS.

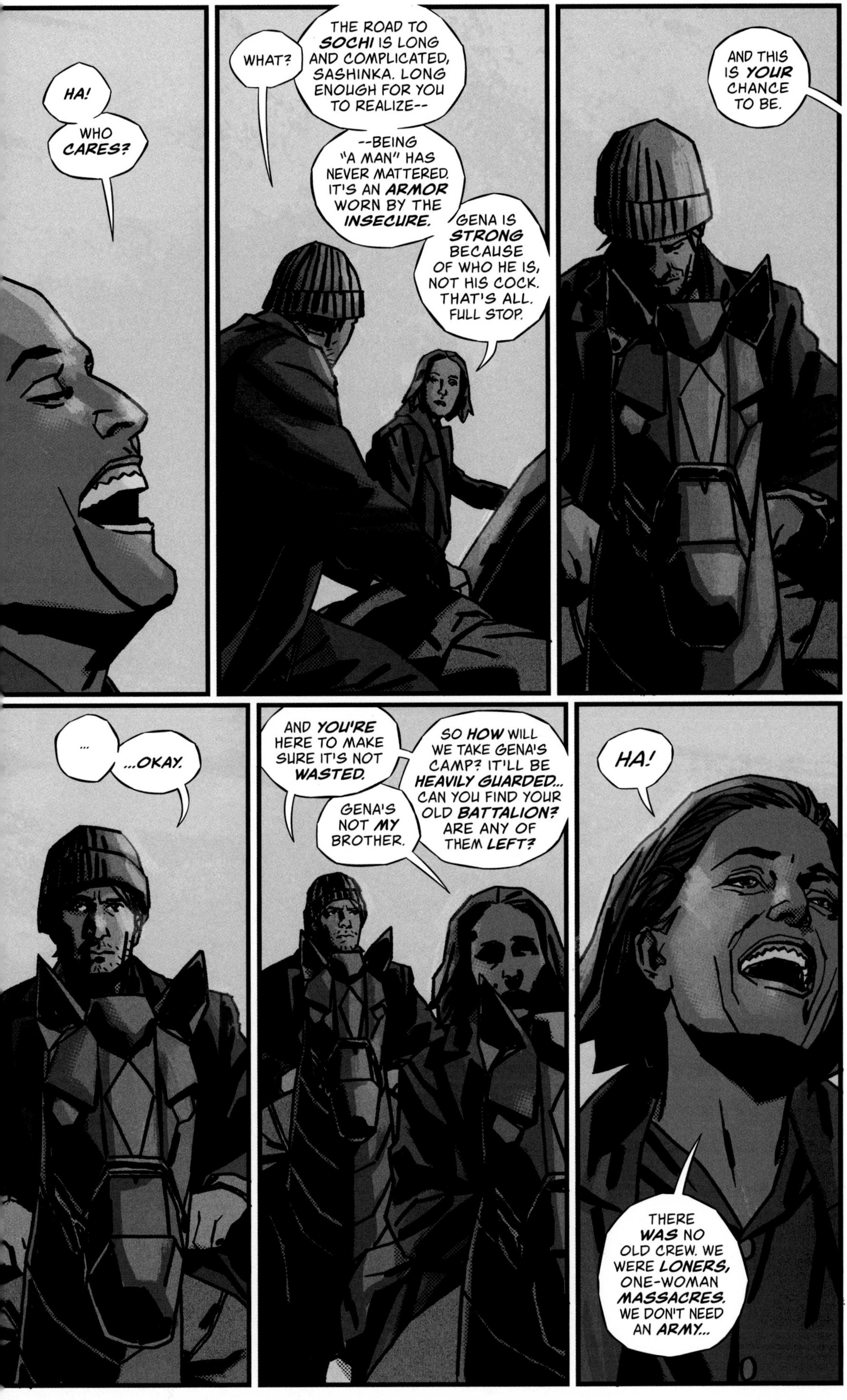
HA!
WHO CARES?
WHAT?
THE ROAD TO SOCHI IS LONG AND COMPLICATED, SASHINKA. LONG ENOUGH FOR YOU TO REALIZE--
--BEING "A MAN" HAS NEVER MATTERED. IT'S AN ARMOR WORN BY THE INSECURE.
GENA IS STRONG BECAUSE OF WHO HE IS, NOT HIS COCK. THAT'S ALL. FULL STOP.
AND THIS IS YOUR CHANCE TO BE.
...
...OKAY.
AND YOU'RE HERE TO MAKE SURE IT'S NOT WASTED.
SO HOW WILL WE TAKE GENA'S CAMP? IT'LL BE HEAVILY GUARDED... CAN YOU FIND YOUR OLD BATTALION? ARE ANY OF THEM LEFT?
GENA'S NOT MY BROTHER.
HA!
THERE WAS NO OLD CREW. WE WERE LONERS, ONE-WOMAN MASSACRES. WE DON'T NEED AN ARMY...

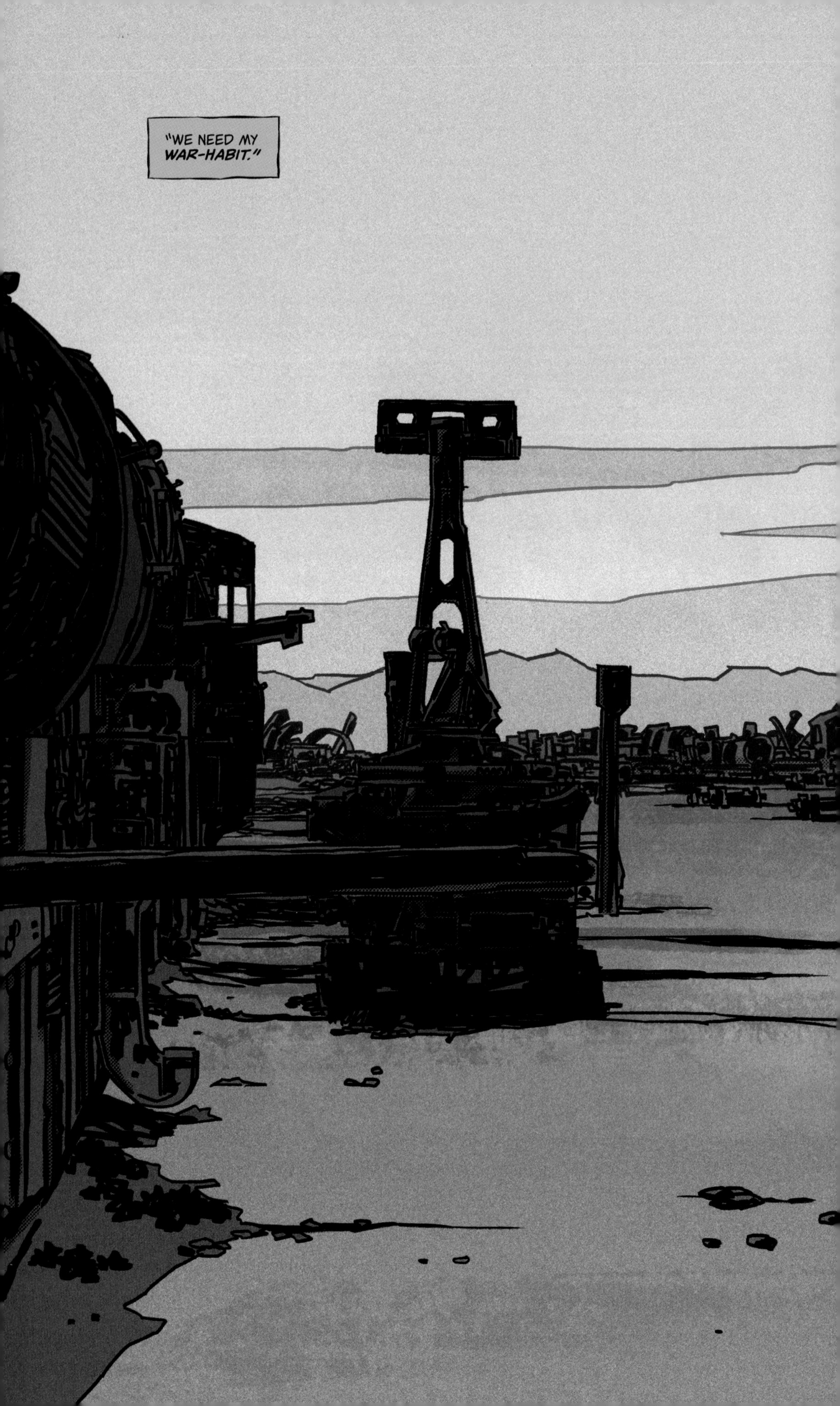
"WE NEED MY WAR-HABIT."

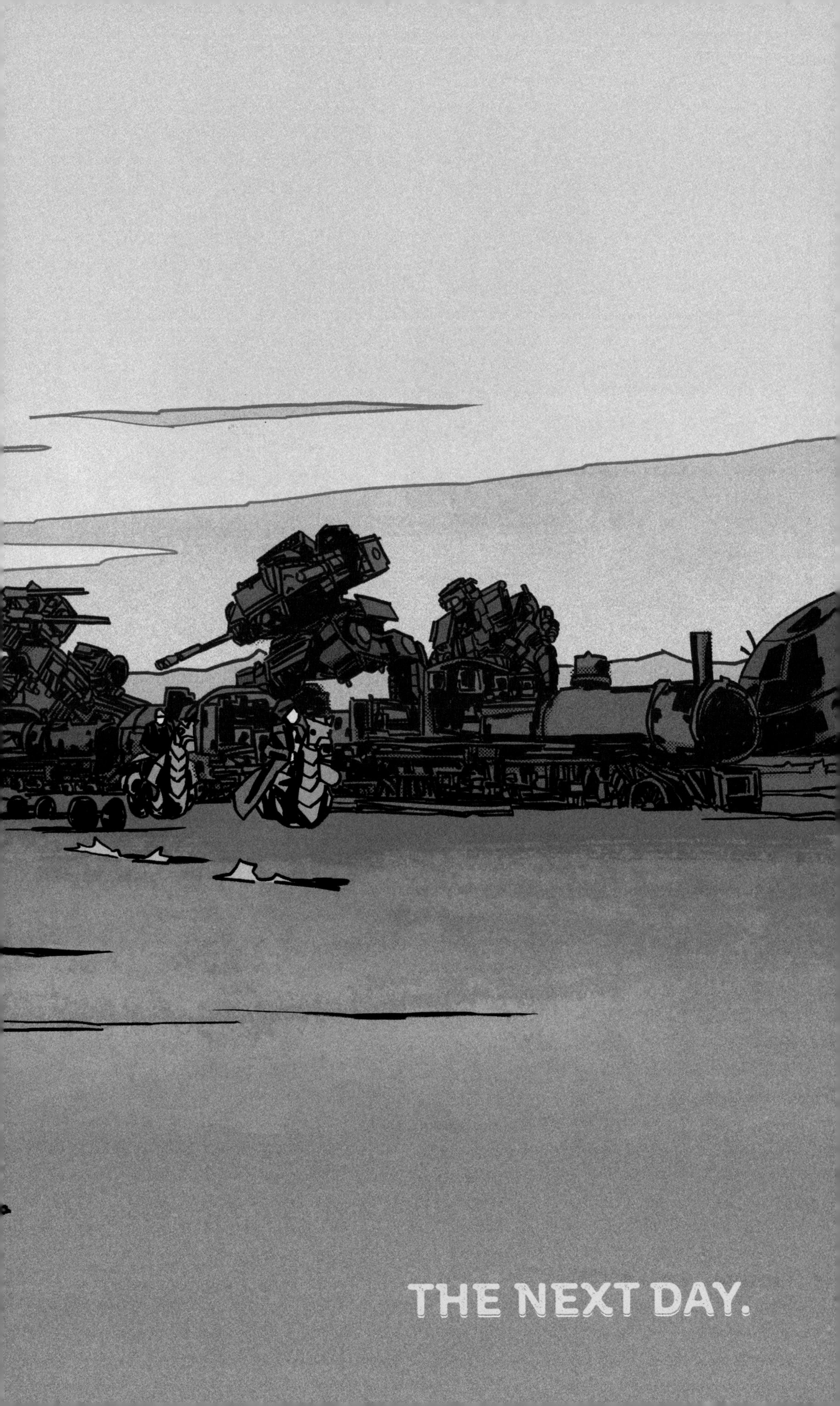
THE NEXT DAY.

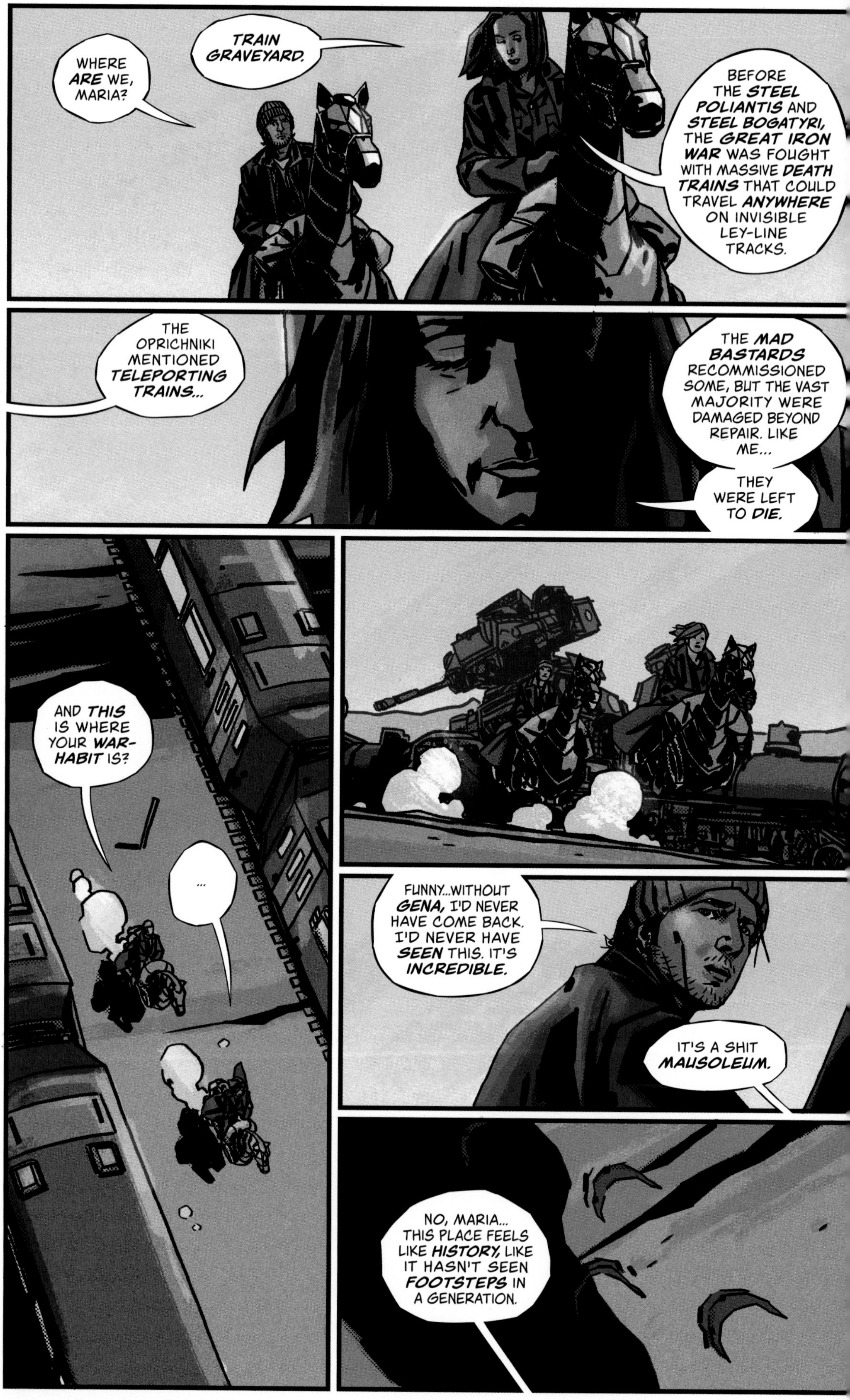

WHERE ARE WE, MARIA?
TRAIN GRAVEYARD.
BEFORE THE STEEL POLIANTIS AND STEEL BOGATYRI, THE GREAT IRON WAR WAS FOUGHT WITH MASSIVE DEATH TRAINS THAT COULD TRAVEL ANYWHERE ON INVISIBLE LEY-LINE TRACKS.
THE OPRICHNIKI MENTIONED TELEPORTING TRAINS...
THE MAD BASTARDS RECOMMISSIONED SOME, BUT THE VAST MAJORITY WERE DAMAGED BEYOND REPAIR. LIKE ME...
THEY WERE LEFT TO DIE.
AND THIS IS WHERE YOUR WAR-HABIT IS?
...
FUNNY...WITHOUT GENA, I'D NEVER HAVE COME BACK. I'D NEVER HAVE SEEN THIS. IT'S INCREDIBLE.
IT'S A SHIT MAUSOLEUM.
NO, MARIA... THIS PLACE FEELS LIKE HISTORY, LIKE IT HASN'T SEEN FOOTSTEPS IN A GENERATION.

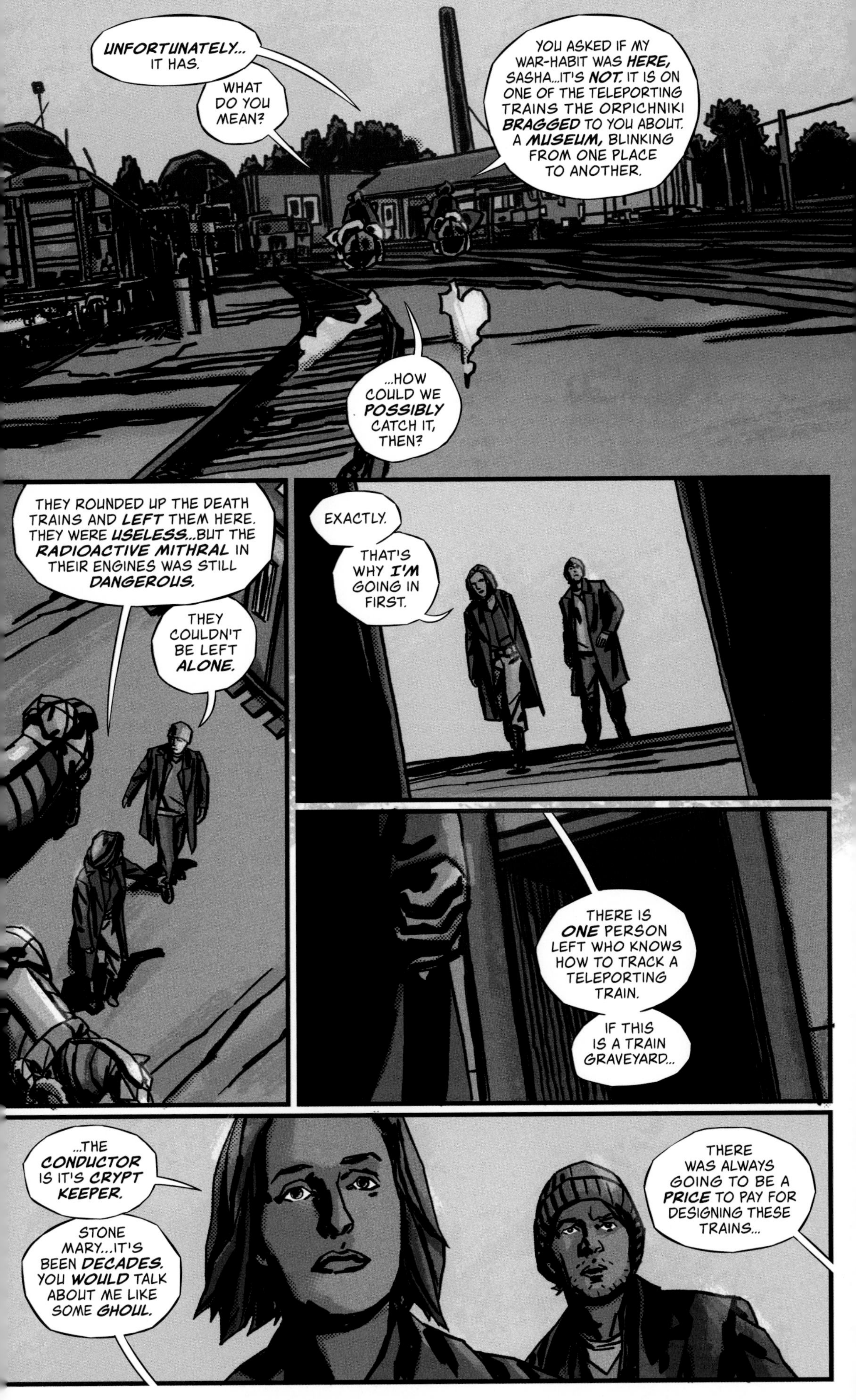
UNFORTUNATELY... IT HAS.
WHAT DO YOU MEAN?
YOU ASKED IF MY WAR-HABIT WAS HERE, SASHA...IT'S NOT. IT IS ON ONE OF THE TELEPORTING TRAINS THE ORPICHNIKI BRAGGED TO YOU ABOUT. A MUSEUM, BLINKING FROM ONE PLACE TO ANOTHER.
...HOW COULD WE POSSIBLY CATCH IT, THEN?
THEY ROUNDED UP THE DEATH TRAINS AND LEFT THEM HERE. THEY WERE USELESS...BUT THE RADIOACTIVE MITHRAL IN THEIR ENGINES WAS STILL DANGEROUS.
THEY COULDN'T BE LEFT ALONE.
EXACTLY.
THAT'S WHY I'M GOING IN FIRST.
THERE IS ONE PERSON LEFT WHO KNOWS HOW TO TRACK A TELEPORTING TRAIN.
IF THIS IS A TRAIN GRAVEYARD...
...THE CONDUCTOR IS IT'S CRYPT KEEPER.
STONE MARY...IT'S BEEN DECADES. YOU WOULD TALK ABOUT ME LIKE SOME GHOUL.
THERE WAS ALWAYS GOING TO BE A PRICE TO PAY FOR DESIGNING THESE TRAINS...

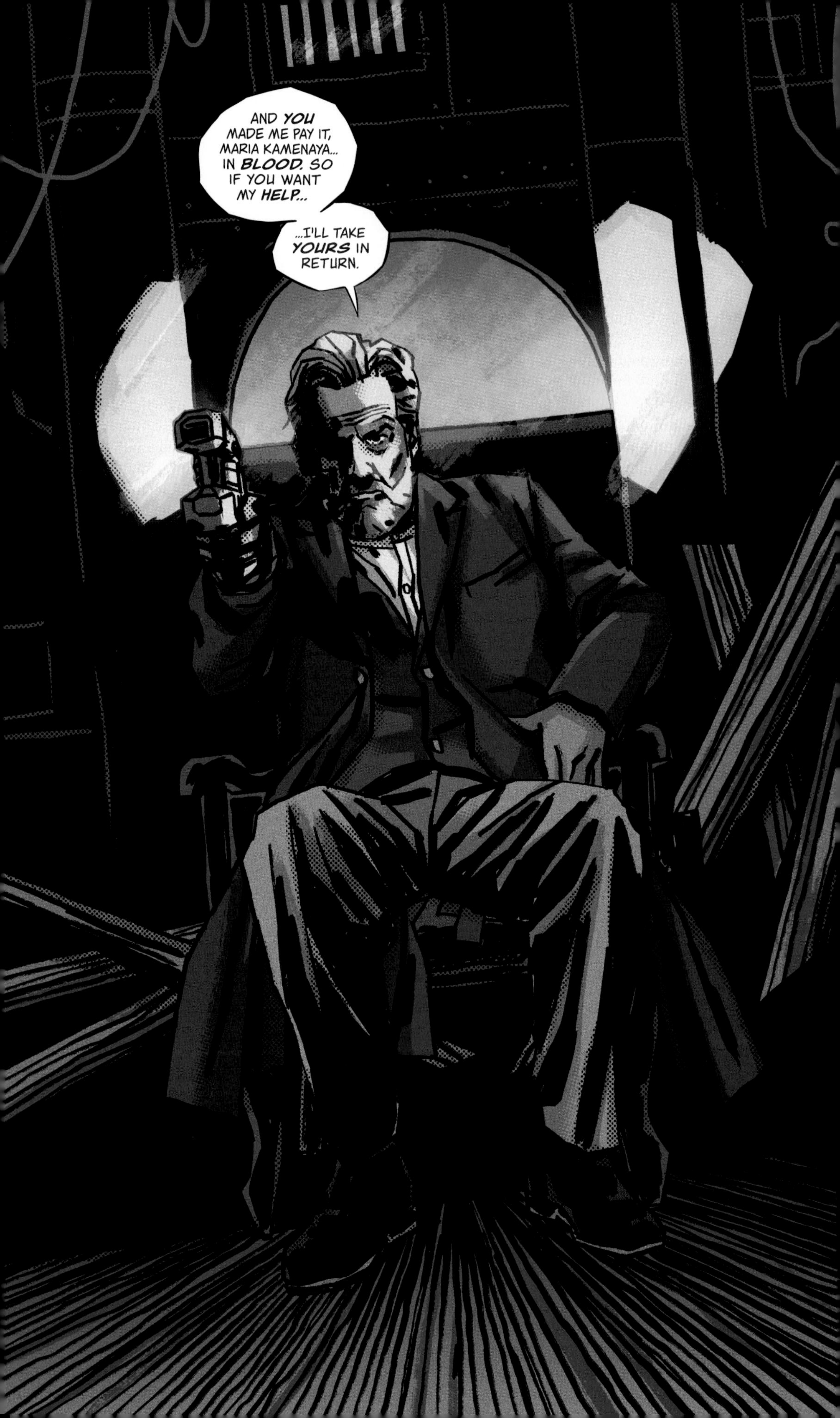
AND *YOU* MADE ME PAY IT, MARIA KAMENAYA... IN *BLOOD*. SO IF YOU WANT MY *HELP*...
...I'LL TAKE *YOURS* IN RETURN.

3

PAY IN BLOOD

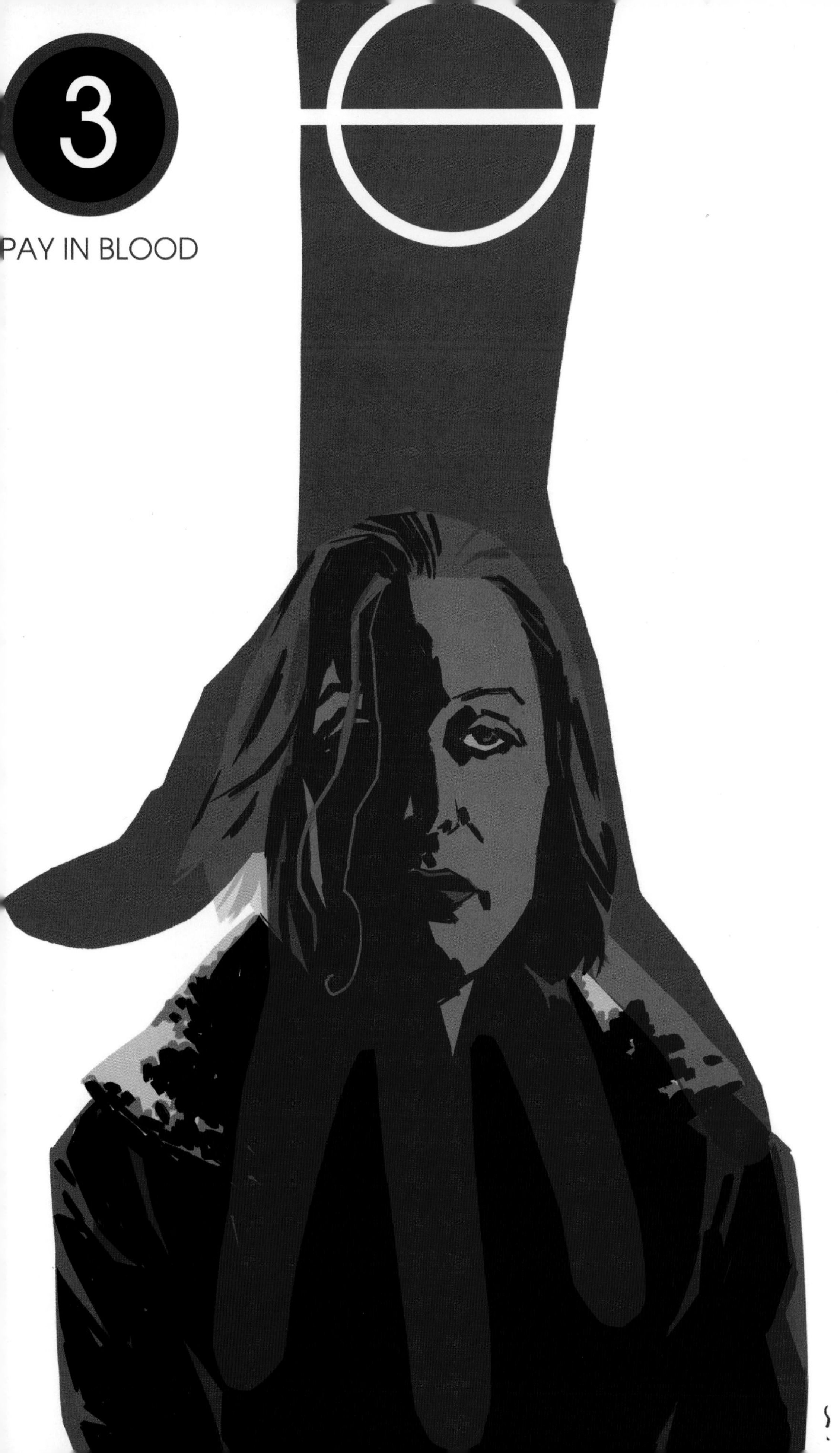

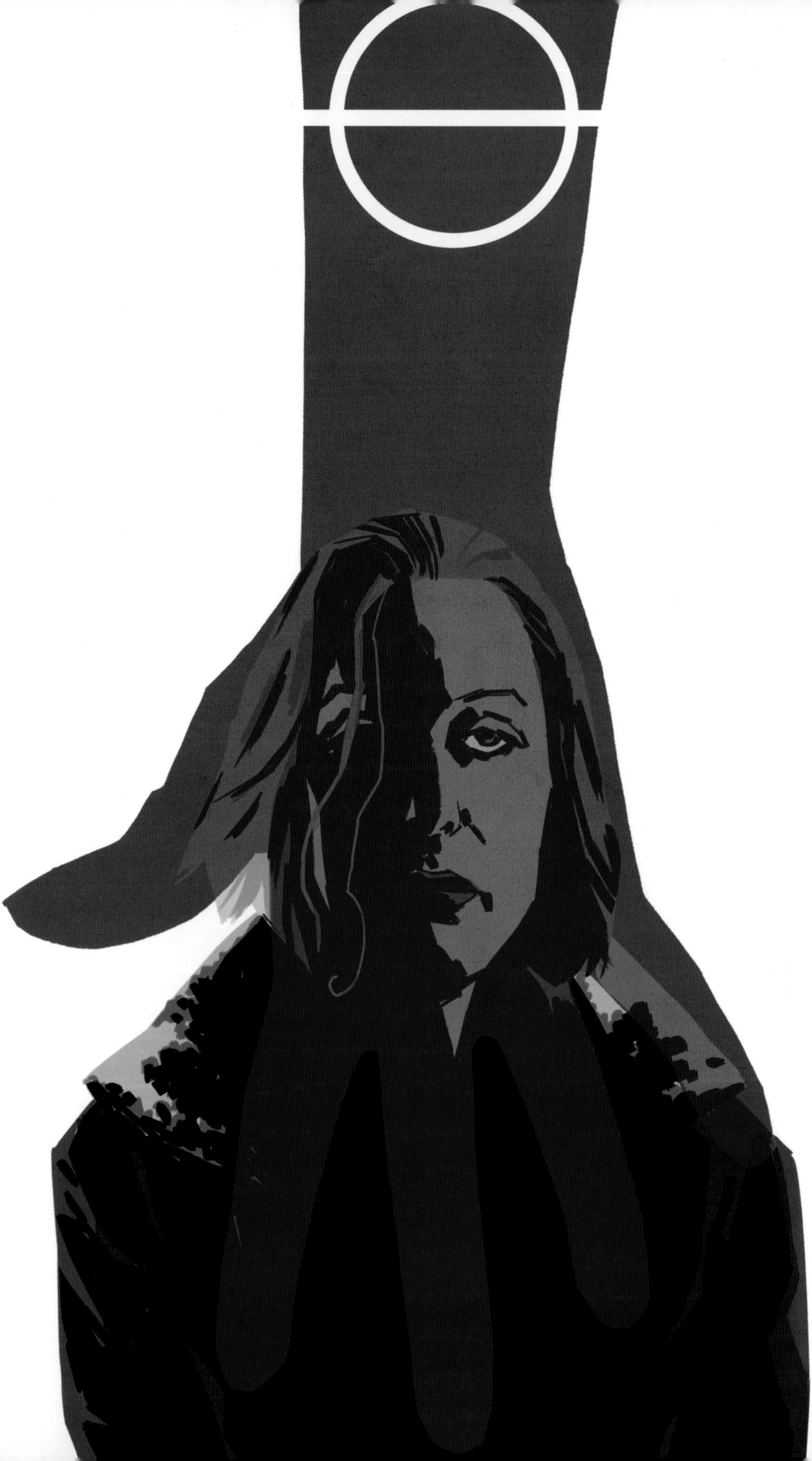

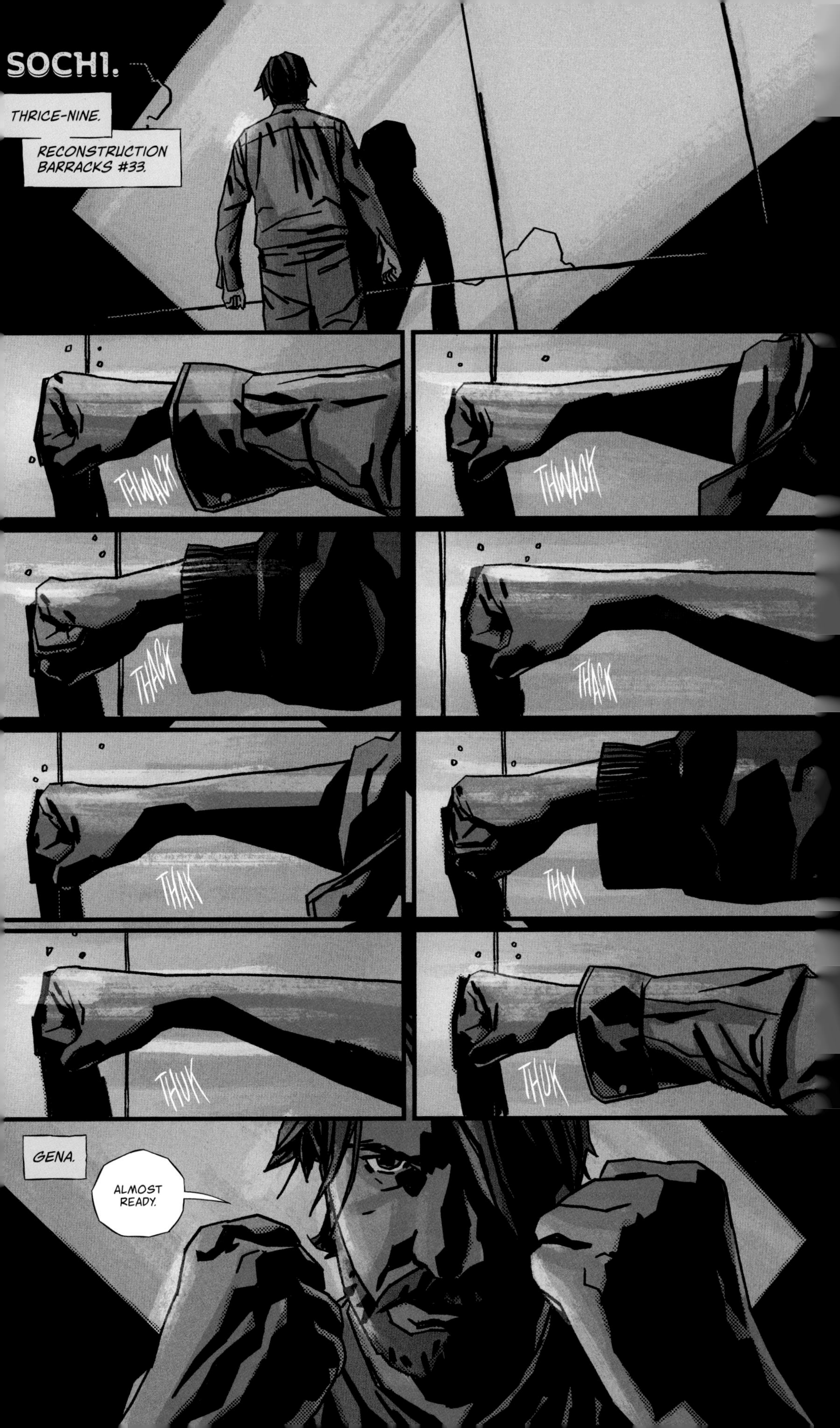
SOCHI.
THRICE-NINE.
RECONSTRUCTION BARRACKS #33.
THWACK
THWACK
THACK
THACK
THAK
THAK
THUK
THUK
GENA.
ALMOST READY.

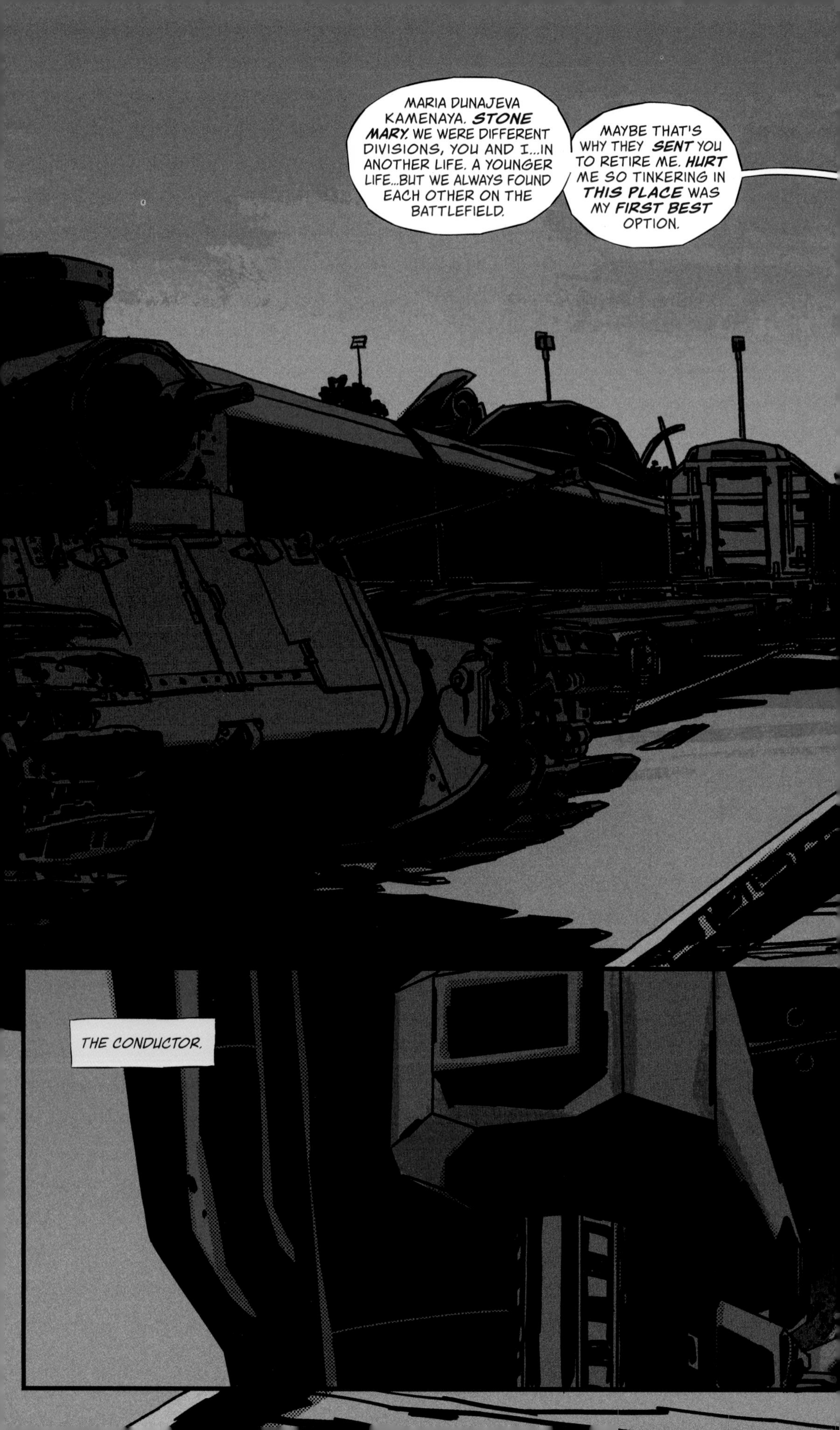
MARIA DUNAJEVA KAMENAYA. STONE MARY. WE WERE DIFFERENT DIVISIONS, YOU AND I...IN ANOTHER LIFE. A YOUNGER LIFE...BUT WE ALWAYS FOUND EACH OTHER ON THE BATTLEFIELD.
MAYBE THAT'S WHY THEY SENT YOU TO RETIRE ME. HURT ME SO TINKERING IN THIS PLACE WAS MY FIRST BEST OPTION.
THE CONDUCTOR.

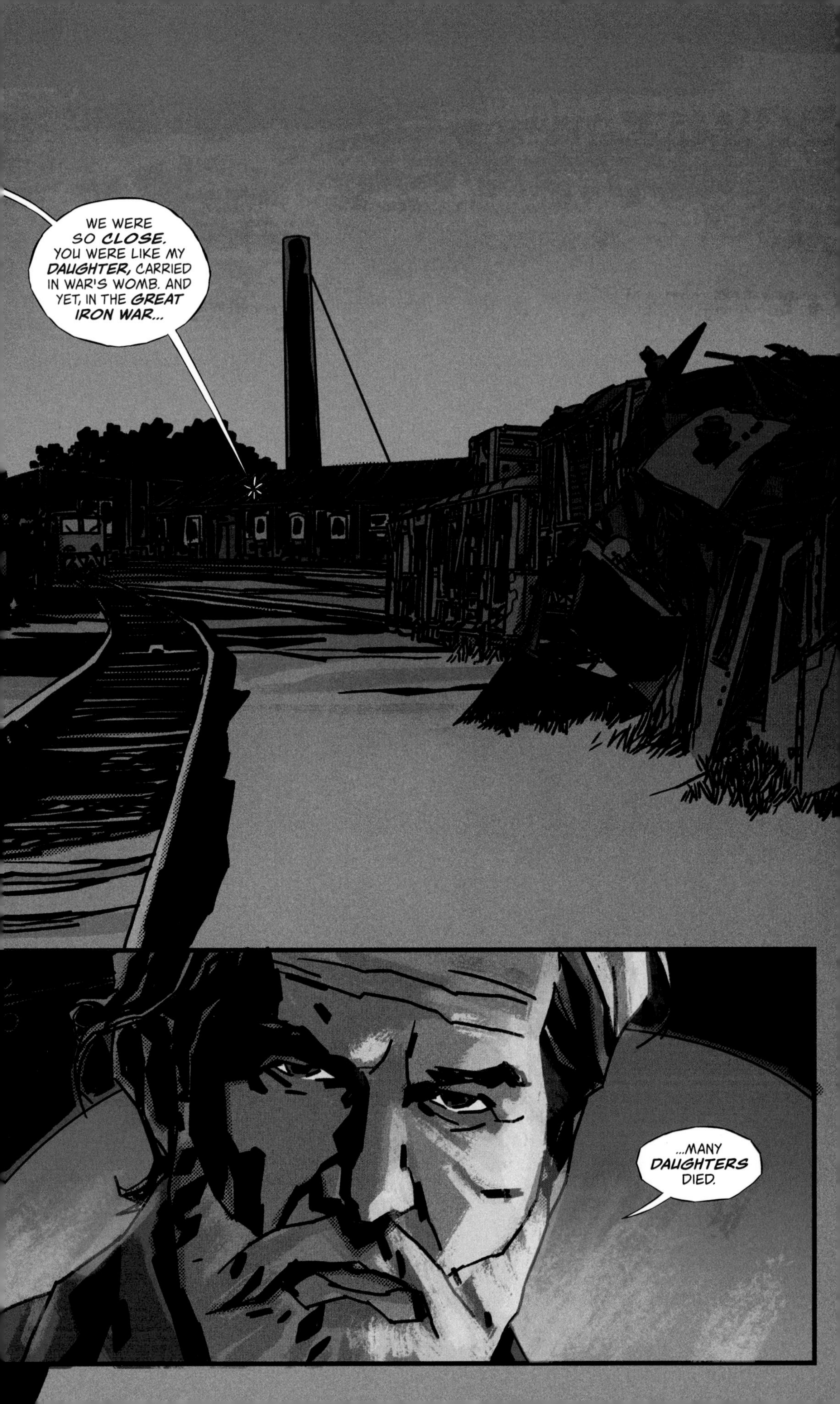
WE WERE SO CLOSE. YOU WERE LIKE MY DAUGHTER, CARRIED IN WAR'S WOMB. AND YET, IN THE GREAT IRON WAR...
...MANY DAUGHTERS DIED.

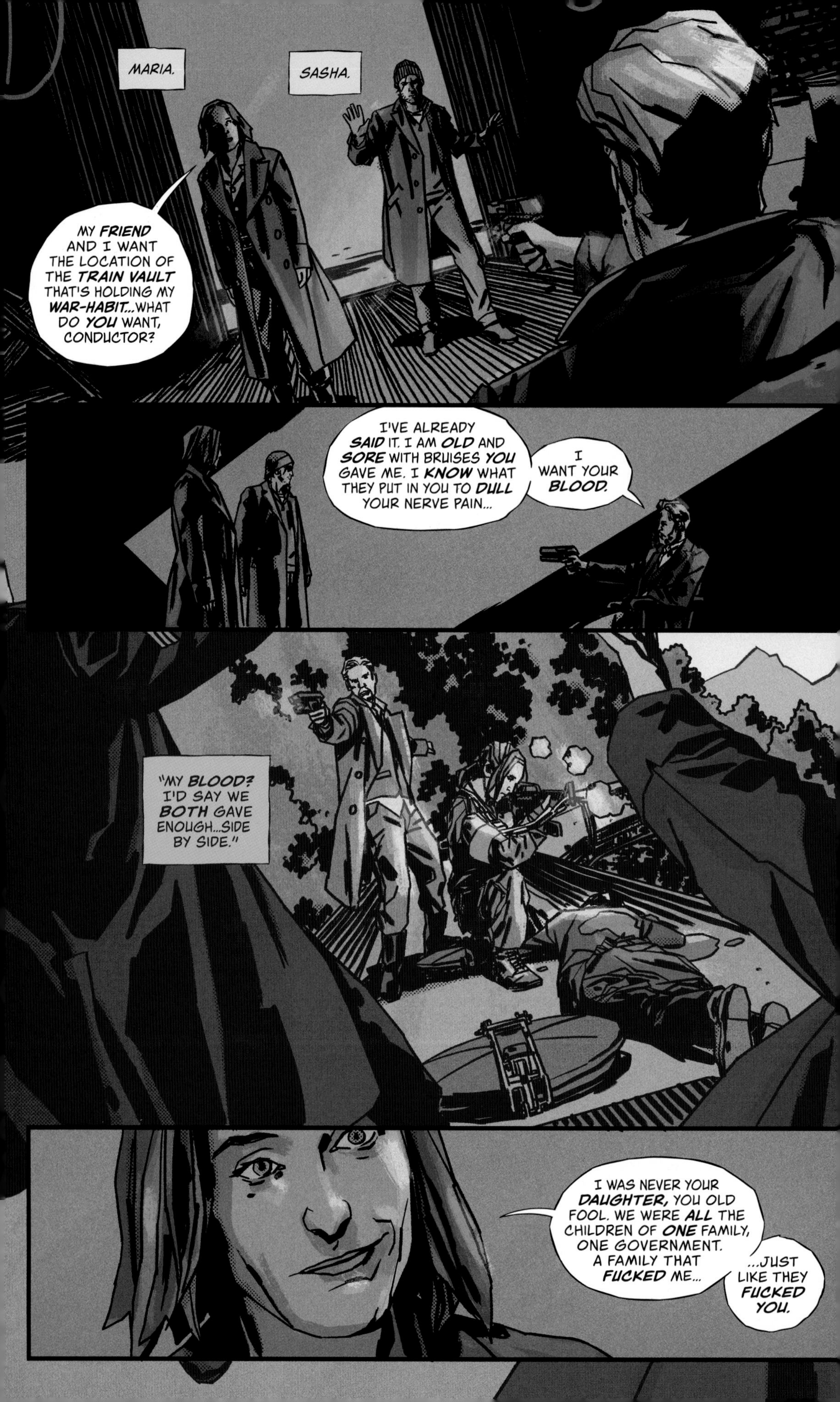

MARIA.
SASHA.
MY FRIEND AND I WANT THE LOCATION OF THE TRAIN VAULT THAT'S HOLDING MY WAR-HABIT...WHAT DO YOU WANT, CONDUCTOR?
I'VE ALREADY SAID IT. I AM OLD AND SORE WITH BRUISES YOU GAVE ME. I KNOW WHAT THEY PUT IN YOU TO DULL YOUR NERVE PAIN...
I WANT YOUR BLOOD.
"MY BLOOD? I'D SAY WE BOTH GAVE ENOUGH...SIDE BY SIDE."
I WAS NEVER YOUR DAUGHTER, YOU OLD FOOL. WE WERE ALL THE CHILDREN OF ONE FAMILY, ONE GOVERNMENT. A FAMILY THAT FUCKED ME...
...JUST LIKE THEY FUCKED YOU.

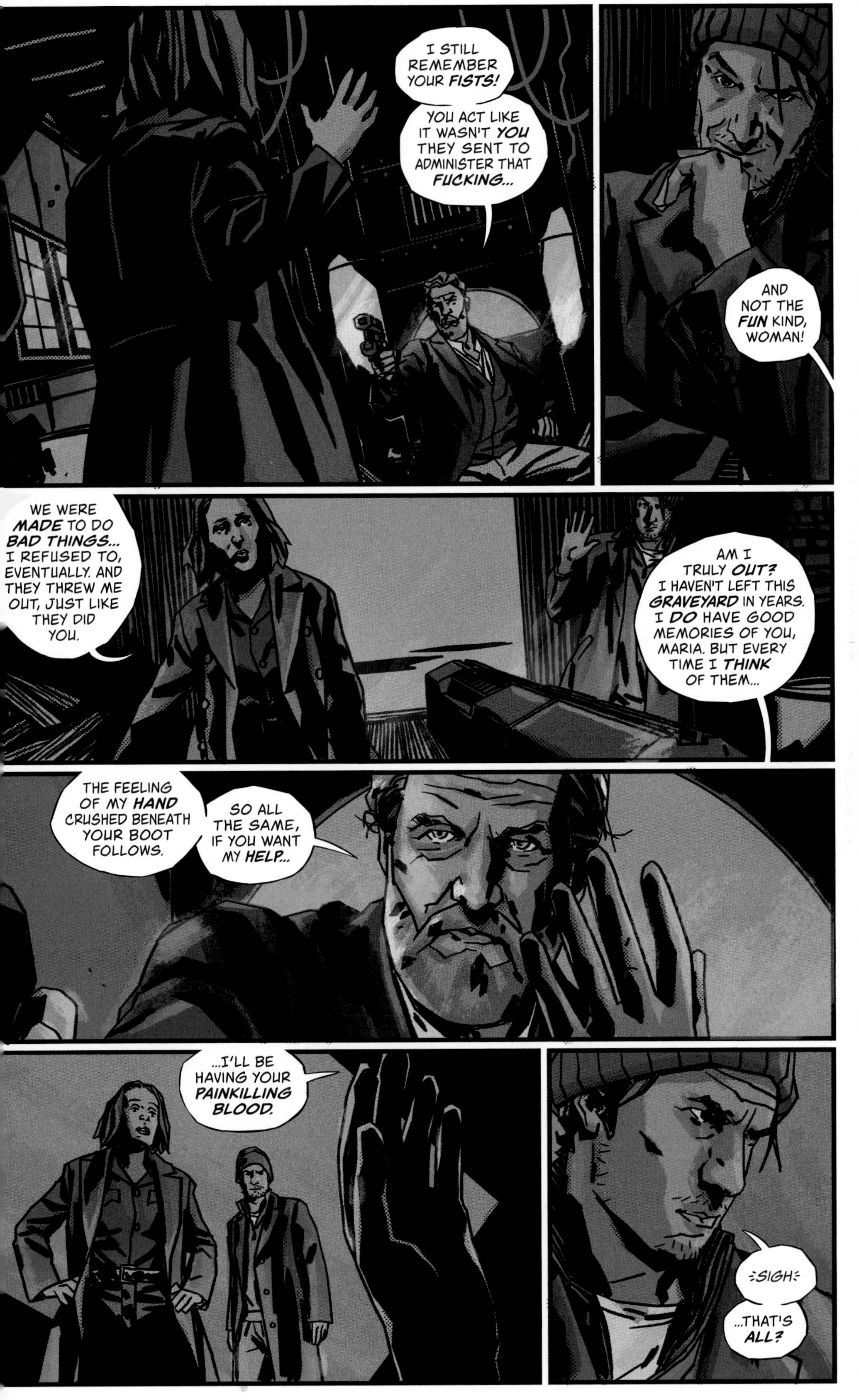
I STILL REMEMBER YOUR FISTS!
YOU ACT LIKE IT WASN'T YOU THEY SENT TO ADMINISTER THAT FUCKING...
AND NOT THE FUN KIND, WOMAN!
WE WERE MADE TO DO BAD THINGS... I REFUSED TO, EVENTUALLY. AND THEY THREW ME OUT, JUST LIKE THEY DID YOU.
AM I TRULY OUT? I HAVEN'T LEFT THIS GRAVEYARD IN YEARS. I DO HAVE GOOD MEMORIES OF YOU, MARIA. BUT EVERY TIME I THINK OF THEM...
THE FEELING OF MY HAND CRUSHED BENEATH YOUR BOOT FOLLOWS.
SO ALL THE SAME, IF YOU WANT MY HELP...
...I'LL BE HAVING YOUR PAINKILLING BLOOD.
SIGH
...THAT'S ALL?

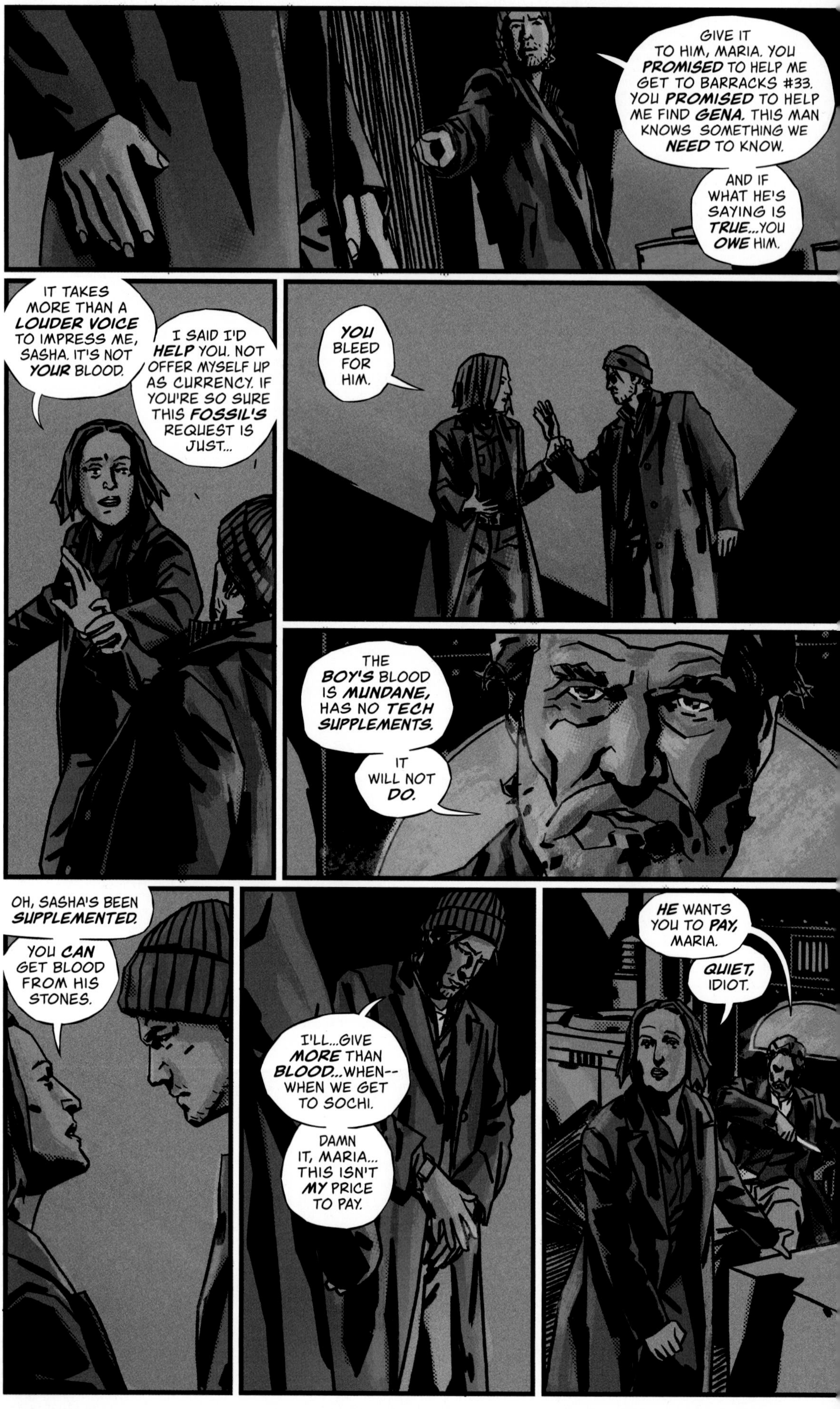
GIVE IT TO HIM, MARIA. YOU PROMISED TO HELP ME GET TO BARRACKS #33. YOU PROMISED TO HELP ME FIND GENA. THIS MAN KNOWS SOMETHING WE NEED TO KNOW.
AND IF WHAT HE'S SAYING IS TRUE...YOU OWE HIM.
IT TAKES MORE THAN A LOUDER VOICE TO IMPRESS ME, SASHA. IT'S NOT YOUR BLOOD.
I SAID I'D HELP YOU. NOT OFFER MYSELF UP AS CURRENCY. IF YOU'RE SO SURE THIS FOSSIL'S REQUEST IS JUST...
YOU BLEED FOR HIM.
THE BOY'S BLOOD IS MUNDANE, HAS NO TECH SUPPLEMENTS.
IT WILL NOT DO.
OH, SASHA'S BEEN SUPPLEMENTED.
YOU CAN GET BLOOD FROM HIS STONES.
I'LL...GIVE MORE THAN BLOOD...WHEN--WHEN WE GET TO SOCHI.
DAMN IT, MARIA... THIS ISN'T MY PRICE TO PAY.
HE WANTS YOU TO PAY, MARIA.
QUIET, IDIOT.

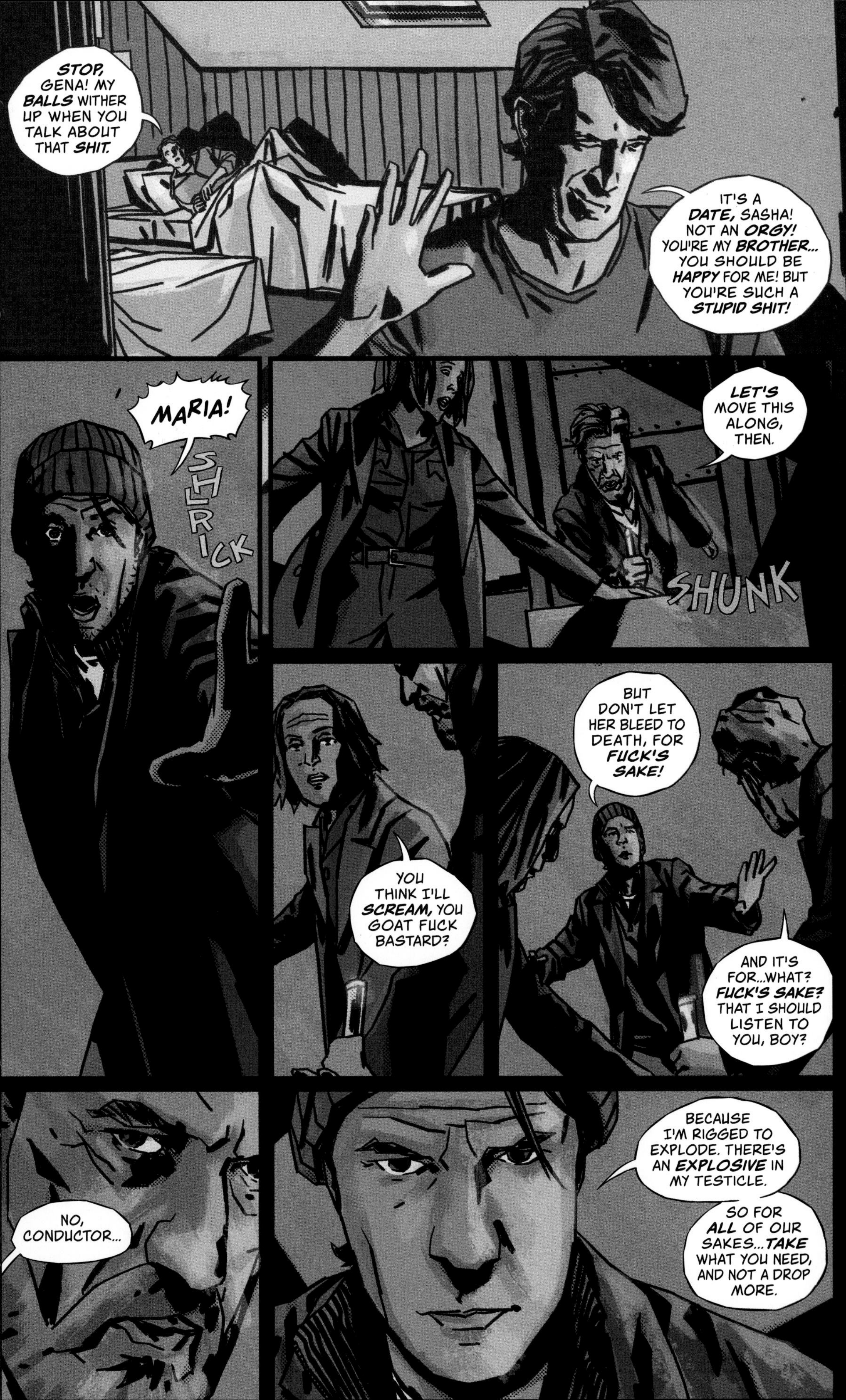
STOP, GENA! MY BALLS WITHER UP WHEN YOU TALK ABOUT THAT SHIT.
IT'S A DATE, SASHA! NOT AN ORGY! YOU'RE MY BROTHER... YOU SHOULD BE HAPPY FOR ME! BUT YOU'RE SUCH A STUPID SHIT!
MARIA!
SHLRICK
LET'S MOVE THIS ALONG, THEN.
SHUNK
YOU THINK I'LL SCREAM, YOU GOAT FUCK BASTARD?
BUT DON'T LET HER BLEED TO DEATH, FOR FUCK'S SAKE!
AND IT'S FOR...WHAT? FUCK'S SAKE? THAT I SHOULD LISTEN TO YOU, BOY?
NO, CONDUCTOR...
BECAUSE I'M RIGGED TO EXPLODE. THERE'S AN EXPLOSIVE IN MY TESTICLE.
SO FOR ALL OF OUR SAKES...TAKE WHAT YOU NEED, AND NOT A DROP MORE.

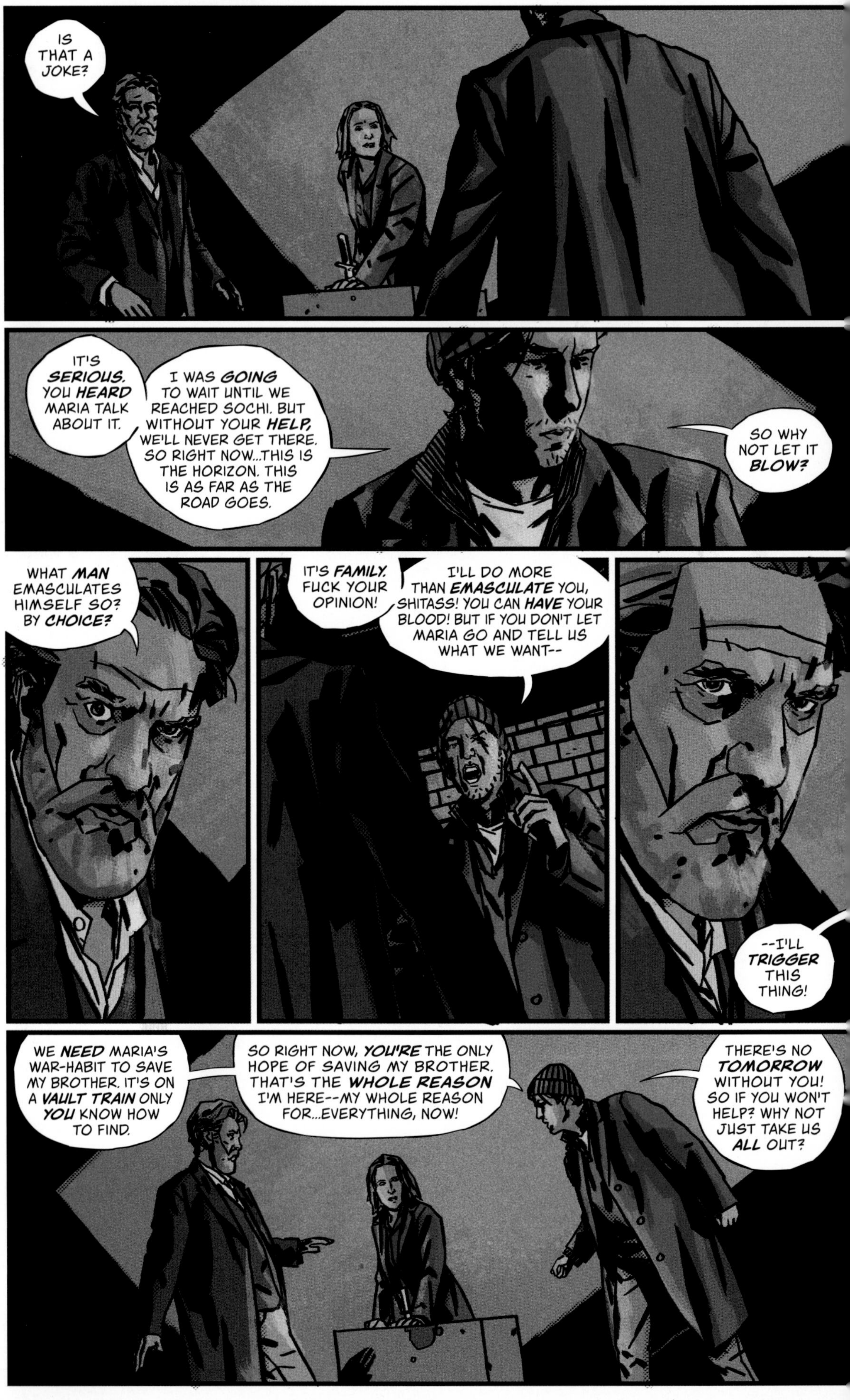
IS THAT A JOKE?
IT'S SERIOUS. YOU HEARD MARIA TALK ABOUT IT.
I WAS GOING TO WAIT UNTIL WE REACHED SOCHI. BUT WITHOUT YOUR HELP, WE'LL NEVER GET THERE. SO RIGHT NOW...THIS IS THE HORIZON. THIS IS AS FAR AS THE ROAD GOES.
SO WHY NOT LET IT BLOW?
WHAT MAN EMASCULATES HIMSELF SO? BY CHOICE?
IT'S FAMILY. FUCK YOUR OPINION!
I'LL DO MORE THAN EMASCULATE YOU, SHITASS! YOU CAN HAVE YOUR BLOOD! BUT IF YOU DON'T LET MARIA GO AND TELL US WHAT WE WANT--
--I'LL TRIGGER THIS THING!
WE NEED MARIA'S WAR-HABIT TO SAVE MY BROTHER. IT'S ON A VAULT TRAIN ONLY YOU KNOW HOW TO FIND.
SO RIGHT NOW, YOU'RE THE ONLY HOPE OF SAVING MY BROTHER. THAT'S THE WHOLE REASON I'M HERE--MY WHOLE REASON FOR...EVERYTHING, NOW!
THERE'S NO TOMORROW WITHOUT YOU! SO IF YOU WON'T HELP? WHY NOT JUST TAKE US ALL OUT?

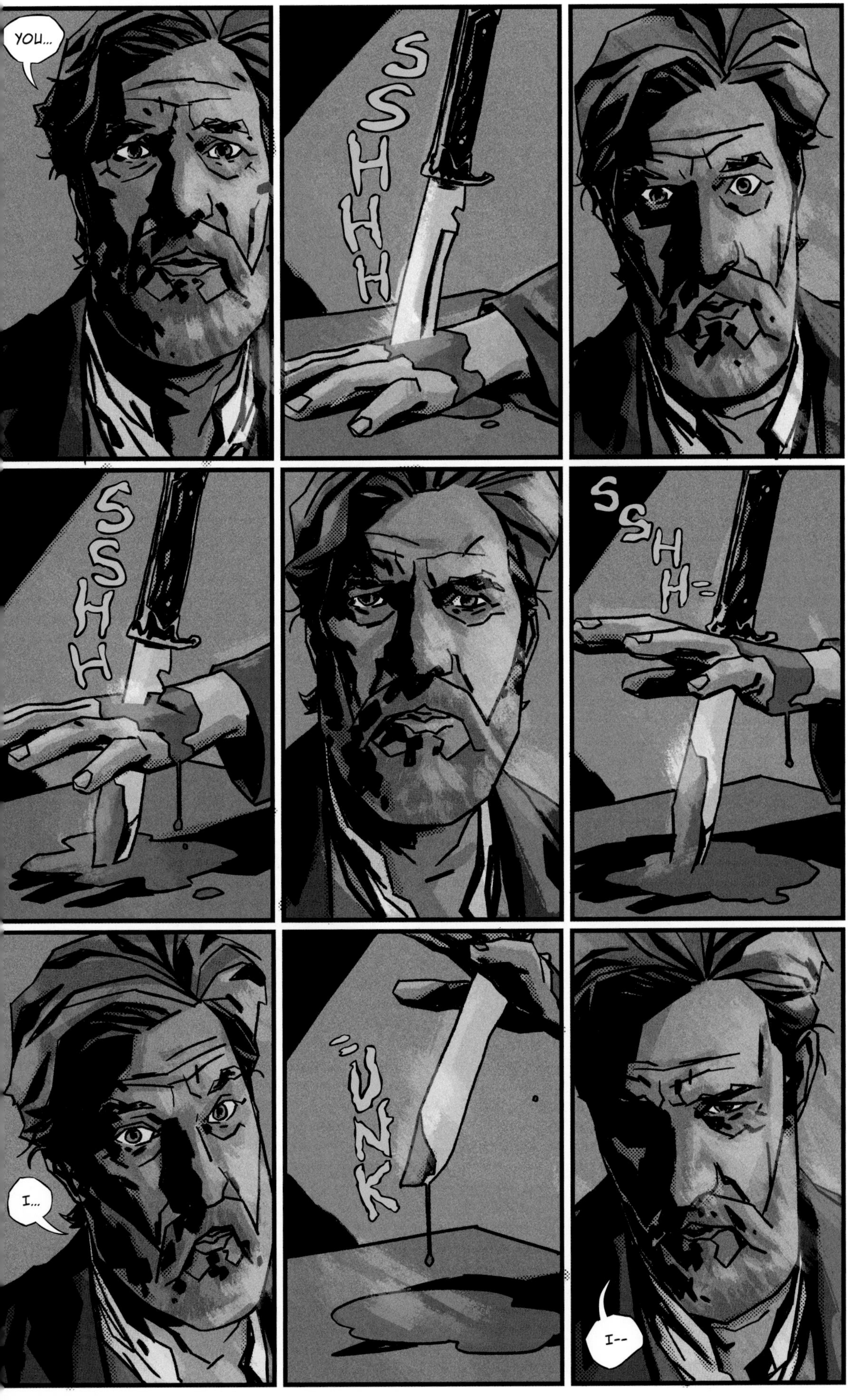

YOU...
SSHHH
SSHHH
SSHH-
I...
-UNK
I--

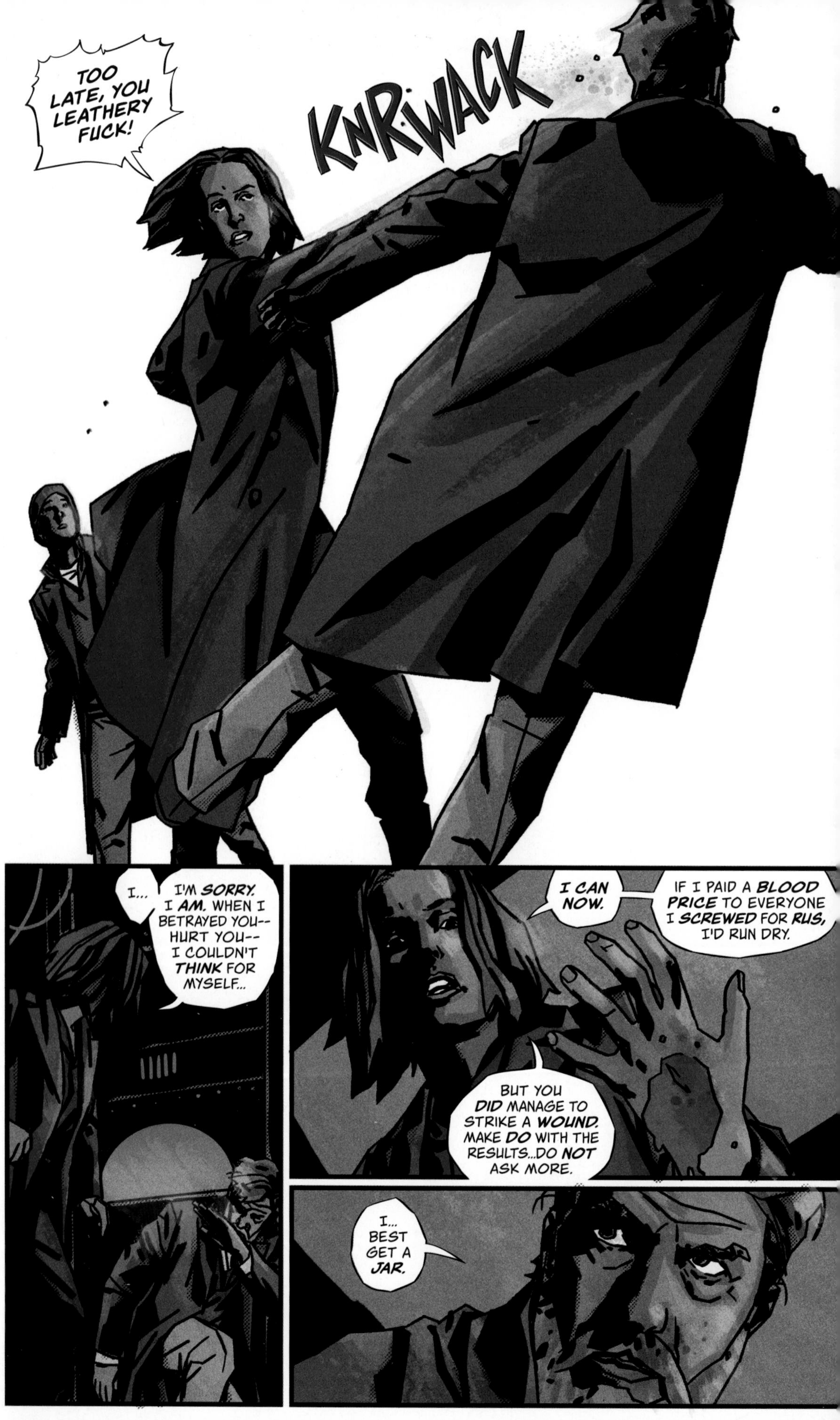
TOO LATE, YOU LEATHERY FUCK!
KNRWACK
I...
I'M SORRY. I AM. WHEN I BETRAYED YOU-- HURT YOU-- I COULDN'T THINK FOR MYSELF...
I CAN NOW.
IF I PAID A BLOOD PRICE TO EVERYONE I SCREWED FOR RUS, I'D RUN DRY.
BUT YOU DID MANAGE TO STRIKE A WOUND. MAKE DO WITH THE RESULTS...DO NOT ASK MORE.
I... BEST GET A JAR.

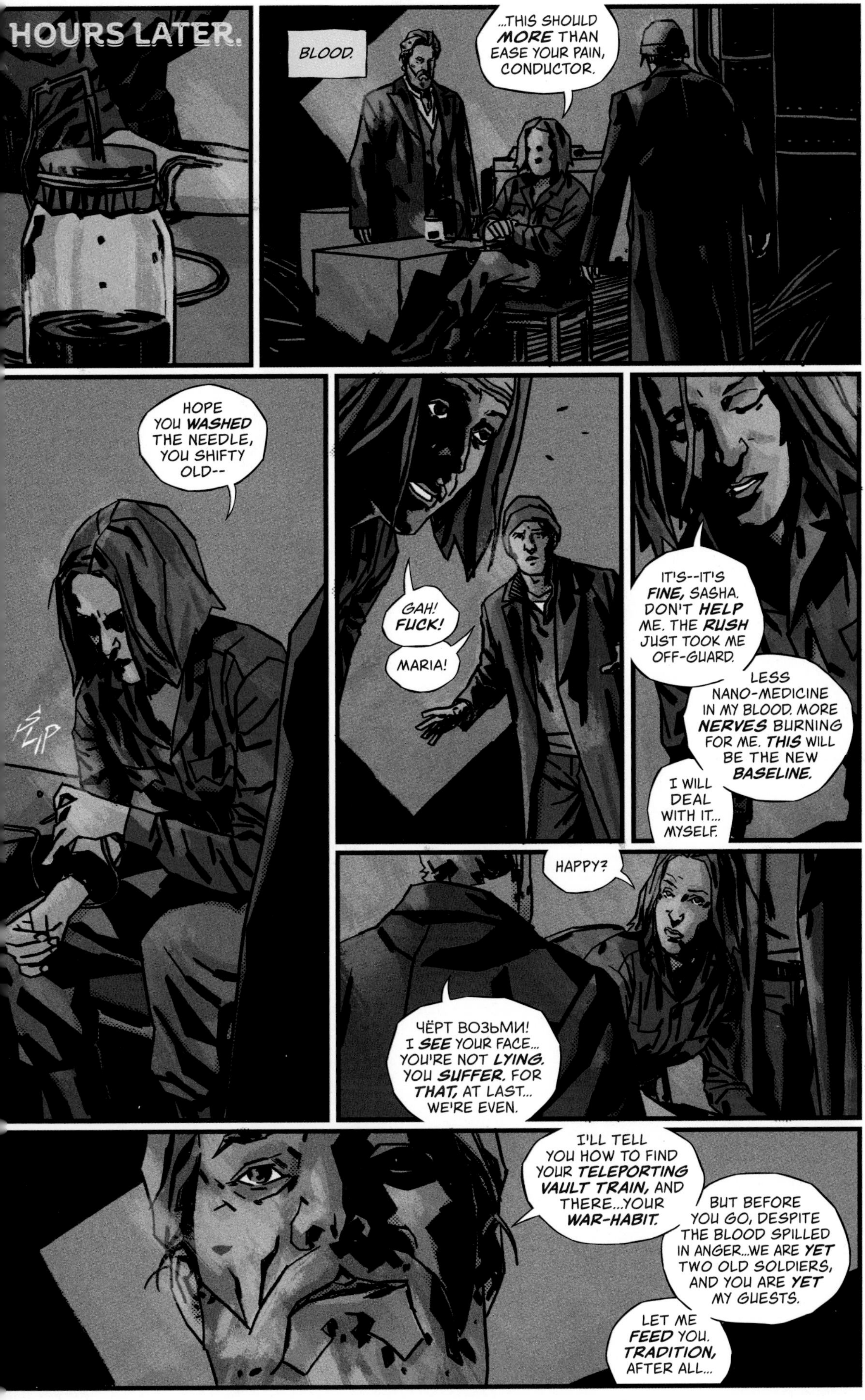
HOURS LATER.
BLOOD.
...THIS SHOULD MORE THAN EASE YOUR PAIN, CONDUCTOR.
HOPE YOU WASHED THE NEEDLE, YOU SHIFTY OLD--
SLIP
GAH! FUCK!
MARIA!
IT'S--IT'S FINE, SASHA. DON'T HELP ME. THE RUSH JUST TOOK ME OFF-GUARD.
LESS NANO-MEDICINE IN MY BLOOD. MORE NERVES BURNING FOR ME. THIS WILL BE THE NEW BASELINE.
I WILL DEAL WITH IT... MYSELF.
HAPPY?
ЧЁРТ ВОЗЬМИ! I SEE YOUR FACE... YOU'RE NOT LYING. YOU SUFFER. FOR THAT, AT LAST... WE'RE EVEN.
I'LL TELL YOU HOW TO FIND YOUR TELEPORTING VAULT TRAIN, AND THERE...YOUR WAR-HABIT.
BUT BEFORE YOU GO, DESPITE THE BLOOD SPILLED IN ANGER...WE ARE YET TWO OLD SOLDIERS, AND YOU ARE YET MY GUESTS.
LET ME FEED YOU. TRADITION, AFTER ALL...

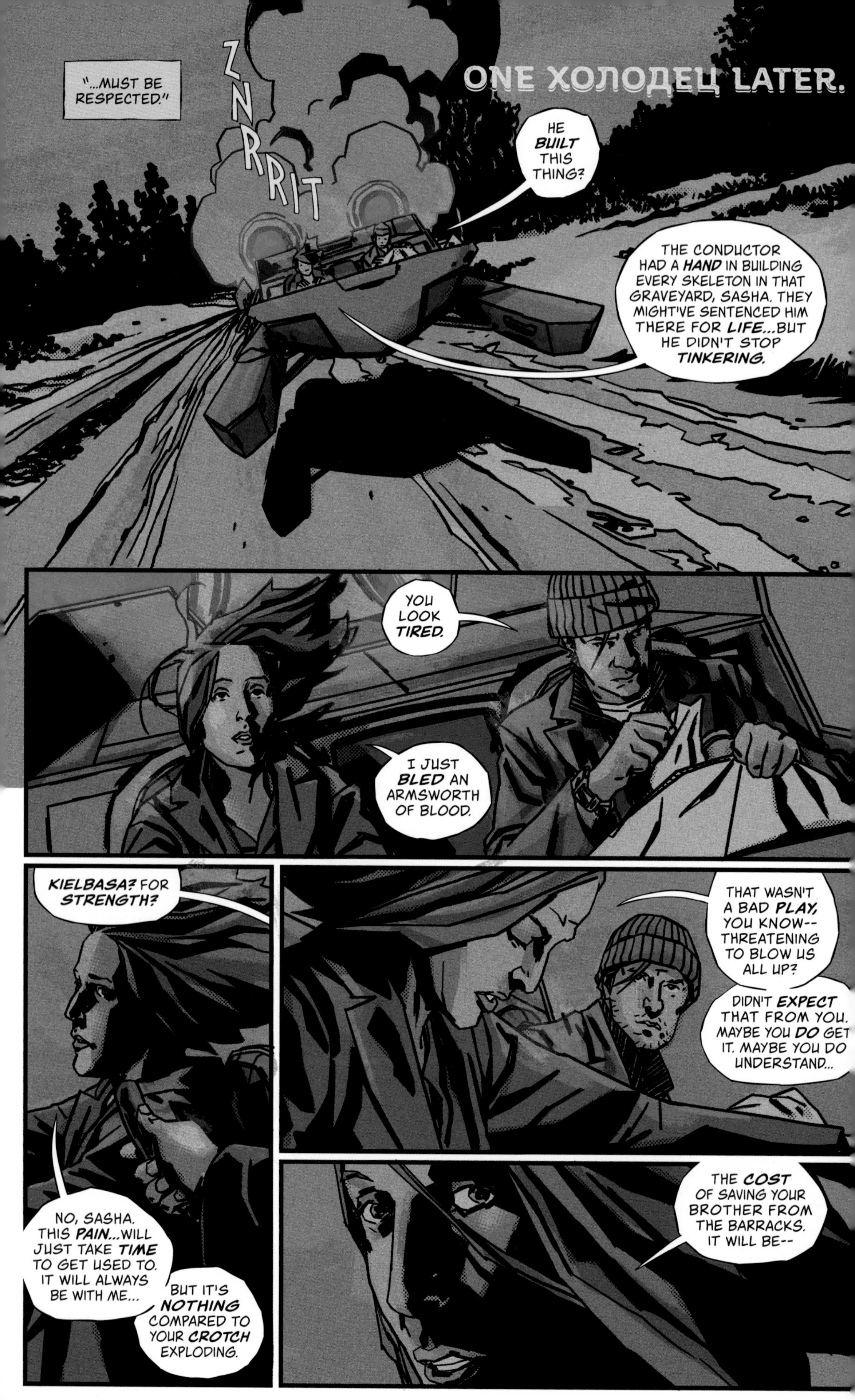
"...MUST BE RESPECTED."
ZNRRRIT
ONE ХОЛОДЕЦ LATER.
HE BUILT THIS THING?
THE CONDUCTOR HAD A HAND IN BUILDING EVERY SKELETON IN THAT GRAVEYARD, SASHA. THEY MIGHT'VE SENTENCED HIM THERE FOR LIFE...BUT HE DIDN'T STOP TINKERING.
YOU LOOK TIRED.
I JUST BLED AN ARMSWORTH OF BLOOD.
KIELBASA? FOR STRENGTH?
NO, SASHA. THIS PAIN...WILL JUST TAKE TIME TO GET USED TO. IT WILL ALWAYS BE WITH ME...
BUT IT'S NOTHING COMPARED TO YOUR CROTCH EXPLODING.
THAT WASN'T A BAD PLAY, YOU KNOW--THREATENING TO BLOW US ALL UP?
DIDN'T EXPECT THAT FROM YOU. MAYBE YOU DO GET IT. MAYBE YOU DO UNDERSTAND...
THE COST OF SAVING YOUR BROTHER FROM THE BARRACKS. IT WILL BE--

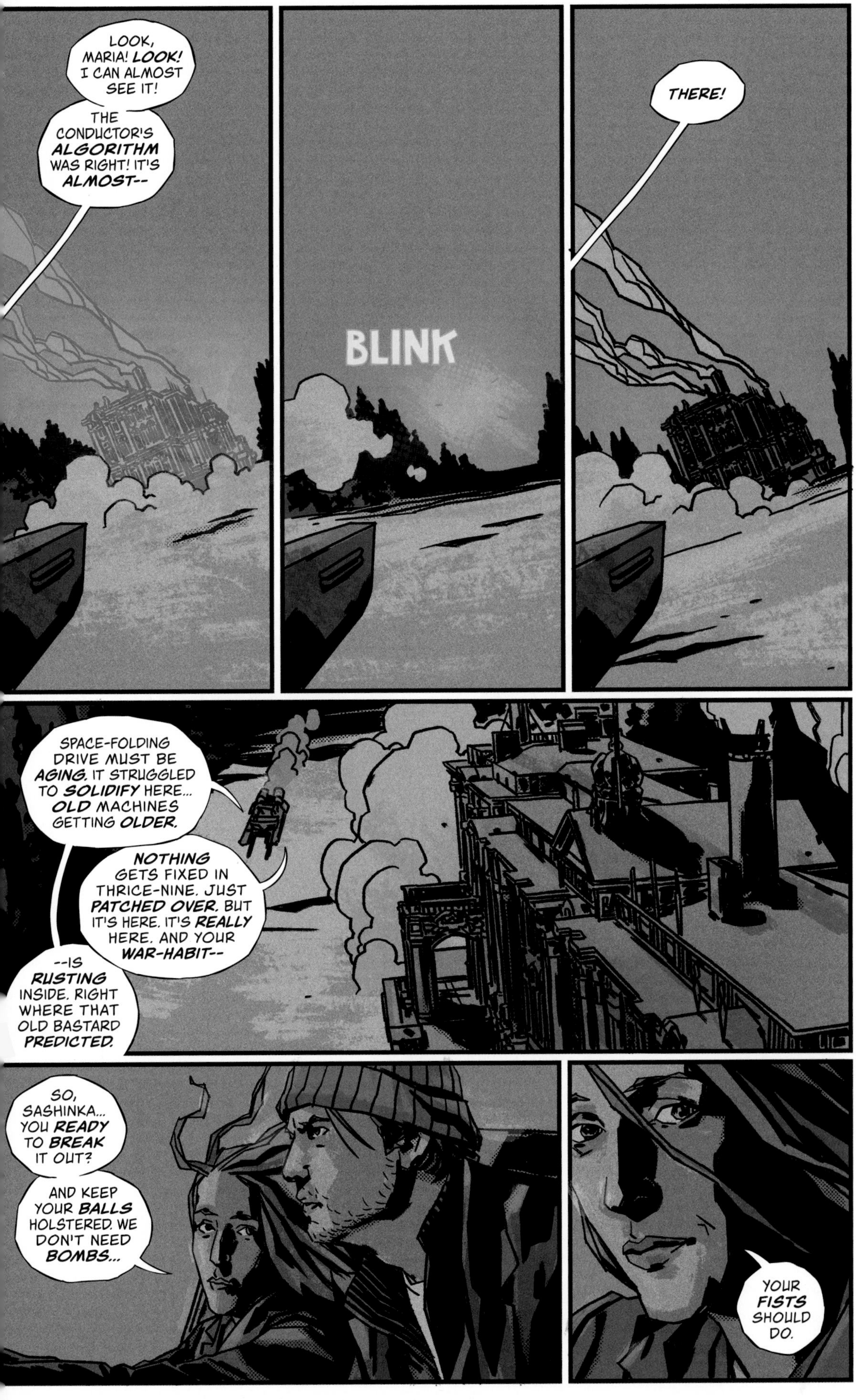

LOOK, MARIA! LOOK! I CAN ALMOST SEE IT!
THE CONDUCTOR'S ALGORITHM WAS RIGHT! IT'S ALMOST--
BLINK
THERE!
SPACE-FOLDING DRIVE MUST BE AGING. IT STRUGGLED TO SOLIDIFY HERE... OLD MACHINES GETTING OLDER.
NOTHING GETS FIXED IN THRICE-NINE. JUST PATCHED OVER. BUT IT'S HERE. IT'S REALLY HERE. AND YOUR WAR-HABIT--
--IS RUSTING INSIDE, RIGHT WHERE THAT OLD BASTARD PREDICTED.
SO, SASHINKA... YOU READY TO BREAK IT OUT?
AND KEEP YOUR BALLS HOLSTERED. WE DON'T NEED BOMBS...
YOUR FISTS SHOULD DO.

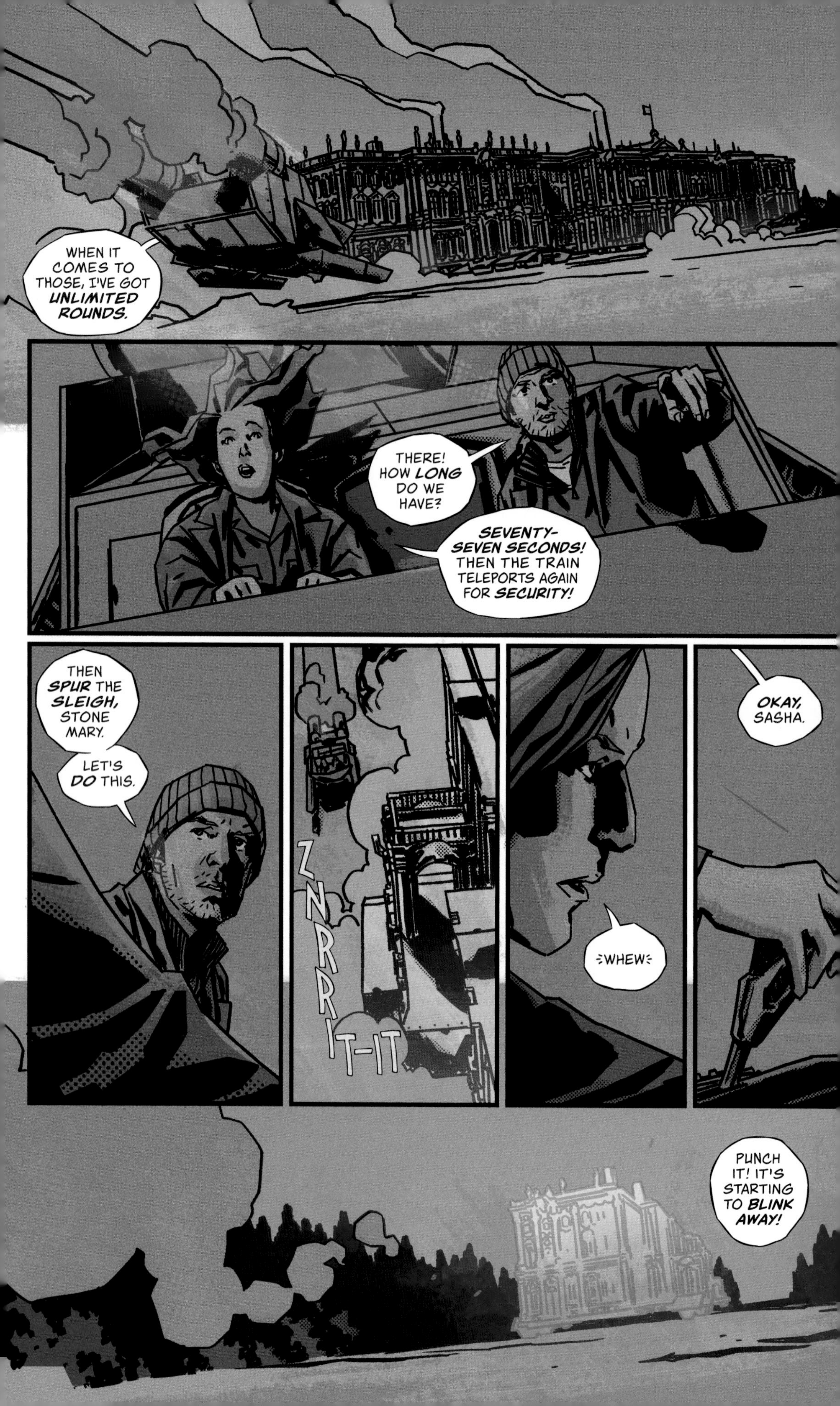

WHEN IT COMES TO THOSE, I'VE GOT UNLIMITED ROUNDS.
THERE! HOW LONG DO WE HAVE?
SEVENTY-SEVEN SECONDS! THEN THE TRAIN TELEPORTS AGAIN FOR SECURITY!
THEN SPUR THE SLEIGH, STONE MARY.
LET'S DO THIS.
ZNRRRIT-IT
OKAY, SASHA.
WHEW
PUNCH IT! IT'S STARTING TO BLINK AWAY!

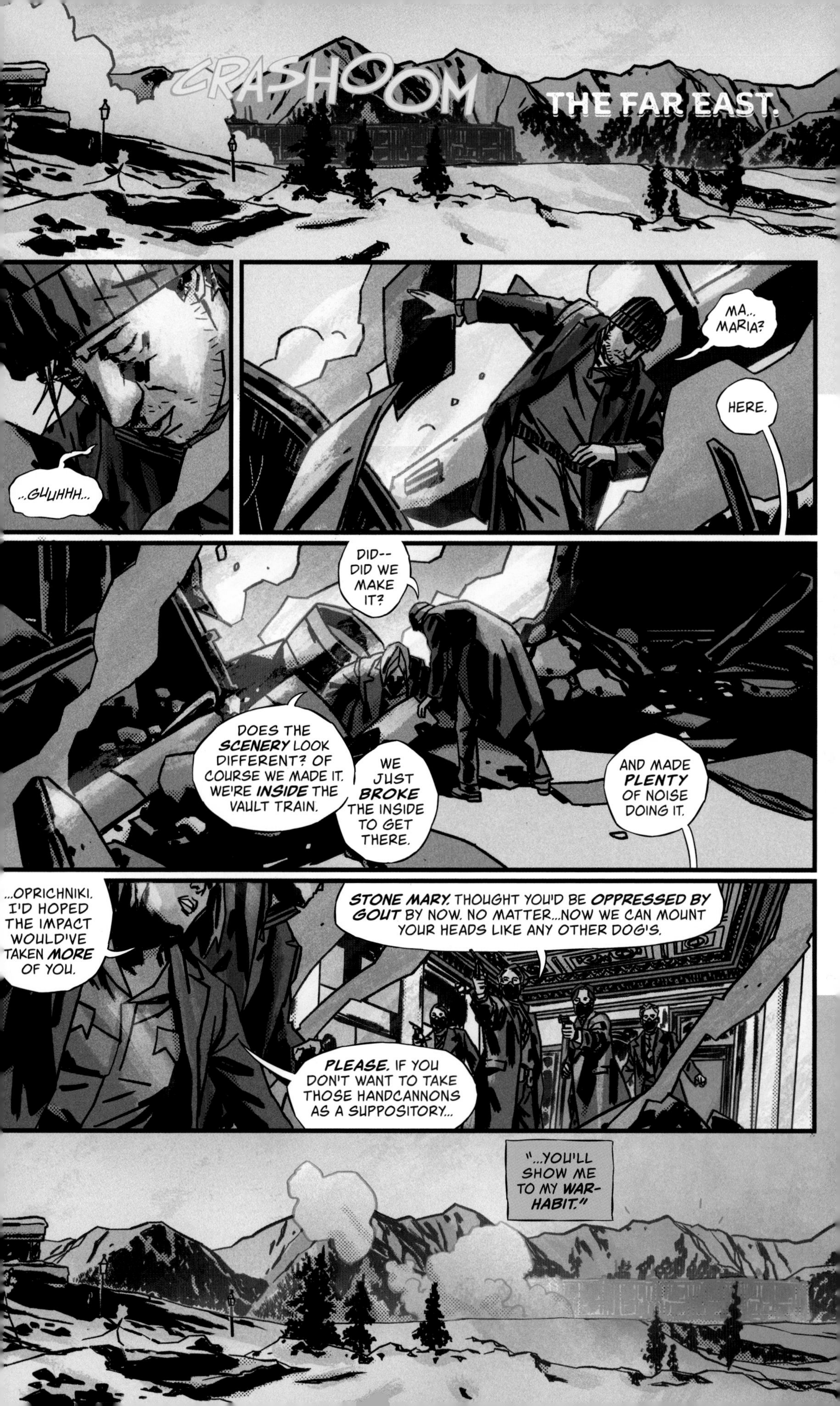
CRASHOOM
THE FAR EAST.
...GUUHHH...
MA... MARIA?
HERE.
DID-- DID WE MAKE IT?
DOES THE SCENERY LOOK DIFFERENT? OF COURSE WE MADE IT. WE'RE INSIDE THE VAULT TRAIN.
WE JUST BROKE THE INSIDE TO GET THERE.
AND MADE PLENTY OF NOISE DOING IT.
...OPRICHNIKI. I'D HOPED THE IMPACT WOULD'VE TAKEN MORE OF YOU.
STONE MARY. THOUGHT YOU'D BE OPPRESSED BY GOUT BY NOW. NO MATTER...NOW WE CAN MOUNT YOUR HEADS LIKE ANY OTHER DOG'S.
PLEASE. IF YOU DON'T WANT TO TAKE THOSE HANDCANNONS AS A SUPPOSITORY...
"...YOU'LL SHOW ME TO MY WAR-HABIT."

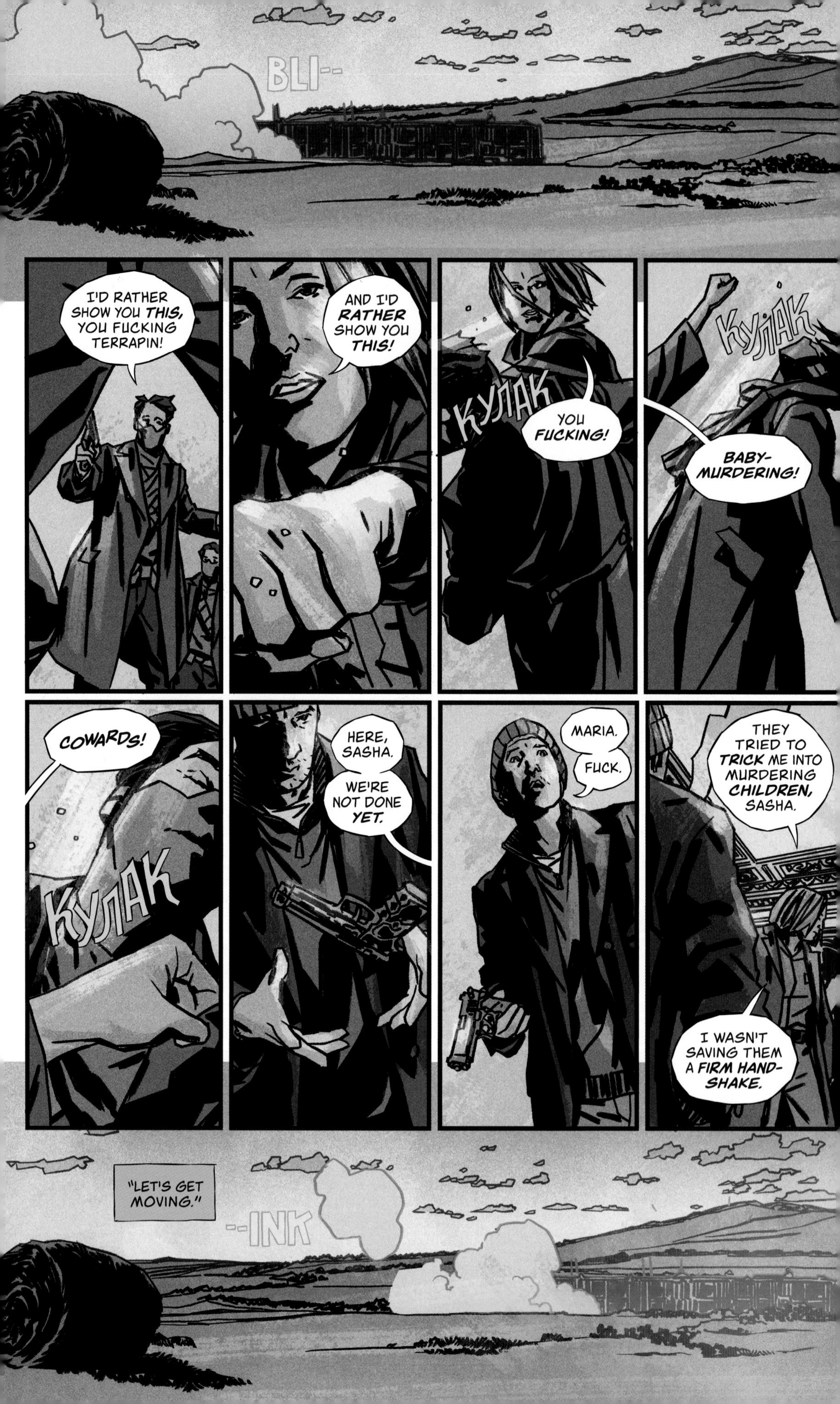
BLI--
I'D RATHER SHOW YOU THIS, YOU FUCKING TERRAPIN!
AND I'D RATHER SHOW YOU THIS!
КУЛАК
YOU FUCKING!
КУЛАК
BABY-MURDERING!
COWARDS!
КУЛАК
HERE, SASHA.
WE'RE NOT DONE YET.
MARIA.
FUCK.
THEY TRIED TO TRICK ME INTO MURDERING CHILDREN, SASHA.
I WASN'T SAVING THEM A FIRM HAND-SHAKE.
"LET'S GET MOVING."
--INK

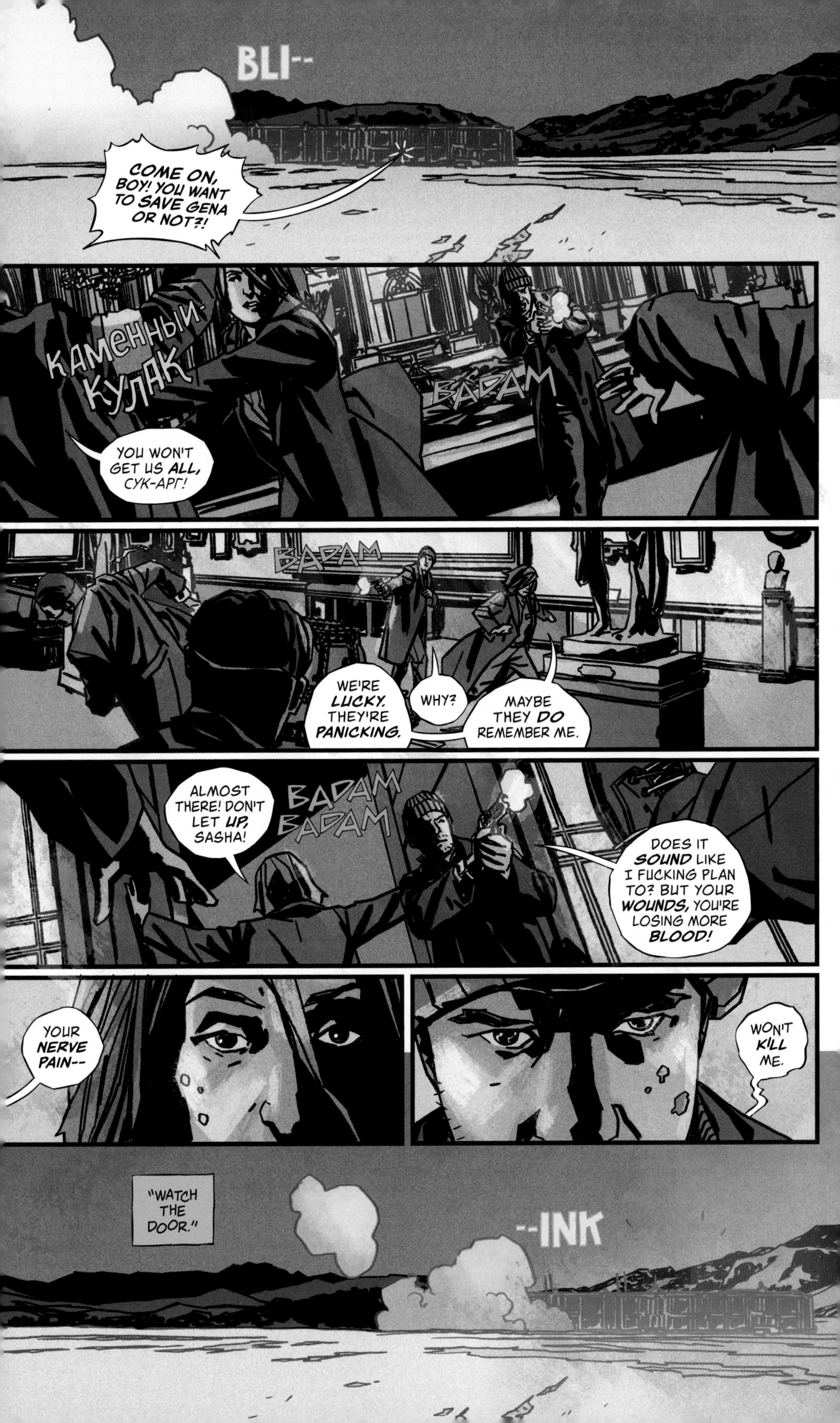
BLI--
COME ON, BOY! YOU WANT TO SAVE GENA OR NOT?!
КАМЕННЫЙ-КУЛАК
BADAM
YOU WON'T GET US ALL, СУК-АРГ!
BADAM
WE'RE LUCKY. THEY'RE PANICKING.
WHY?
MAYBE THEY DO REMEMBER ME.
ALMOST THERE! DON'T LET UP, SASHA!
BADAM BADAM
DOES IT SOUND LIKE I FUCKING PLAN TO? BUT YOUR WOUNDS, YOU'RE LOSING MORE BLOOD!
YOUR NERVE PAIN--
WON'T KILL ME.
"WATCH THE DOOR."
--INK

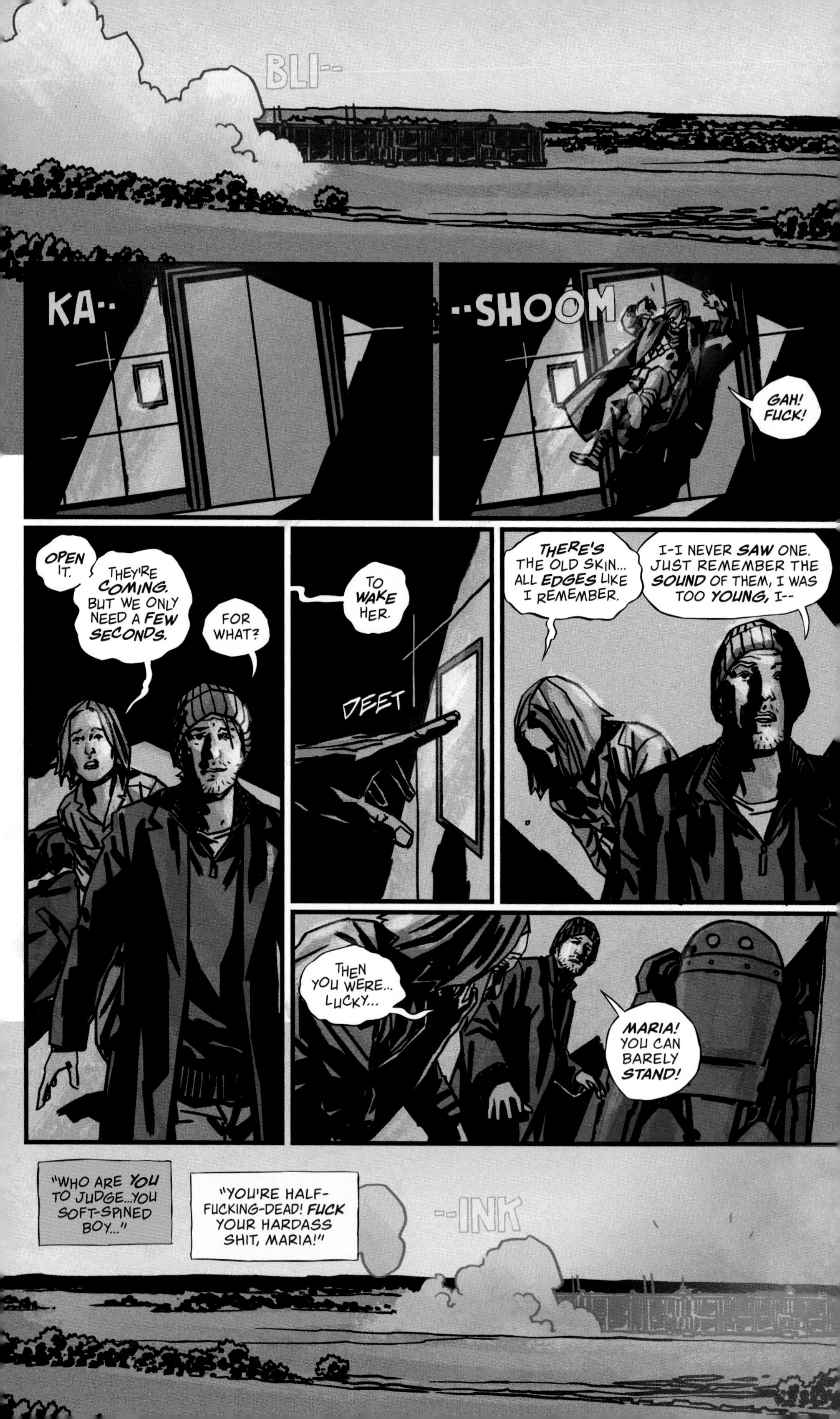
BLI--
KA--
--SHOOM
GAH! FUCK!
OPEN IT.
THEY'RE COMING. BUT WE ONLY NEED A FEW SECONDS.
FOR WHAT?
TO WAKE HER.
DEET
THERE'S THE OLD SKIN... ALL EDGES LIKE I REMEMBER.
I-I NEVER SAW ONE. JUST REMEMBER THE SOUND OF THEM, I WAS TOO YOUNG, I--
THEN YOU WERE... LUCKY...
MARIA! YOU CAN BARELY STAND!
"WHO ARE YOU TO JUDGE...YOU SOFT-SPINED BOY..."
"YOU'RE HALF-FUCKING-DEAD! FUCK YOUR HARDASS SHIT, MARIA!"
--INK

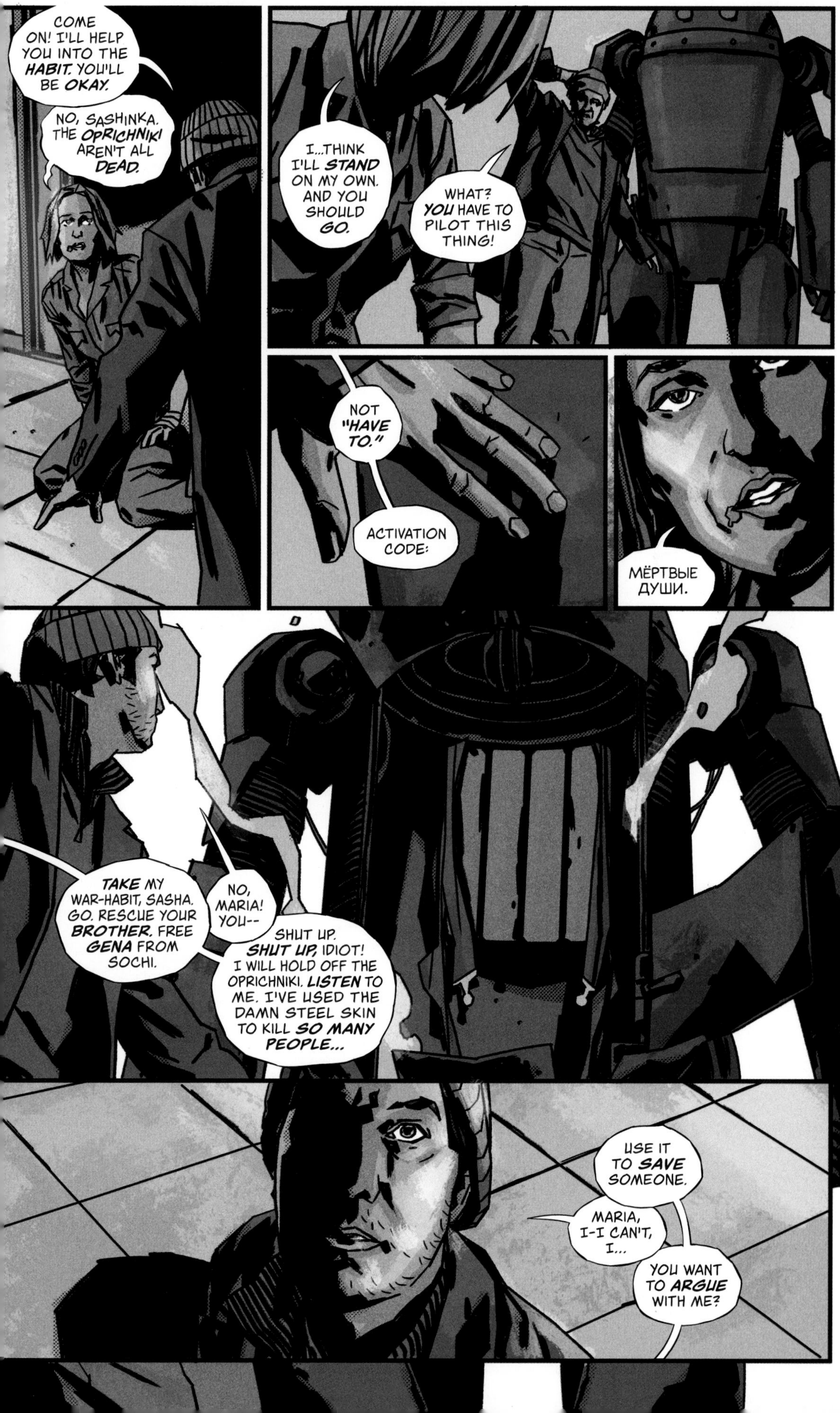
COME ON! I'LL HELP YOU INTO THE HABIT. YOU'LL BE OKAY.
NO, SASHINKA. THE OPRICHNIKI AREN'T ALL DEAD.
I...THINK I'LL STAND ON MY OWN. AND YOU SHOULD GO.
WHAT? YOU HAVE TO PILOT THIS THING!
NOT "HAVE TO."
ACTIVATION CODE:
МЁРТВЫЕ ДУШИ.
TAKE MY WAR-HABIT, SASHA. GO. RESCUE YOUR BROTHER. FREE GENA FROM SOCHI.
NO, MARIA! YOU--
SHUT UP. SHUT UP, IDIOT! I WILL HOLD OFF THE OPRICHNIKI. LISTEN TO ME. I'VE USED THE DAMN STEEL SKIN TO KILL SO MANY PEOPLE...
USE IT TO SAVE SOMEONE.
MARIA, I-I CAN'T, I...
YOU WANT TO ARGUE WITH ME?

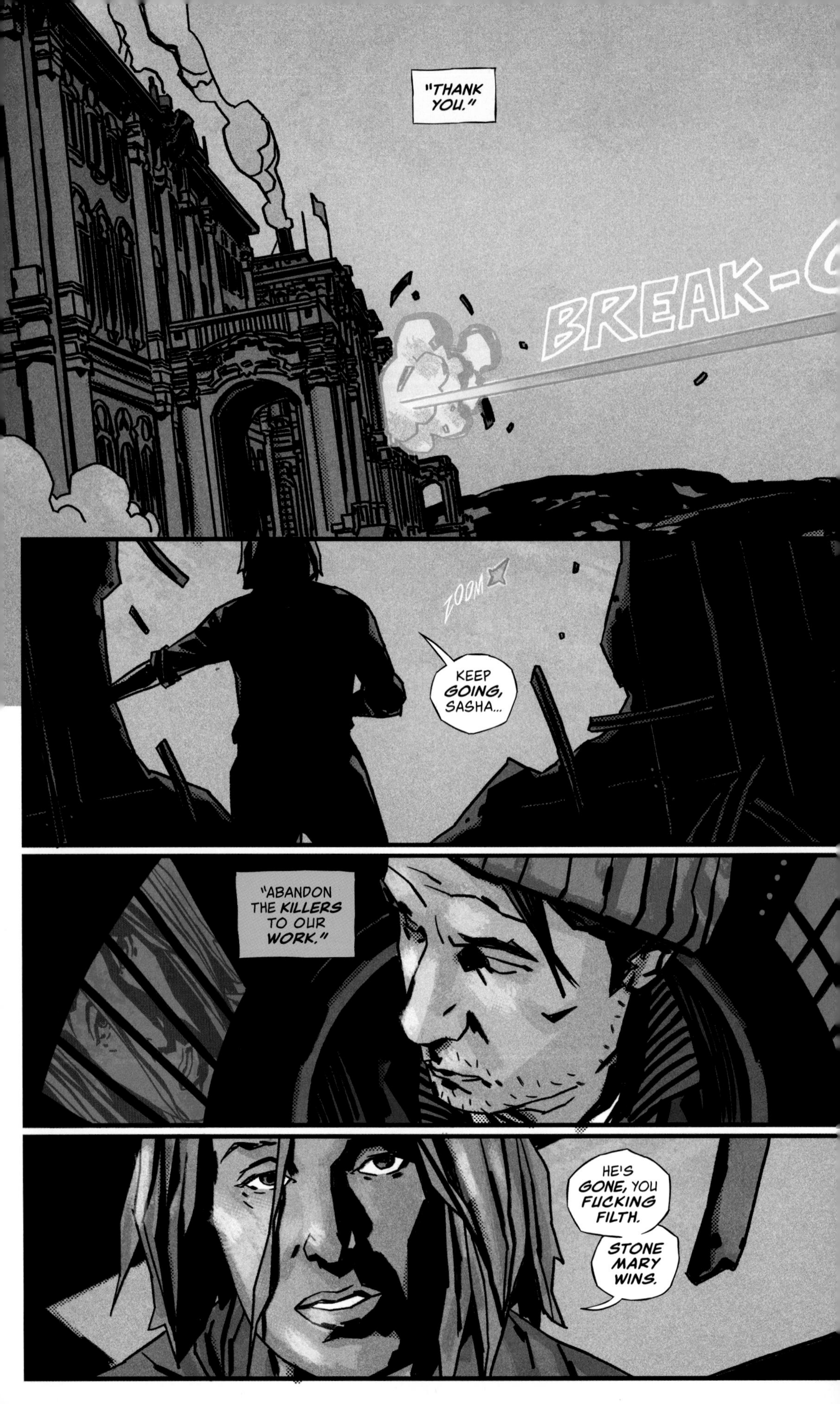
"THANK YOU."
BREAK-
ZOOM
KEEP GOING, SASHA...
"ABANDON THE KILLERS TO OUR WORK."
HE'S GONE, YOU FUCKING FILTH.
STONE MARY WINS.

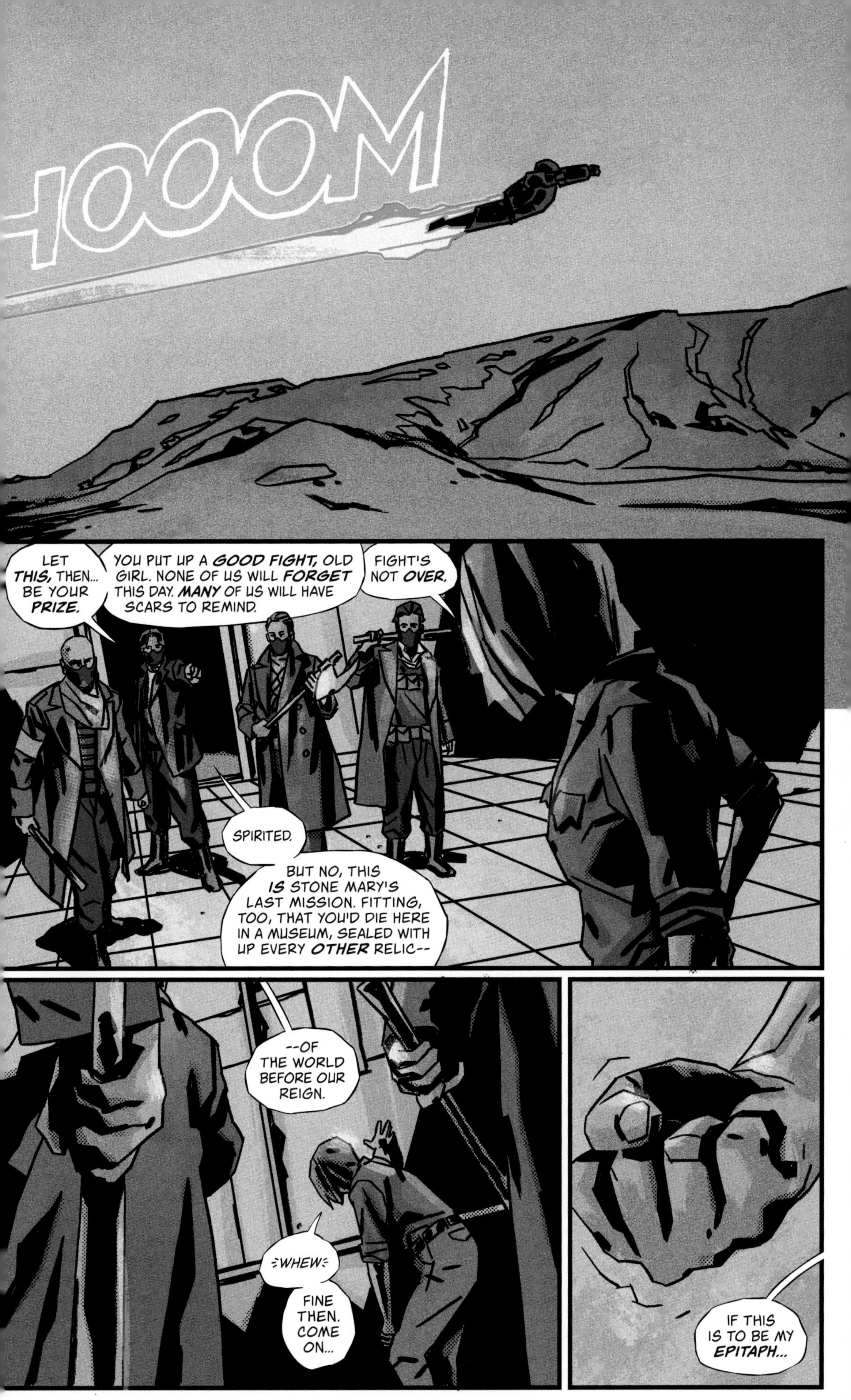
FWOOOM
LET THIS, THEN... BE YOUR PRIZE.
YOU PUT UP A GOOD FIGHT, OLD GIRL. NONE OF US WILL FORGET THIS DAY. MANY OF US WILL HAVE SCARS TO REMIND.
FIGHT'S NOT OVER.
SPIRITED.
BUT NO, THIS IS STONE MARY'S LAST MISSION. FITTING, TOO, THAT YOU'D DIE HERE IN A MUSEUM, SEALED UP WITH EVERY OTHER RELIC--
--OF THE WORLD BEFORE OUR REIGN.
WHEW
FINE THEN. COME ON...
IF THIS IS TO BE MY EPITAPH...

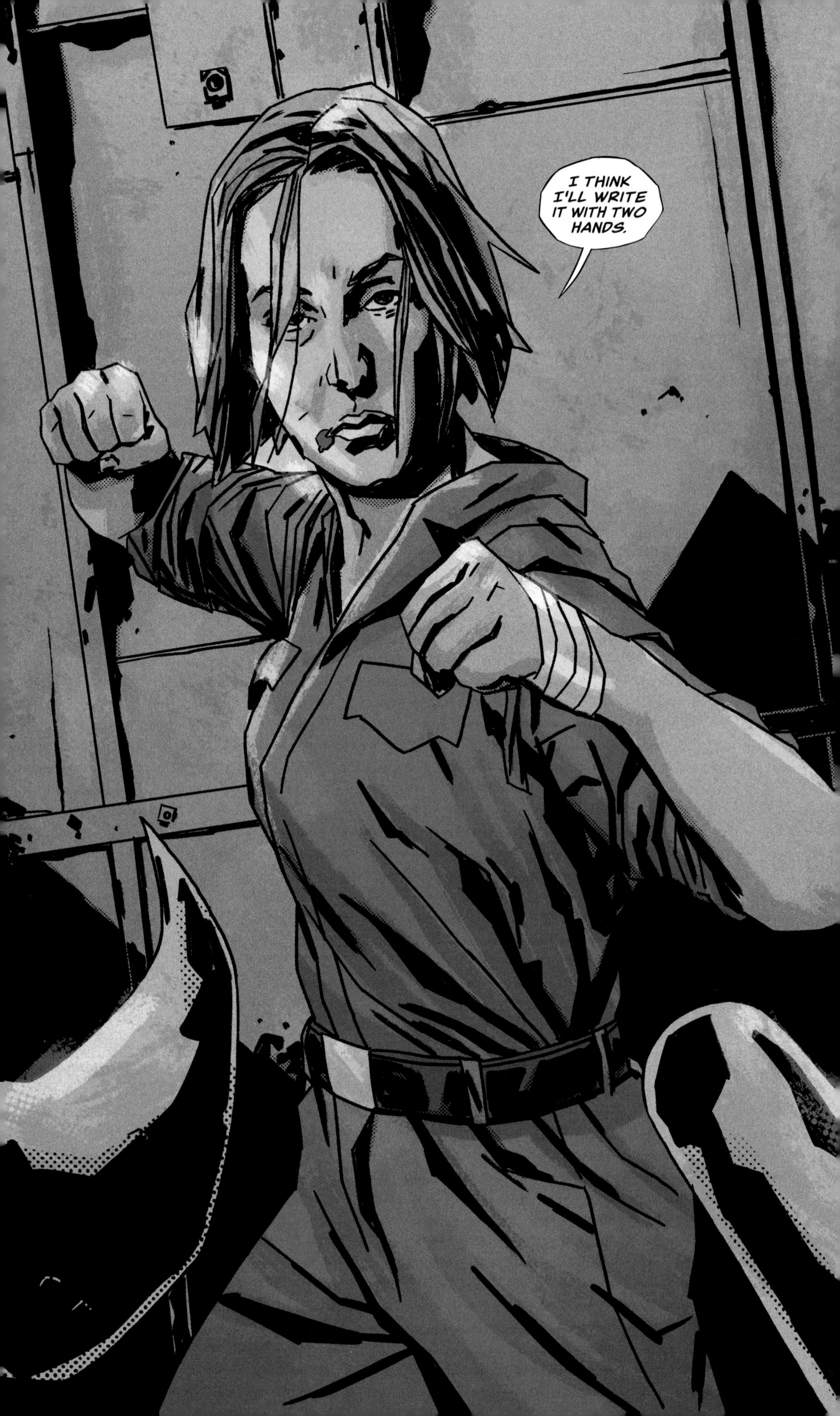
I THINK I'LL WRITE IT WITH TWO HANDS.

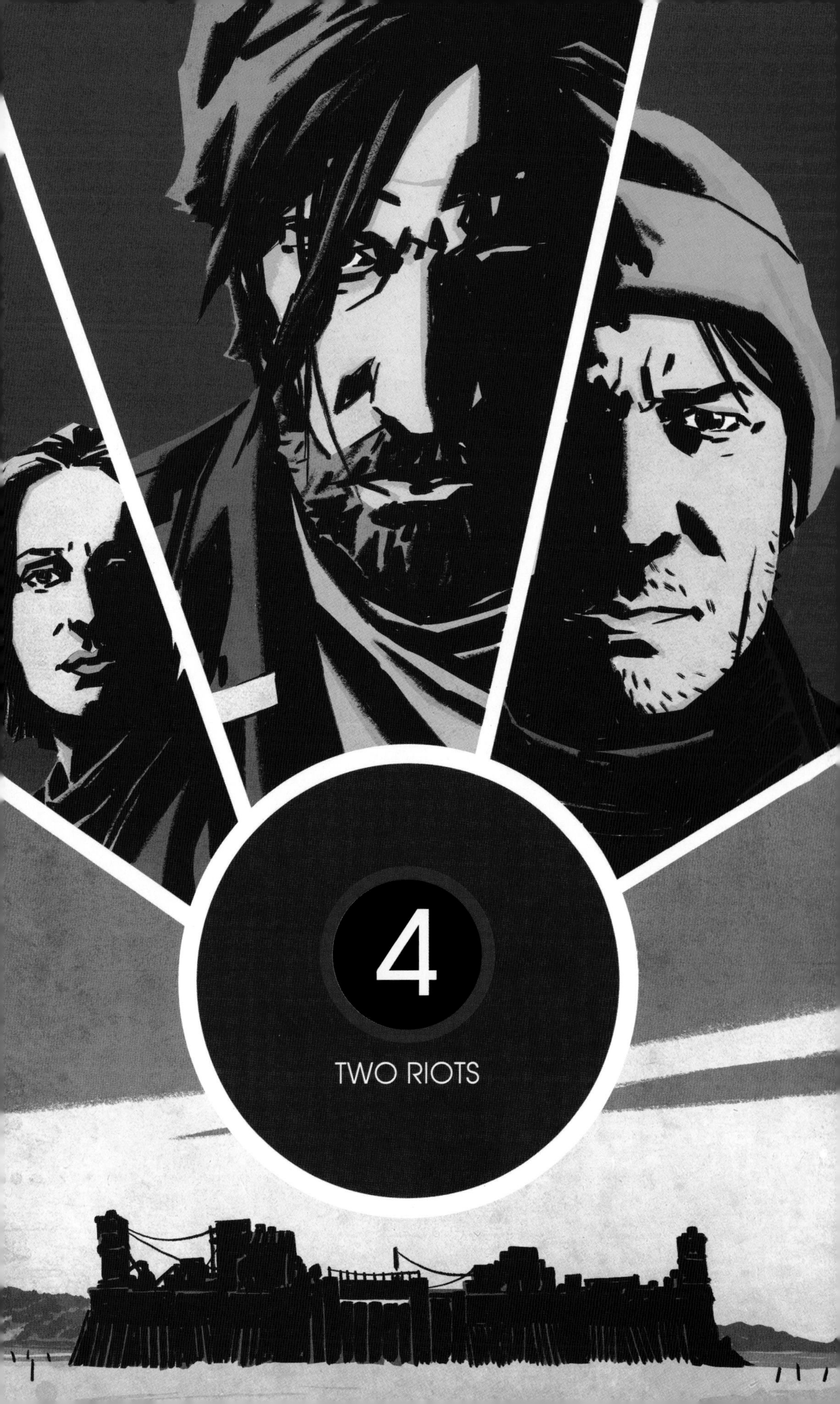
4
TWO RIOTS

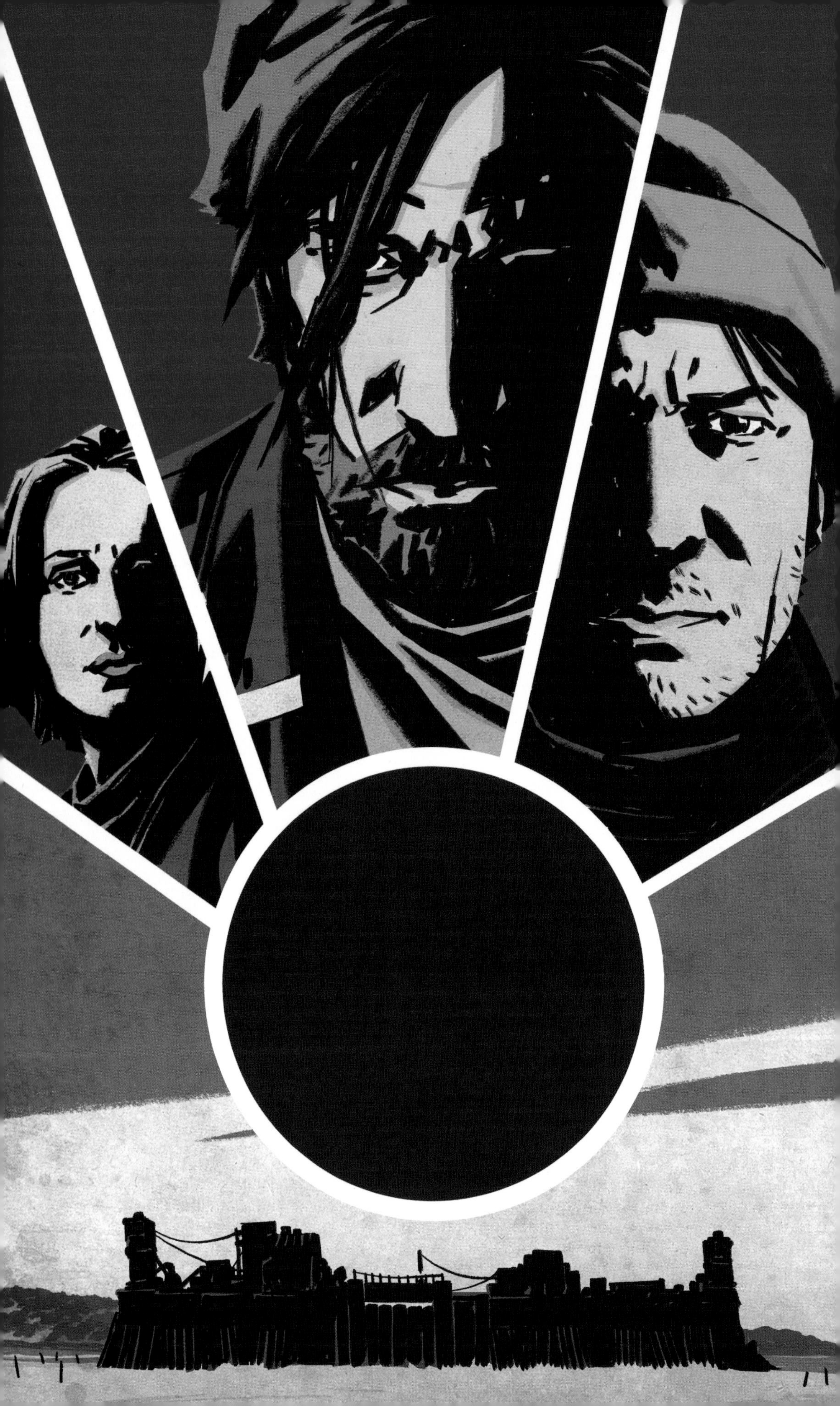

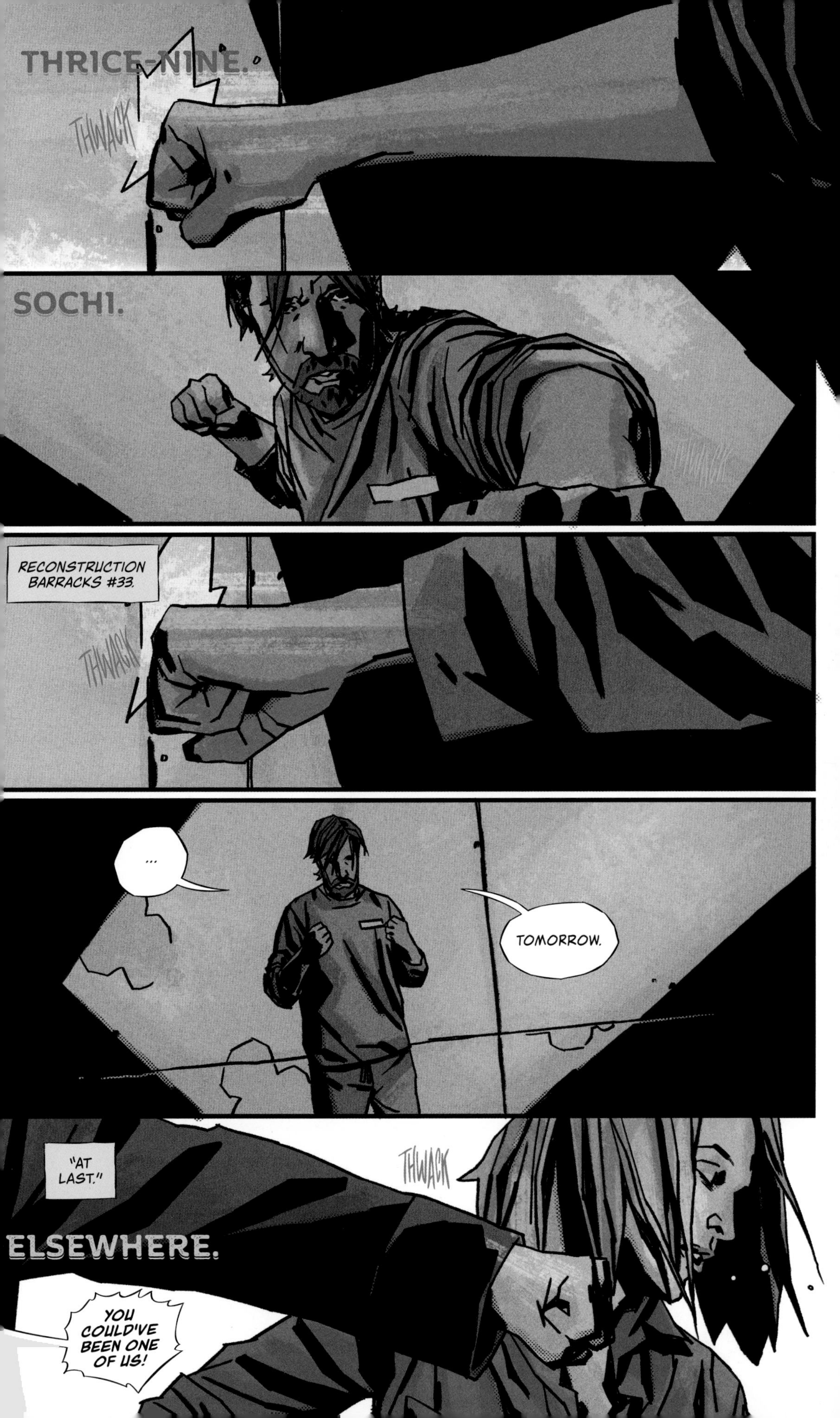
THRICE-NINE.
THWACK
SOCHI.
THWACK
RECONSTRUCTION BARRACKS #33.
THWACK
...
TOMORROW.
"AT LAST."
THWACK
ELSEWHERE.
YOU COULD'VE BEEN ONE OF US!

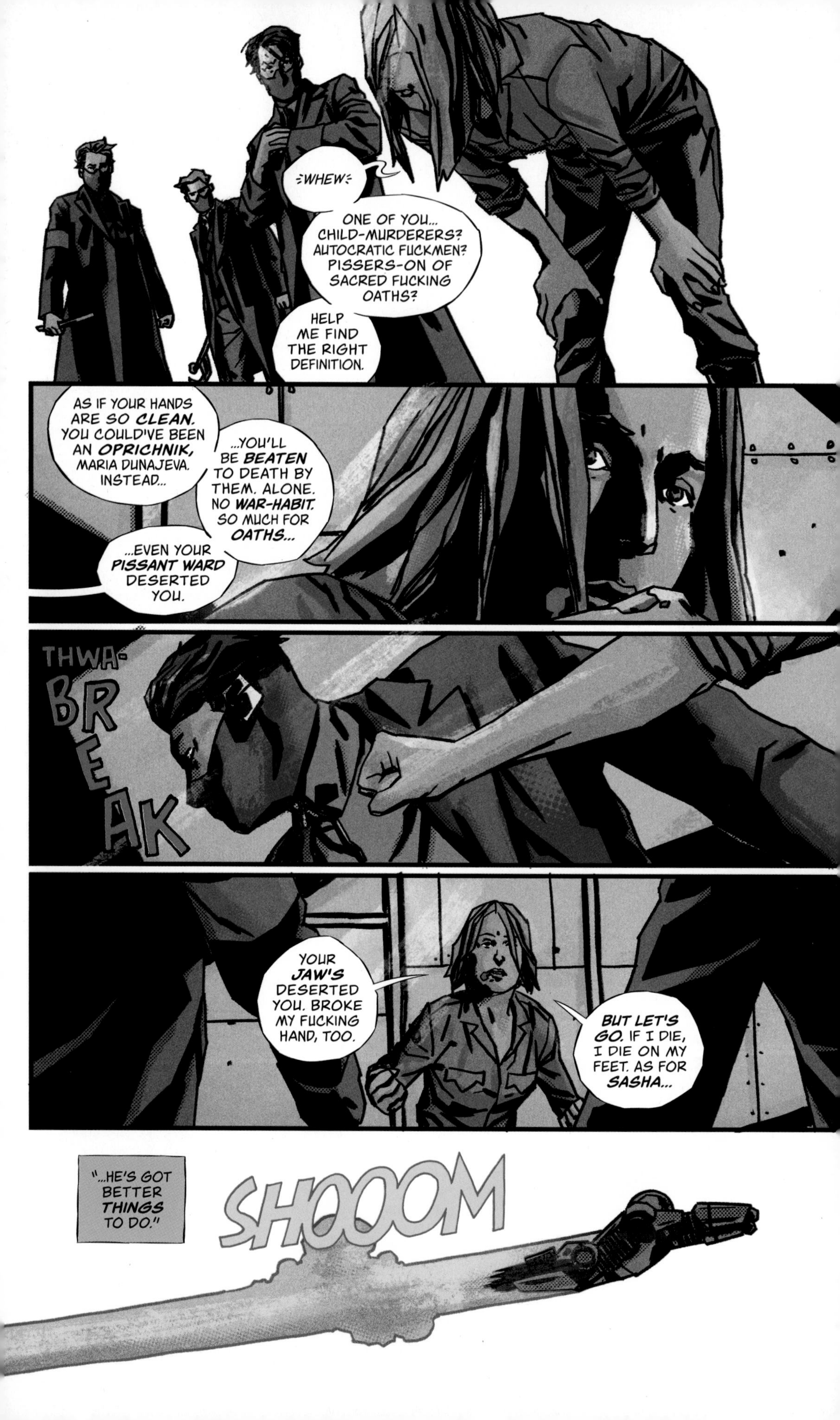

WHEW
ONE OF YOU... CHILD-MURDERERS? AUTOCRATIC FUCKMEN? PISSERS-ON OF SACRED FUCKING OATHS?
HELP ME FIND THE RIGHT DEFINITION.
AS IF YOUR HANDS ARE SO CLEAN. YOU COULD'VE BEEN AN OPRICHNIK, MARIA DUNAJEVA. INSTEAD...
...YOU'LL BE BEATEN TO DEATH BY THEM. ALONE. NO WAR-HABIT. SO MUCH FOR OATHS...
...EVEN YOUR PISSANT WARD DESERTED YOU.
THWA-BREAK
YOUR JAW'S DESERTED YOU. BROKE MY FUCKING HAND, TOO.
BUT LET'S GO. IF I DIE, I DIE ON MY FEET. AS FOR SASHA...
"...HE'S GOT BETTER THINGS TO DO."
SHOOOM

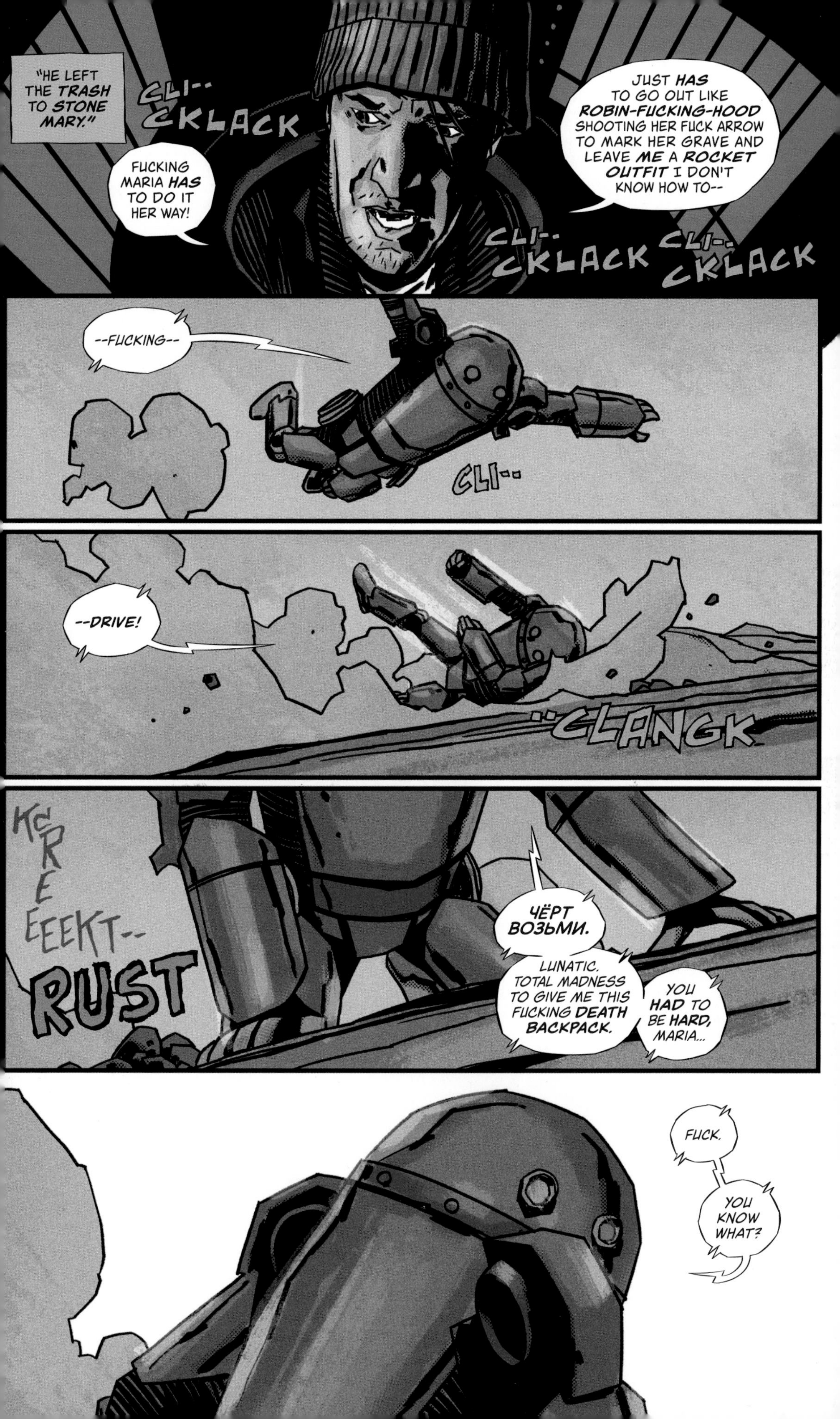
"HE LEFT THE TRASH TO STONE MARY."
CLI-- CKLACK
FUCKING MARIA HAS TO DO IT HER WAY!
JUST HAS TO GO OUT LIKE ROBIN-FUCKING-HOOD SHOOTING HER FUCK ARROW TO MARK HER GRAVE AND LEAVE ME A ROCKET OUTFIT I DON'T KNOW HOW TO--
CLI-- CKLACK CLI-- CKLACK
--FUCKING--
CLI--
--DRIVE!
--CLANGK
KCREEEEKT--
RUST
ЧЁРТ ВОЗЬМИ.
LUNATIC. TOTAL MADNESS TO GIVE ME THIS FUCKING DEATH BACKPACK.
YOU HAD TO BE HARD, MARIA...
FUCK.
YOU KNOW WHAT?

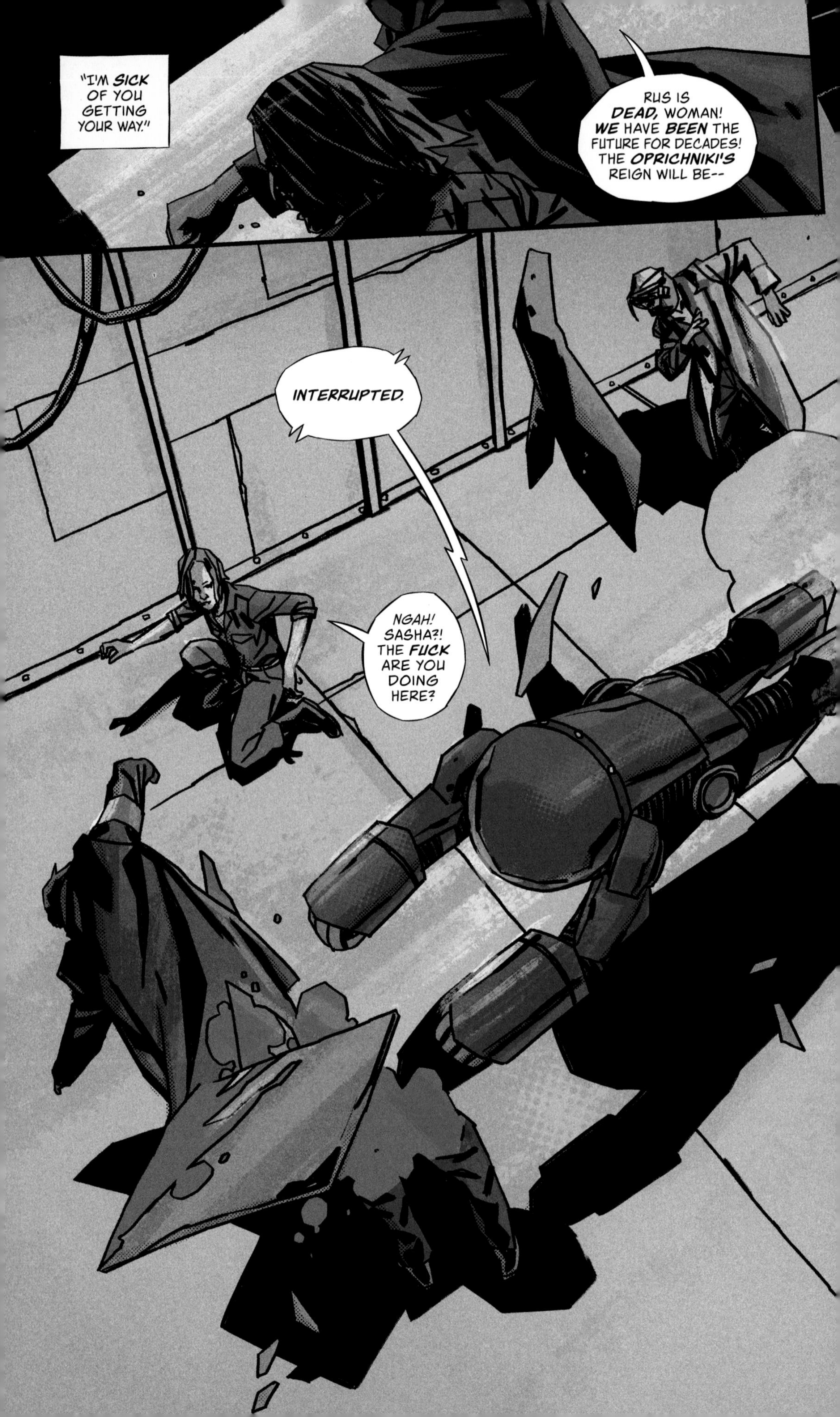
"I'M SICK OF YOU GETTING YOUR WAY."
RUS IS DEAD, WOMAN! WE HAVE BEEN THE FUTURE FOR DECADES! THE OPRICHNIKI'S REIGN WILL BE--
INTERRUPTED.
NGAH! SASHA?! THE FUCK ARE YOU DOING HERE?

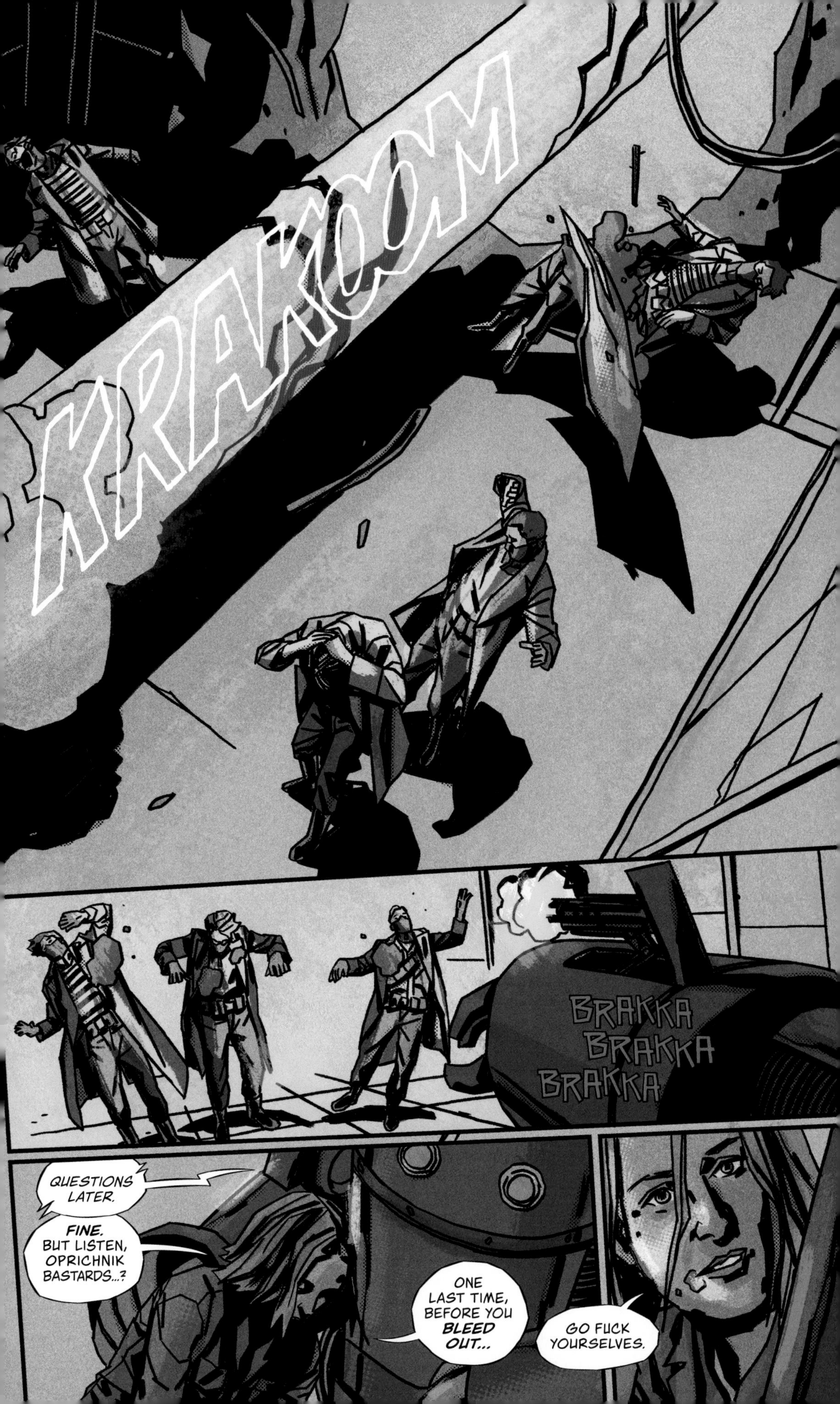
KRAKOOM
BRAKKA BRAKKA BRAKKA
QUESTIONS LATER.
FINE. BUT LISTEN, OPRICHNIK BASTARDS...?
ONE LAST TIME, BEFORE YOU BLEED OUT...
GO FUCK YOURSELVES.

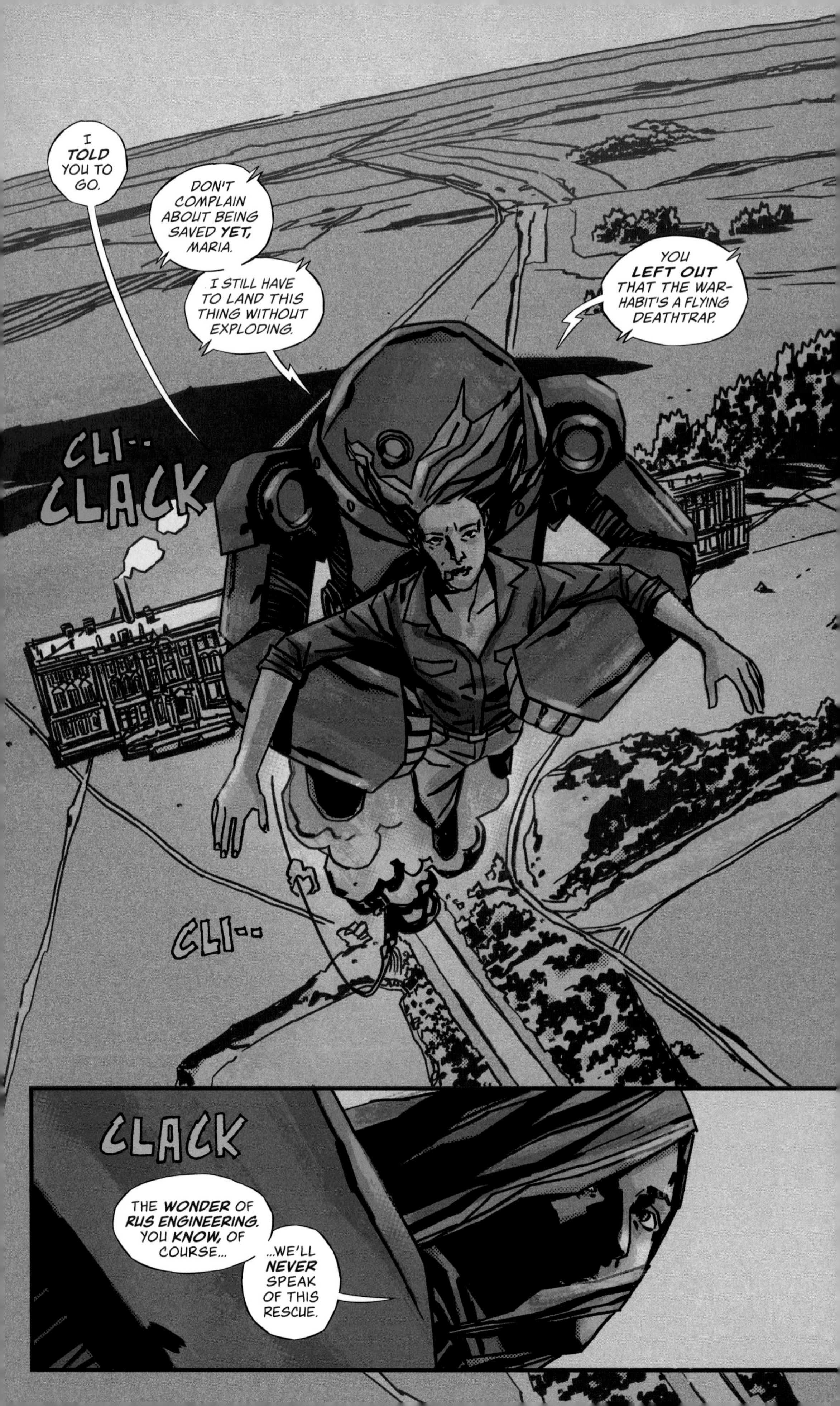
I TOLD YOU TO GO.
DON'T COMPLAIN ABOUT BEING SAVED YET, MARIA.
I STILL HAVE TO LAND THIS THING WITHOUT EXPLODING.
YOU LEFT OUT THAT THE WAR-HABIT'S A FLYING DEATHTRAP.
CLI-- CLACK
CLI--
CLACK
THE WONDER OF RUS ENGINEERING. YOU KNOW, OF COURSE...
...WE'LL NEVER SPEAK OF THIS RESCUE.

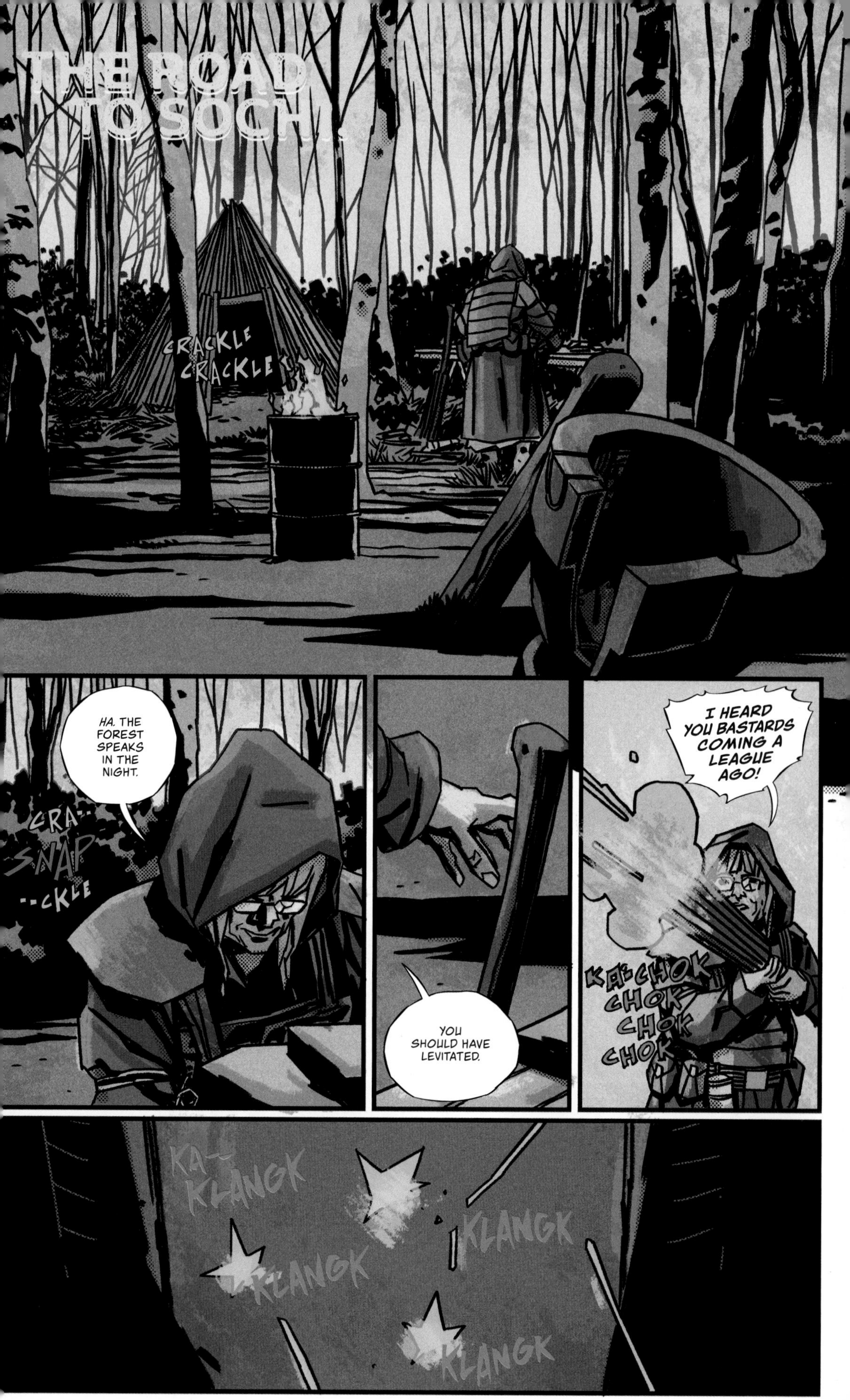
THE ROAD TO SOCHI.
CRACKLE CRACKLE
HA. THE FOREST SPEAKS IN THE NIGHT.
CRA--SNAP--CKLE
YOU SHOULD HAVE LEVITATED.
I HEARD YOU BASTARDS COMING A LEAGUE AGO!
KA-CHOK CHOK CHOK CHOK
KA-KLANGK
KLANGK
KLANGK
KLANGK

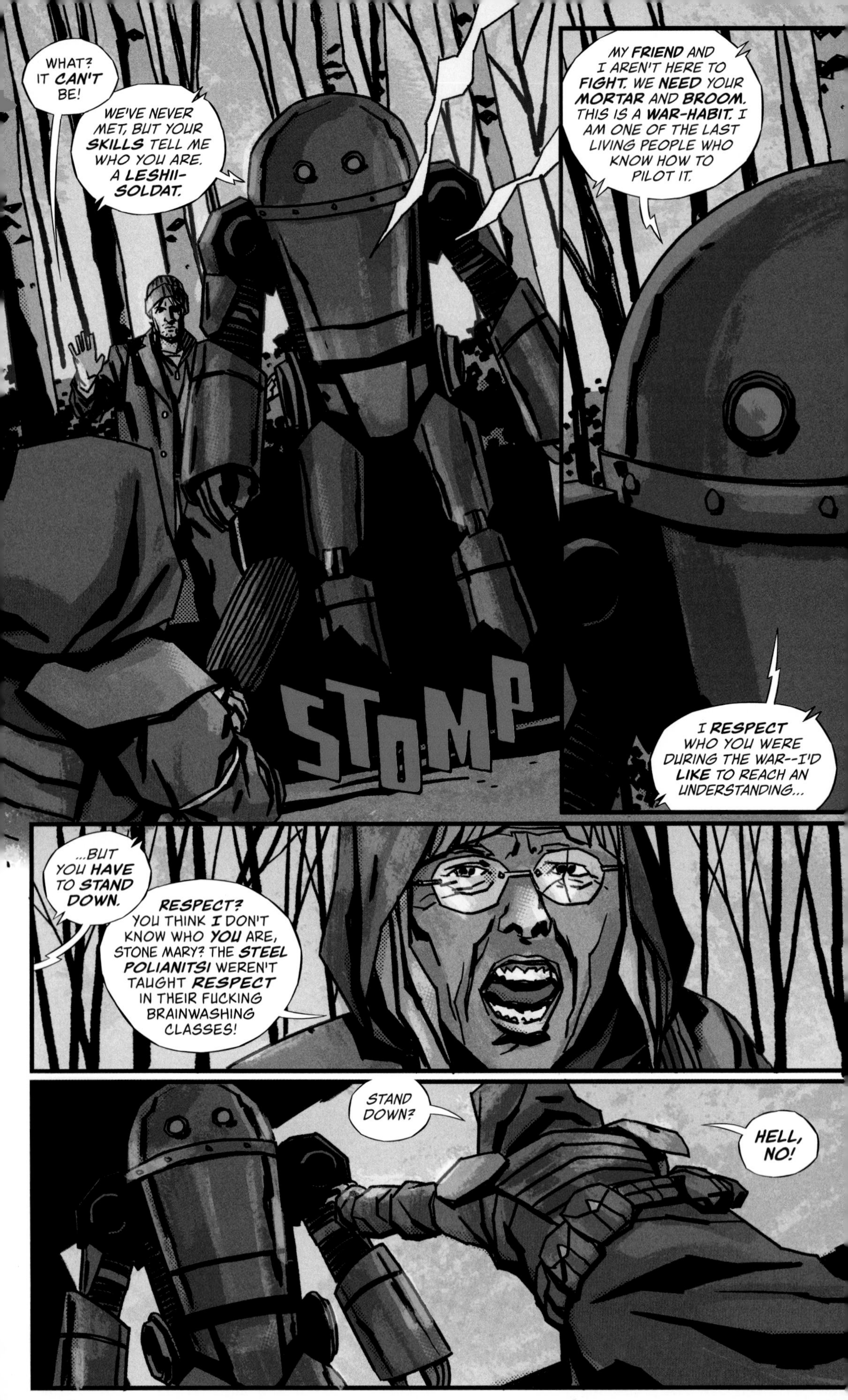
WHAT? IT CAN'T BE!
WE'VE NEVER MET, BUT YOUR SKILLS TELL ME WHO YOU ARE. A LESHII-SOLDAT.
MY FRIEND AND I AREN'T HERE TO FIGHT. WE NEED YOUR MORTAR AND BROOM. THIS IS A WAR-HABIT. I AM ONE OF THE LAST LIVING PEOPLE WHO KNOW HOW TO PILOT IT.
STOMP
I RESPECT WHO YOU WERE DURING THE WAR--I'D LIKE TO REACH AN UNDERSTANDING...
...BUT YOU HAVE TO STAND DOWN.
RESPECT? YOU THINK I DON'T KNOW WHO YOU ARE, STONE MARY? THE STEEL POLIANITSI WEREN'T TAUGHT RESPECT IN THEIR FUCKING BRAINWASHING CLASSES!
STAND DOWN?
HELL, NO!

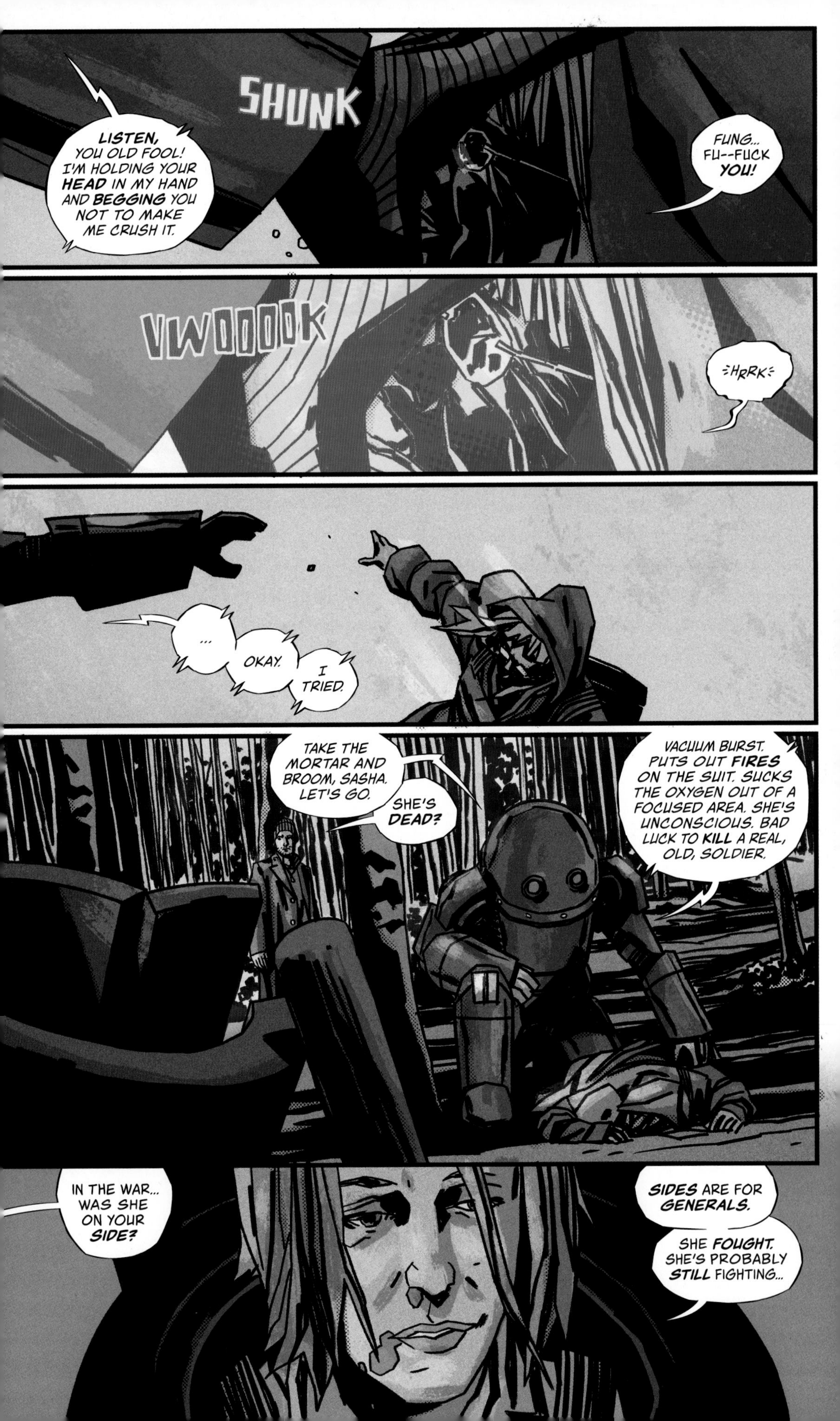
LISTEN, YOU OLD FOOL! I'M HOLDING YOUR HEAD IN MY HAND AND BEGGING YOU NOT TO MAKE ME CRUSH IT.
SHUNK
FUNG... FU--FUCK YOU!
VWOOOOK
HRRK
...
OKAY.
I TRIED.
TAKE THE MORTAR AND BROOM, SASHA. LET'S GO.
SHE'S DEAD?
VACUUM BURST. PUTS OUT FIRES ON THE SUIT. SUCKS THE OXYGEN OUT OF A FOCUSED AREA. SHE'S UNCONSCIOUS. BAD LUCK TO KILL A REAL, OLD, SOLDIER.
IN THE WAR... WAS SHE ON YOUR SIDE?
SIDES ARE FOR GENERALS.
SHE FOUGHT. SHE'S PROBABLY STILL FIGHTING...

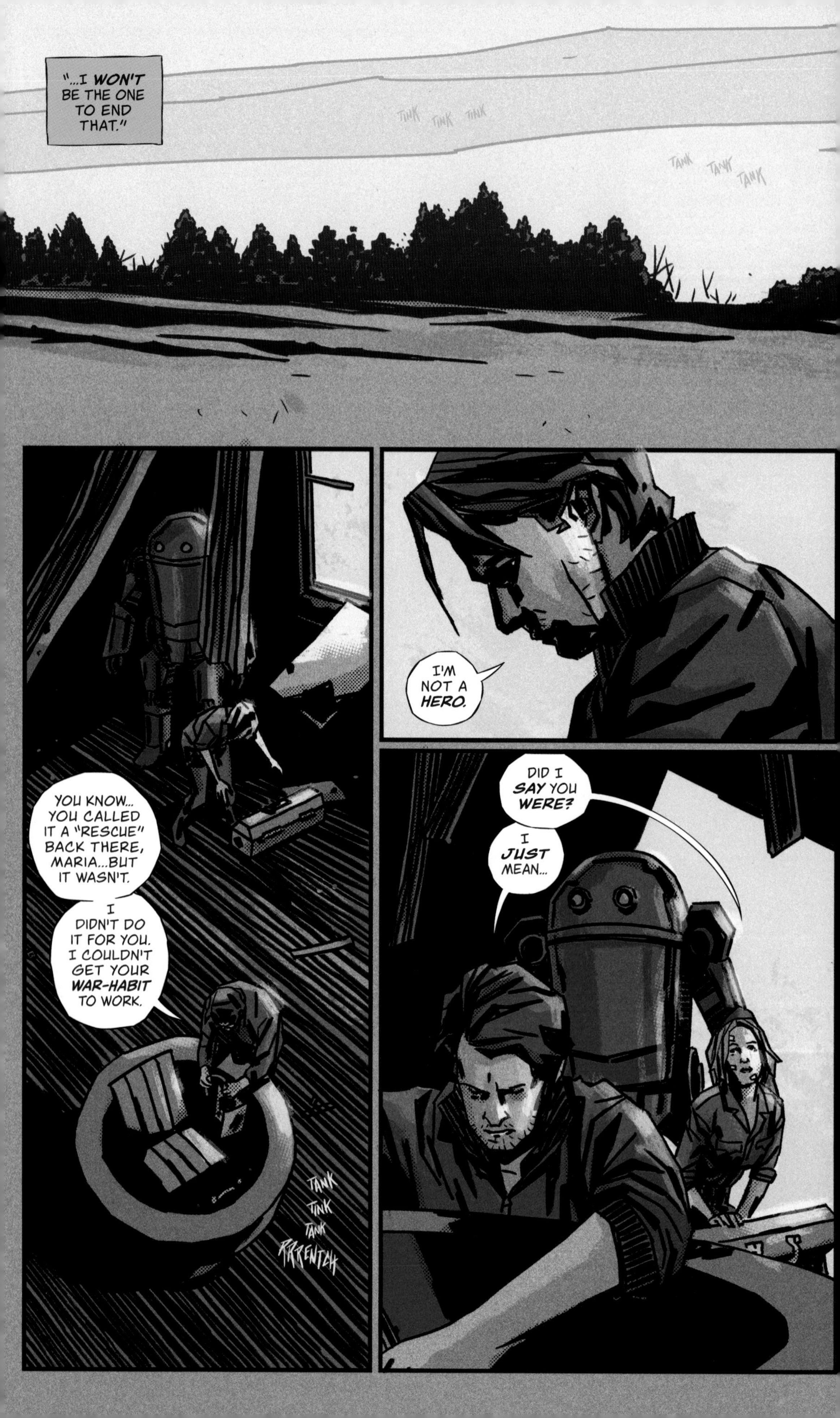
"...I WON'T BE THE ONE TO END THAT."
TINK TINK TINK
TANK TANK TANK
YOU KNOW... YOU CALLED IT A "RESCUE" BACK THERE, MARIA...BUT IT WASN'T.
I DIDN'T DO IT FOR YOU. I COULDN'T GET YOUR WAR-HABIT TO WORK.
TANK TINK TANK RRRENTCH
I'M NOT A HERO.
DID I SAY YOU WERE?
I JUST MEAN...

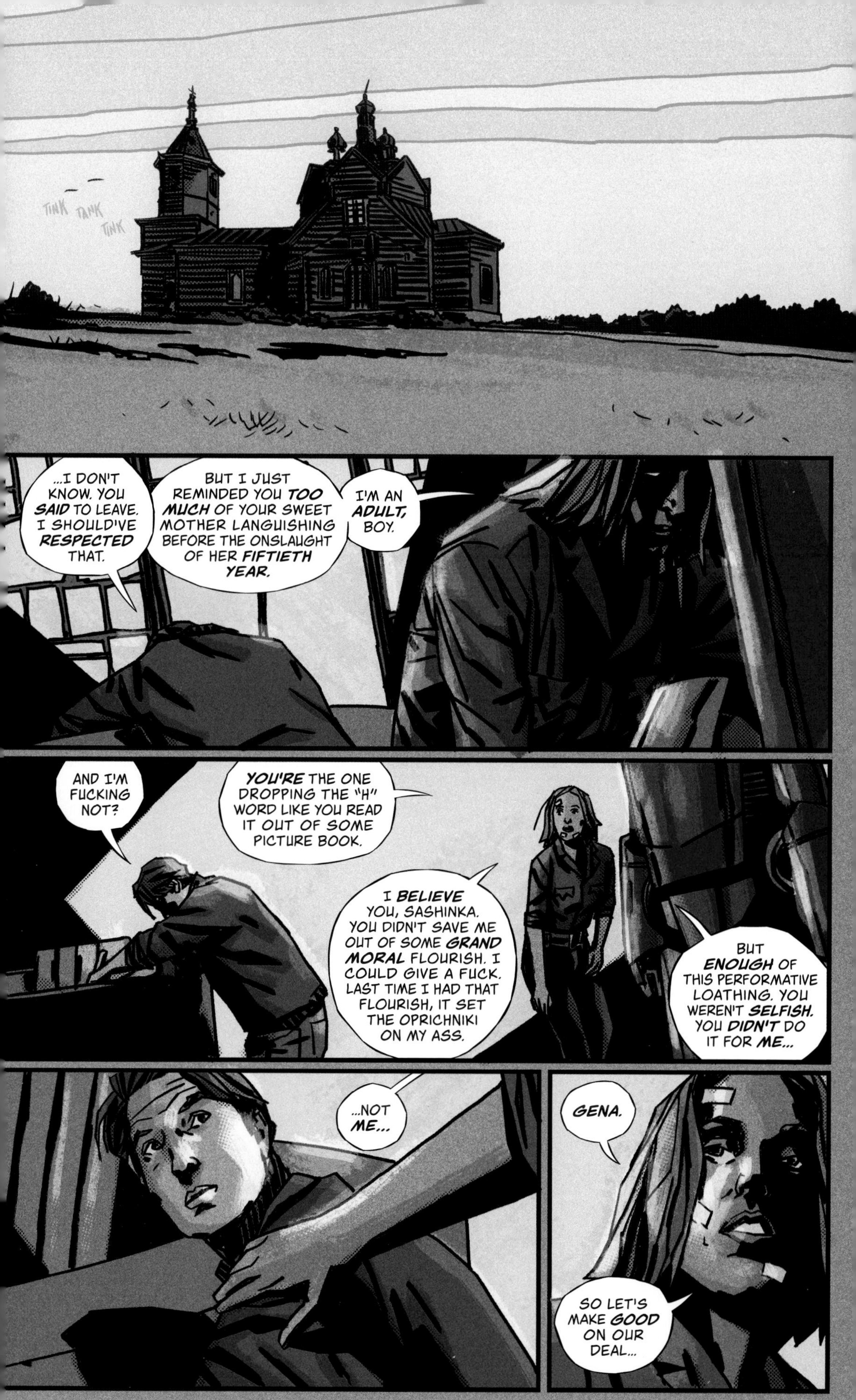
TINK TANK TINK
...I DON'T KNOW. YOU SAID TO LEAVE. I SHOULD'VE RESPECTED THAT.
BUT I JUST REMINDED YOU TOO MUCH OF YOUR SWEET MOTHER LANGUISHING BEFORE THE ONSLAUGHT OF HER FIFTIETH YEAR.
I'M AN ADULT, BOY.
AND I'M FUCKING NOT?
YOU'RE THE ONE DROPPING THE "H" WORD LIKE YOU READ IT OUT OF SOME PICTURE BOOK.
I BELIEVE YOU, SASHINKA. YOU DIDN'T SAVE ME OUT OF SOME GRAND MORAL FLOURISH. I COULD GIVE A FUCK. LAST TIME I HAD THAT FLOURISH, IT SET THE OPRICHNIKI ON MY ASS.
BUT ENOUGH OF THIS PERFORMATIVE LOATHING. YOU WEREN'T SELFISH. YOU DIDN'T DO IT FOR ME...
...NOT ME...
GENA.
SO LET'S MAKE GOOD ON OUR DEAL...

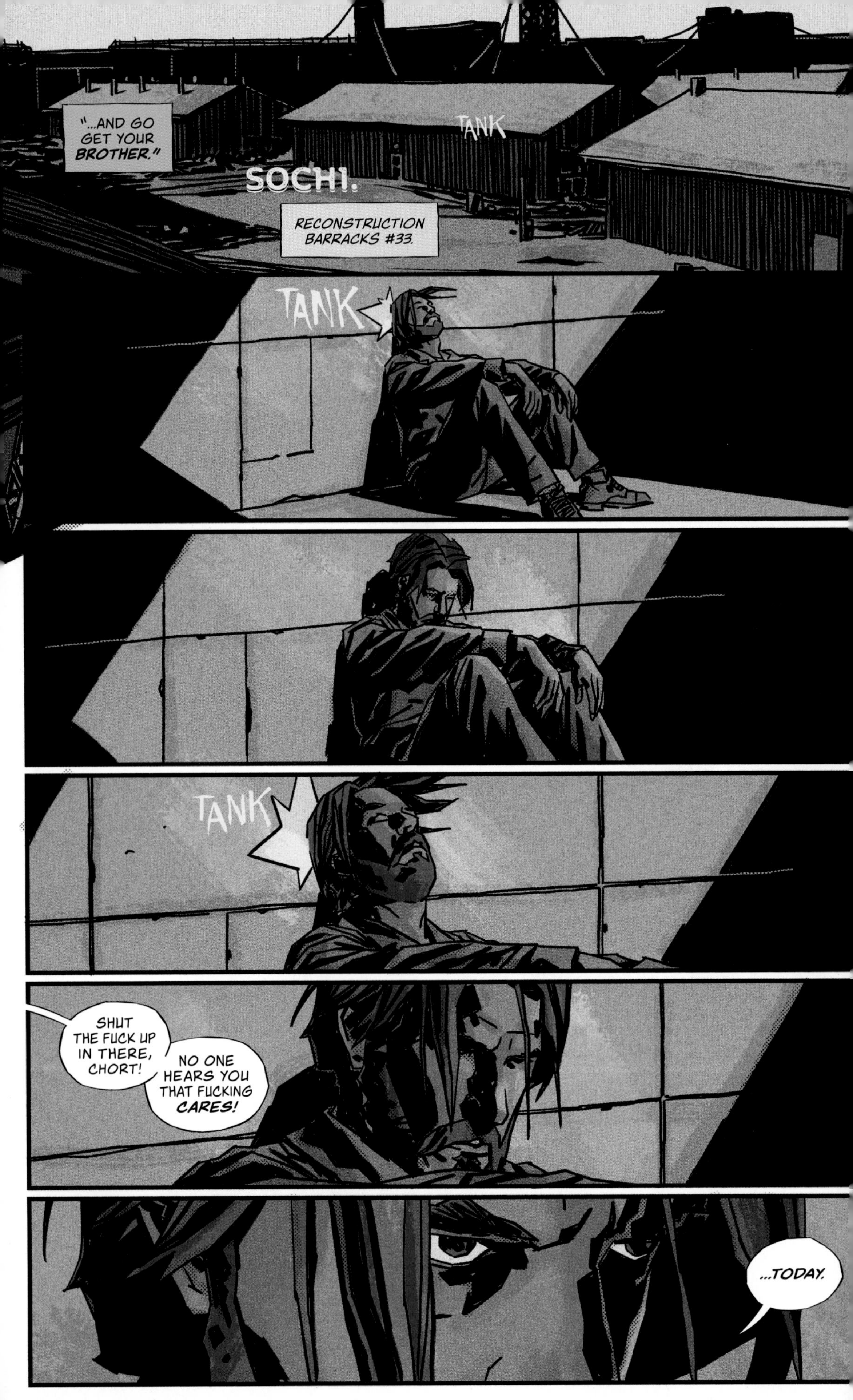
"...AND GO GET YOUR BROTHER."
TANK
SOCHI.
RECONSTRUCTION BARRACKS #33.
TANK
TANK
SHUT THE FUCK UP IN THERE, CHORT!
NO ONE HEARS YOU THAT FUCKING CARES!
...TODAY.

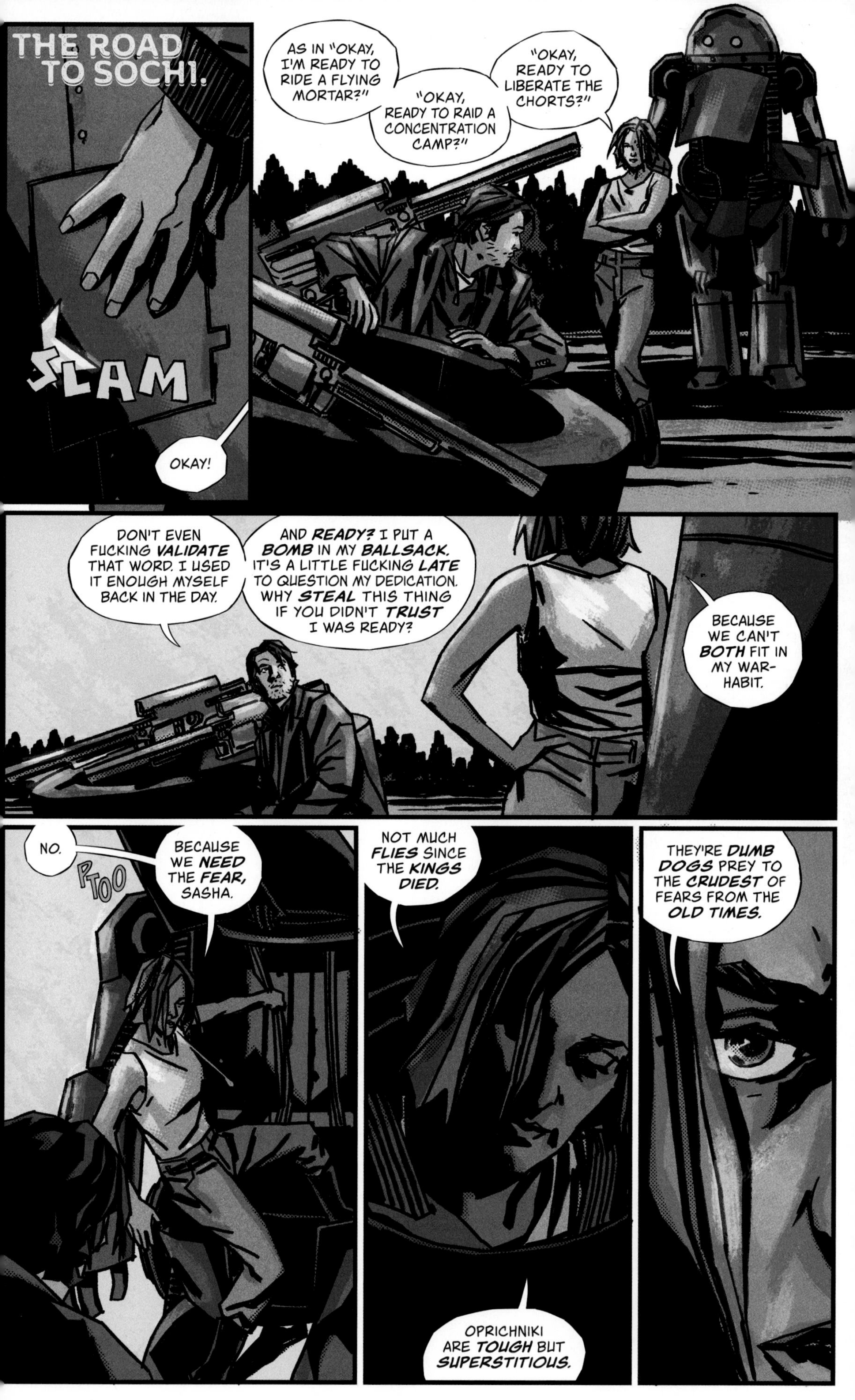
THE ROAD TO SOCHI.
SLAM
OKAY!
AS IN "OKAY, I'M READY TO RIDE A FLYING MORTAR?"
"OKAY, READY TO RAID A CONCENTRATION CAMP?"
"OKAY, READY TO LIBERATE THE CHORTS?"
DON'T EVEN FUCKING VALIDATE THAT WORD. I USED IT ENOUGH MYSELF BACK IN THE DAY.
AND READY? I PUT A BOMB IN MY BALLSACK. IT'S A LITTLE FUCKING LATE TO QUESTION MY DEDICATION. WHY STEAL THIS THING IF YOU DIDN'T TRUST I WAS READY?
BECAUSE WE CAN'T BOTH FIT IN MY WAR-HABIT.
NO.
PTOO
BECAUSE WE NEED THE FEAR, SASHA.
NOT MUCH FLIES SINCE THE KINGS DIED.
OPRICHNIKI ARE TOUGH BUT SUPERSTITIOUS.
THEY'RE DUMB DOGS PREY TO THE CRUDEST OF FEARS FROM THE OLD TIMES.

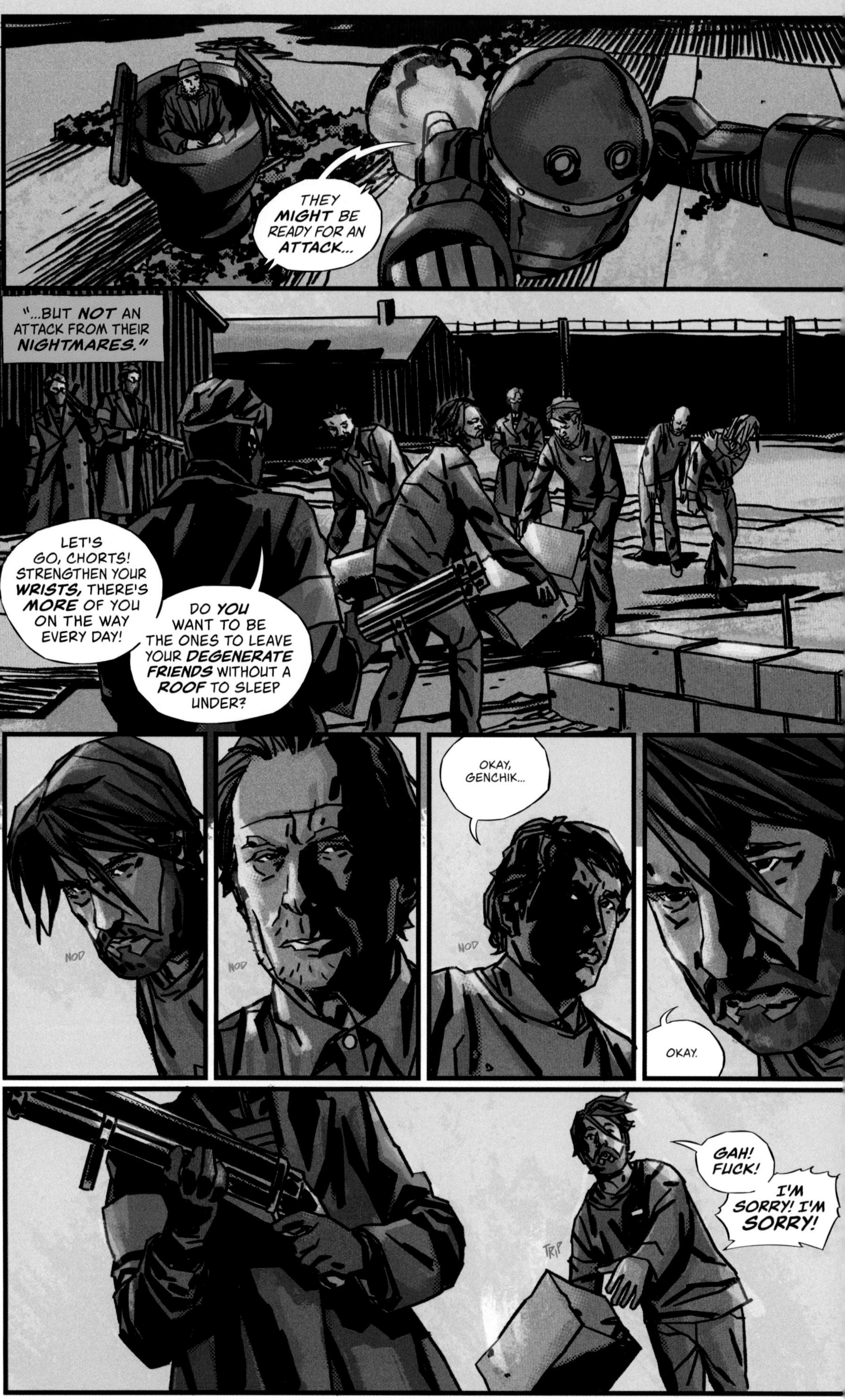
THEY MIGHT BE READY FOR AN ATTACK...
"...BUT NOT AN ATTACK FROM THEIR NIGHTMARES."
LET'S GO, CHORTS! STRENGTHEN YOUR WRISTS, THERE'S MORE OF YOU ON THE WAY EVERY DAY!
DO YOU WANT TO BE THE ONES TO LEAVE YOUR DEGENERATE FRIENDS WITHOUT A ROOF TO SLEEP UNDER?
NOD
NOD
OKAY, GENCHIK...
NOD
OKAY.
TRIP
GAH! FUCK!
I'M SORRY! I'M SORRY!

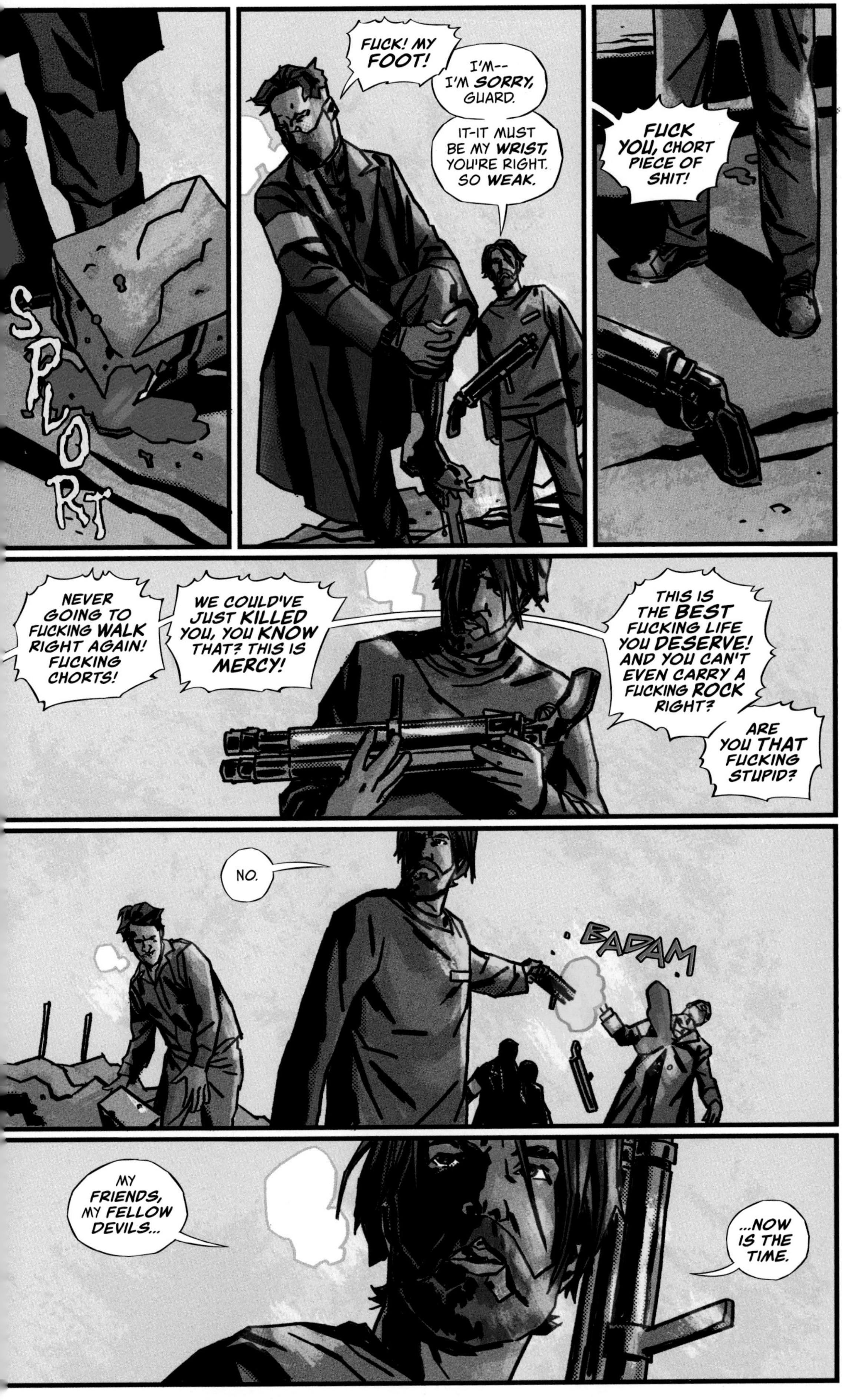
SPLORT
FUCK! MY FOOT!
I'M-- I'M SORRY, GUARD.
IT-IT MUST BE MY WRIST, YOU'RE RIGHT. SO WEAK.
FUCK YOU, CHORT PIECE OF SHIT!
NEVER GOING TO FUCKING WALK RIGHT AGAIN! FUCKING CHORTS!
WE COULD'VE JUST KILLED YOU, YOU KNOW THAT? THIS IS MERCY!
THIS IS THE BEST FUCKING LIFE YOU DESERVE! AND YOU CAN'T EVEN CARRY A FUCKING ROCK RIGHT?
ARE YOU THAT FUCKING STUPID?
NO.
BADAM
MY FRIENDS, MY FELLOW DEVILS...
...NOW IS THE TIME.

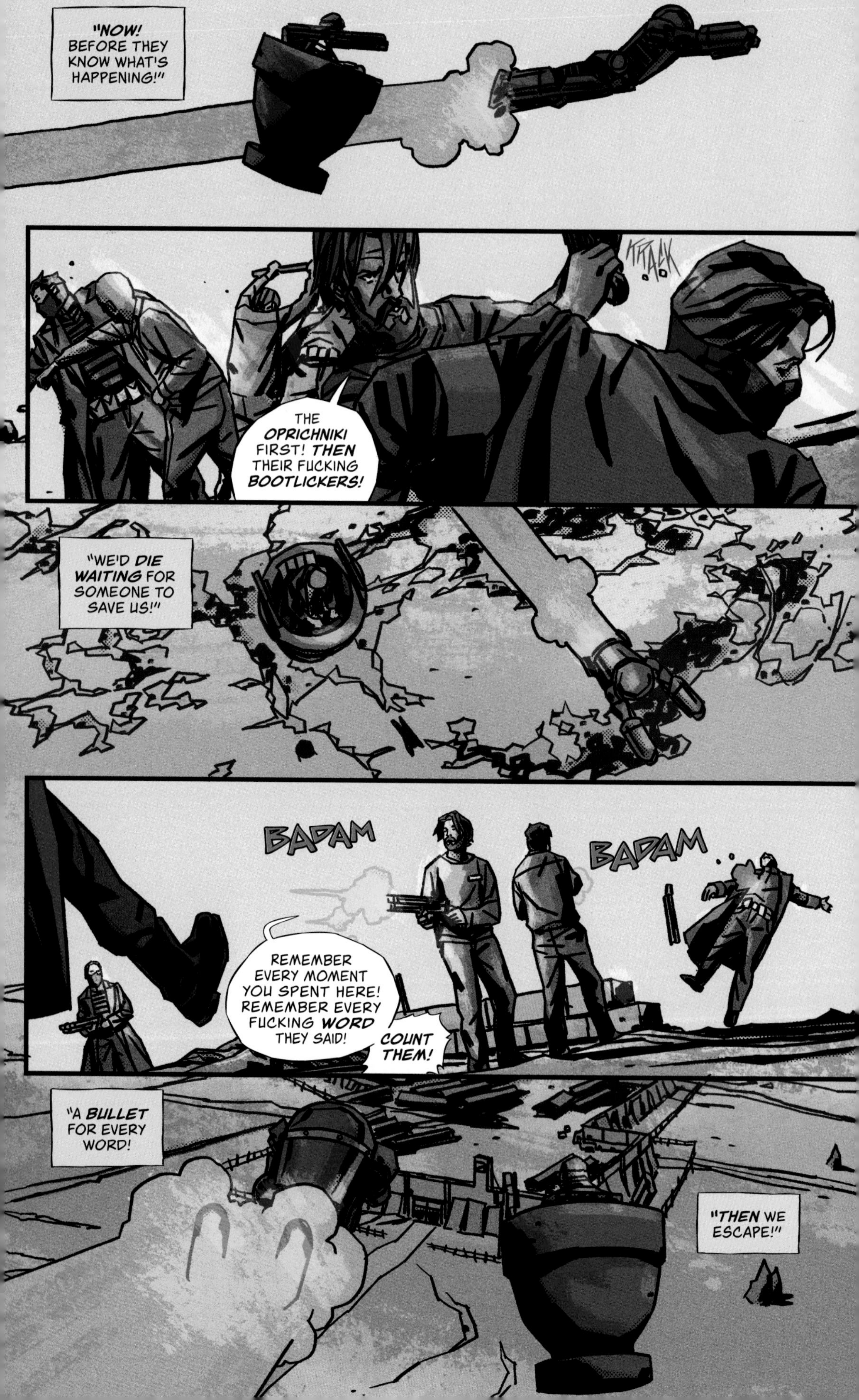
"NOW! BEFORE THEY KNOW WHAT'S HAPPENING!"
KRACK
THE OPRICHNIKI FIRST! THEN THEIR FUCKING BOOTLICKERS!
"WE'D DIE WAITING FOR SOMEONE TO SAVE US!"
BADAM
BADAM
REMEMBER EVERY MOMENT YOU SPENT HERE! REMEMBER EVERY FUCKING WORD THEY SAID!
COUNT THEM!
"A BULLET FOR EVERY WORD!
"THEN WE ESCAPE!"

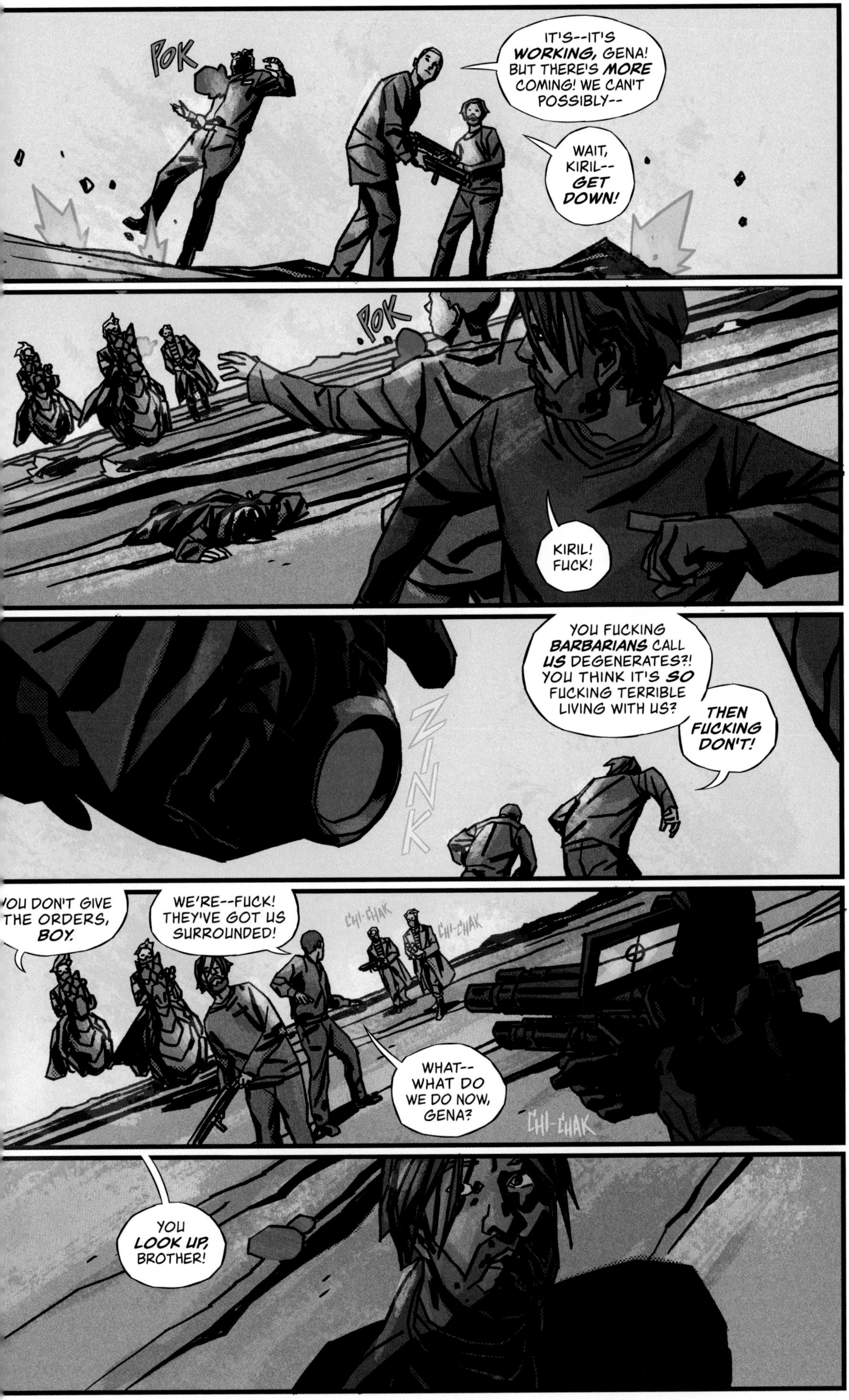
POK
IT'S--IT'S WORKING, GENA! BUT THERE'S MORE COMING! WE CAN'T POSSIBLY--
WAIT, KIRIL-- GET DOWN!
POK
KIRIL! FUCK!
YOU FUCKING BARBARIANS CALL US DEGENERATES?! YOU THINK IT'S SO FUCKING TERRIBLE LIVING WITH US?
THEN FUCKING DON'T!
ZINK
YOU DON'T GIVE THE ORDERS, BOY.
WE'RE--FUCK! THEY'VE GOT US SURROUNDED!
CHI-CHAK
CHI-CHAK
WHAT-- WHAT DO WE DO NOW, GENA?
CHI-CHAK
YOU LOOK UP, BROTHER!

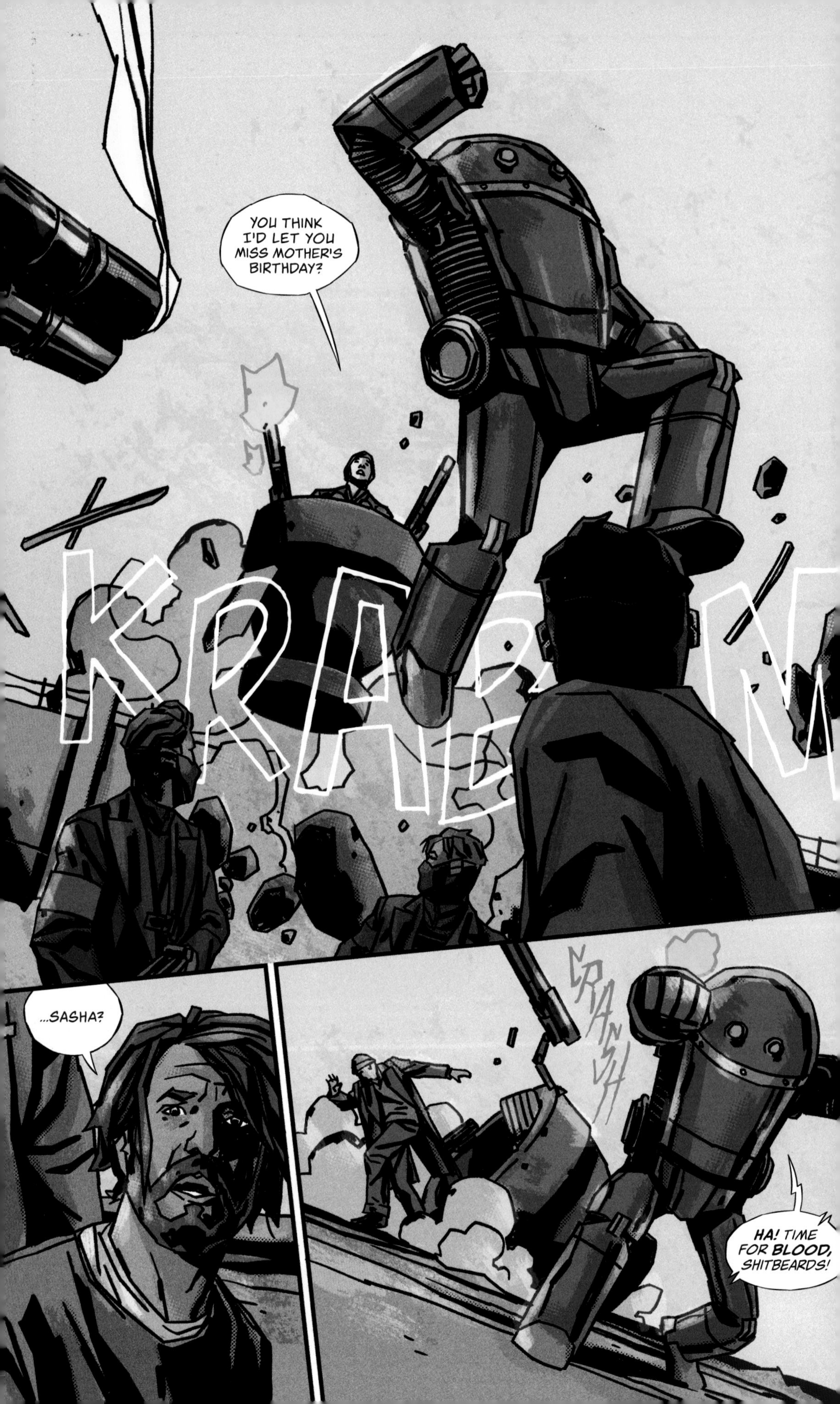
YOU THINK I'D LET YOU MISS MOTHER'S BIRTHDAY?
KRABOOM
...SASHA?
CRASH
HA! TIME FOR BLOOD, SHITBEARDS!

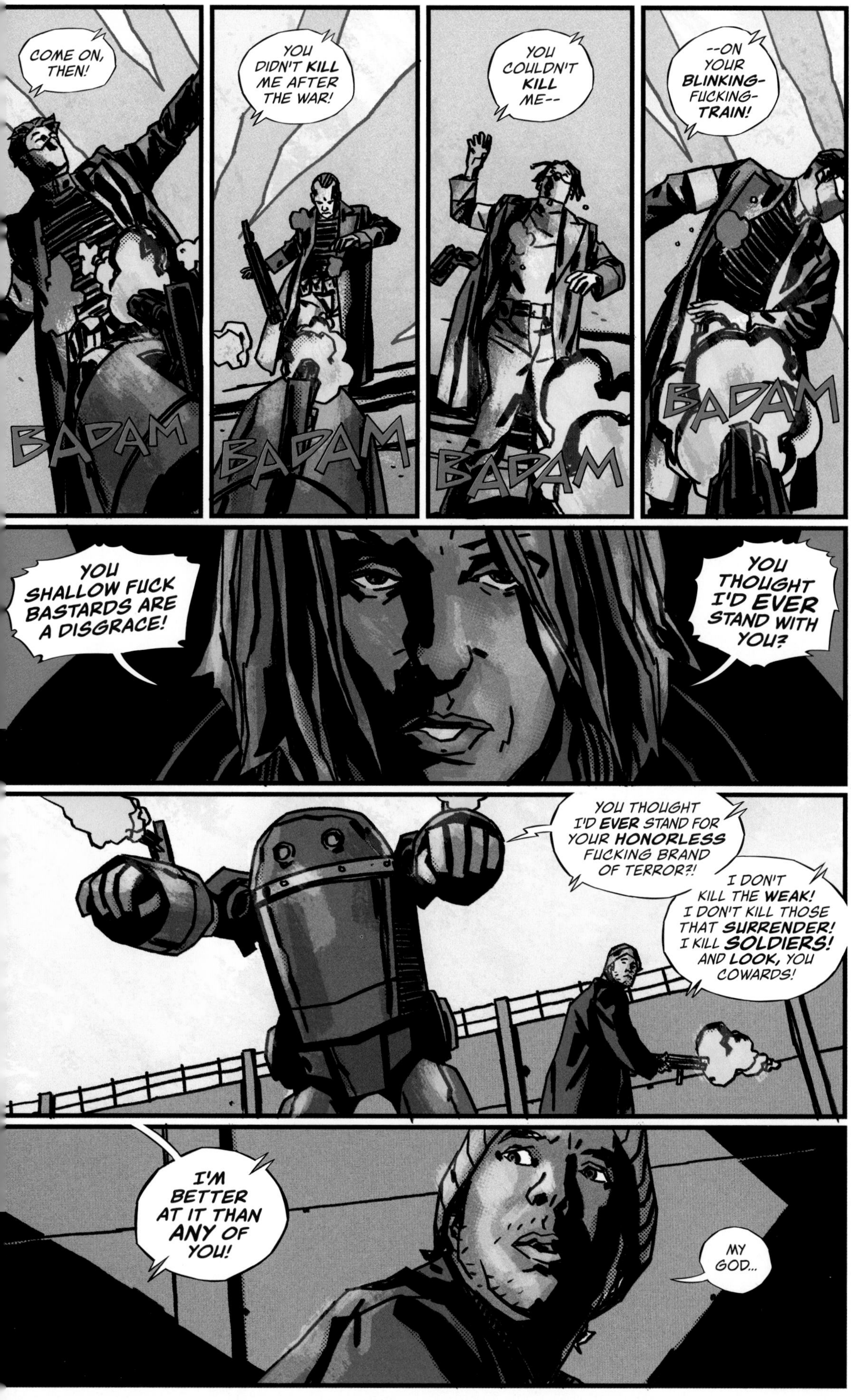
COME ON, THEN!
BADAM
YOU DIDN'T KILL ME AFTER THE WAR!
BADAM
YOU COULDN'T KILL ME--
BADAM
--ON YOUR BLINKING-FUCKING-TRAIN!
BADAM
YOU SHALLOW FUCK BASTARDS ARE A DISGRACE!
YOU THOUGHT I'D EVER STAND WITH YOU?
YOU THOUGHT I'D EVER STAND FOR YOUR HONORLESS FUCKING BRAND OF TERROR?!
I DON'T KILL THE WEAK! I DON'T KILL THOSE THAT SURRENDER! I KILL SOLDIERS! AND LOOK, YOU COWARDS!
I'M BETTER AT IT THAN ANY OF YOU!
MY GOD...

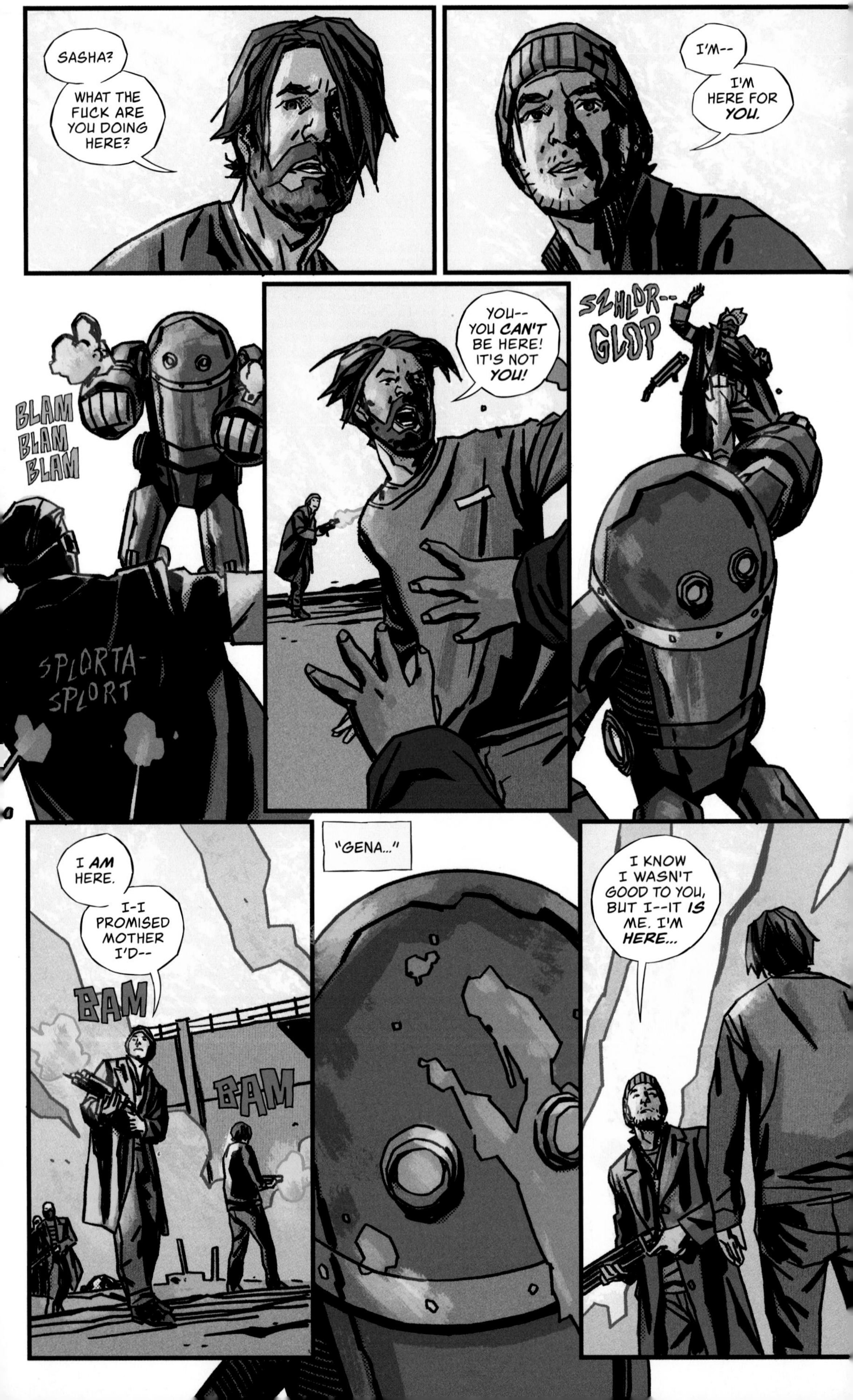
SASHA?
WHAT THE FUCK ARE YOU DOING HERE?
I'M--
I'M HERE FOR YOU.
BLAM BLAM BLAM
YOU-- YOU CAN'T BE HERE! IT'S NOT YOU!
SZHLOR-- GLOP
SPLORTA-SPLORT
I AM HERE.
I-I PROMISED MOTHER I'D--
BAM
BAM
"GENA..."
I KNOW I WASN'T GOOD TO YOU, BUT I--IT IS ME. I'M HERE...

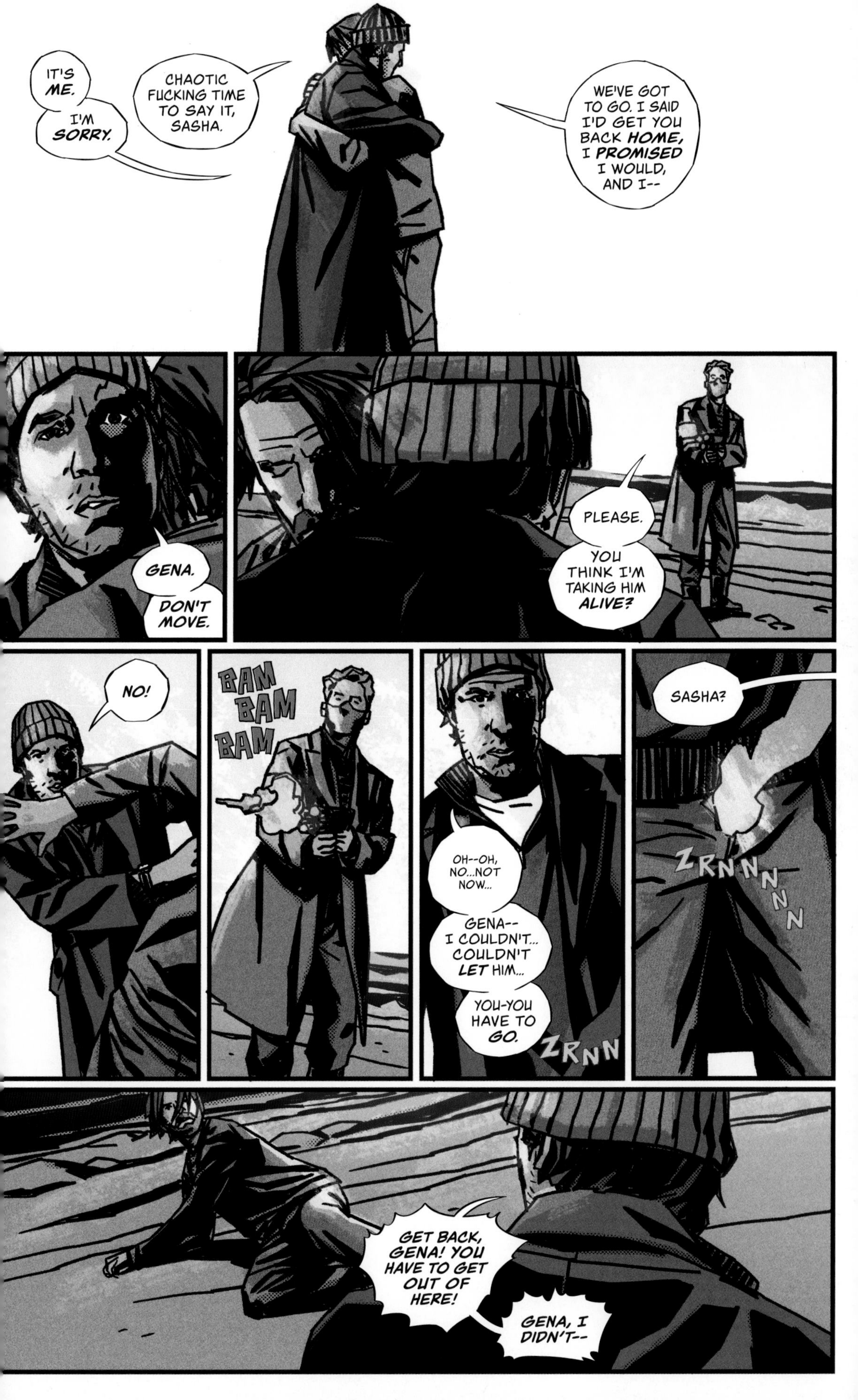
IT'S ME.
I'M SORRY.
CHAOTIC FUCKING TIME TO SAY IT, SASHA.
WE'VE GOT TO GO. I SAID I'D GET YOU BACK HOME, I PROMISED I WOULD, AND I--
GENA.
DON'T MOVE.
PLEASE.
YOU THINK I'M TAKING HIM ALIVE?
NO!
BAM BAM BAM
OH--OH, NO...NOT NOW...
GENA-- I COULDN'T... COULDN'T LET HIM...
YOU-YOU HAVE TO GO.
ZRNN
SASHA?
ZRNNNNNN
GET BACK, GENA! YOU HAVE TO GET OUT OF HERE!
GENA, I DIDN'T--

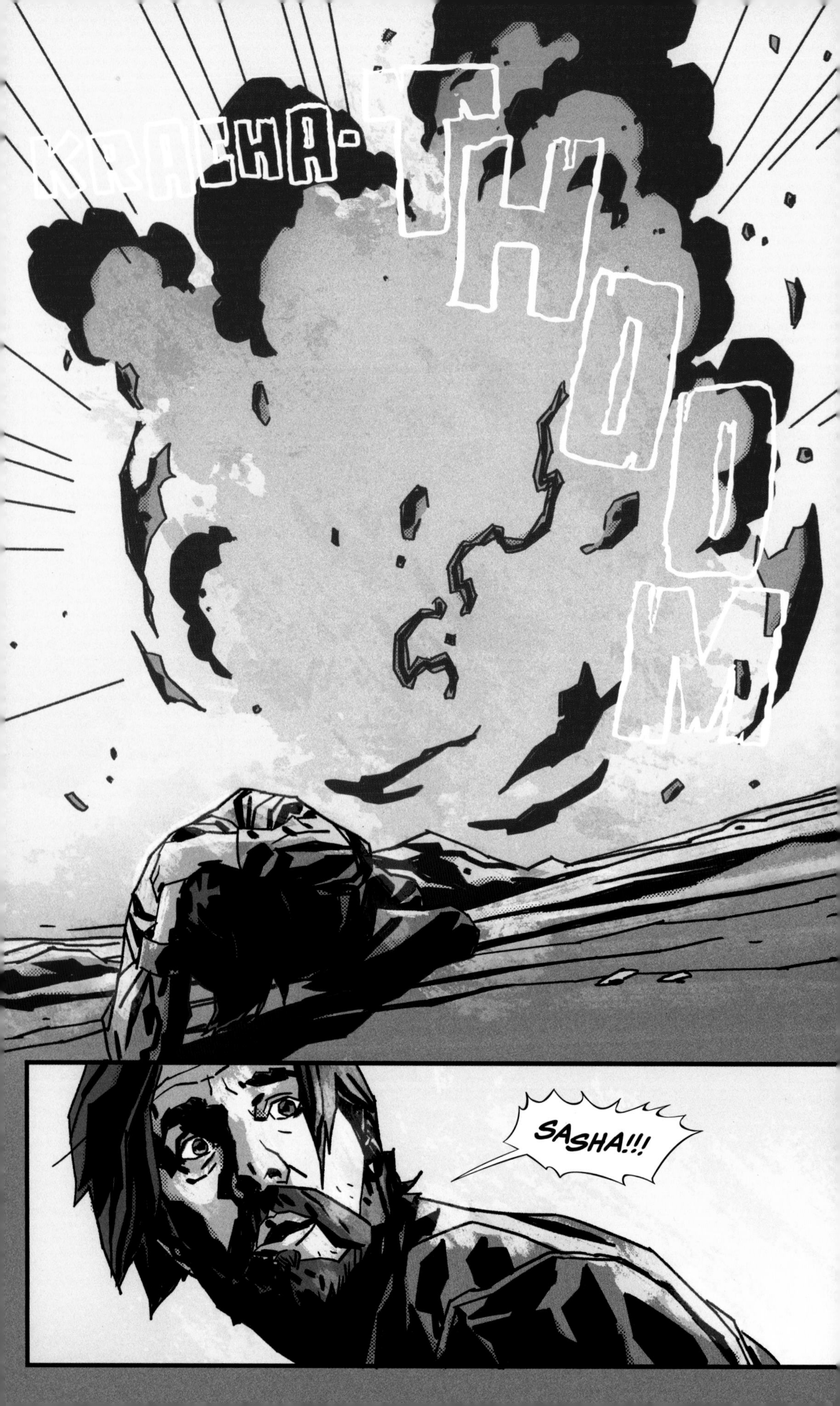
KRACHA-THOOM
SASHA!!!

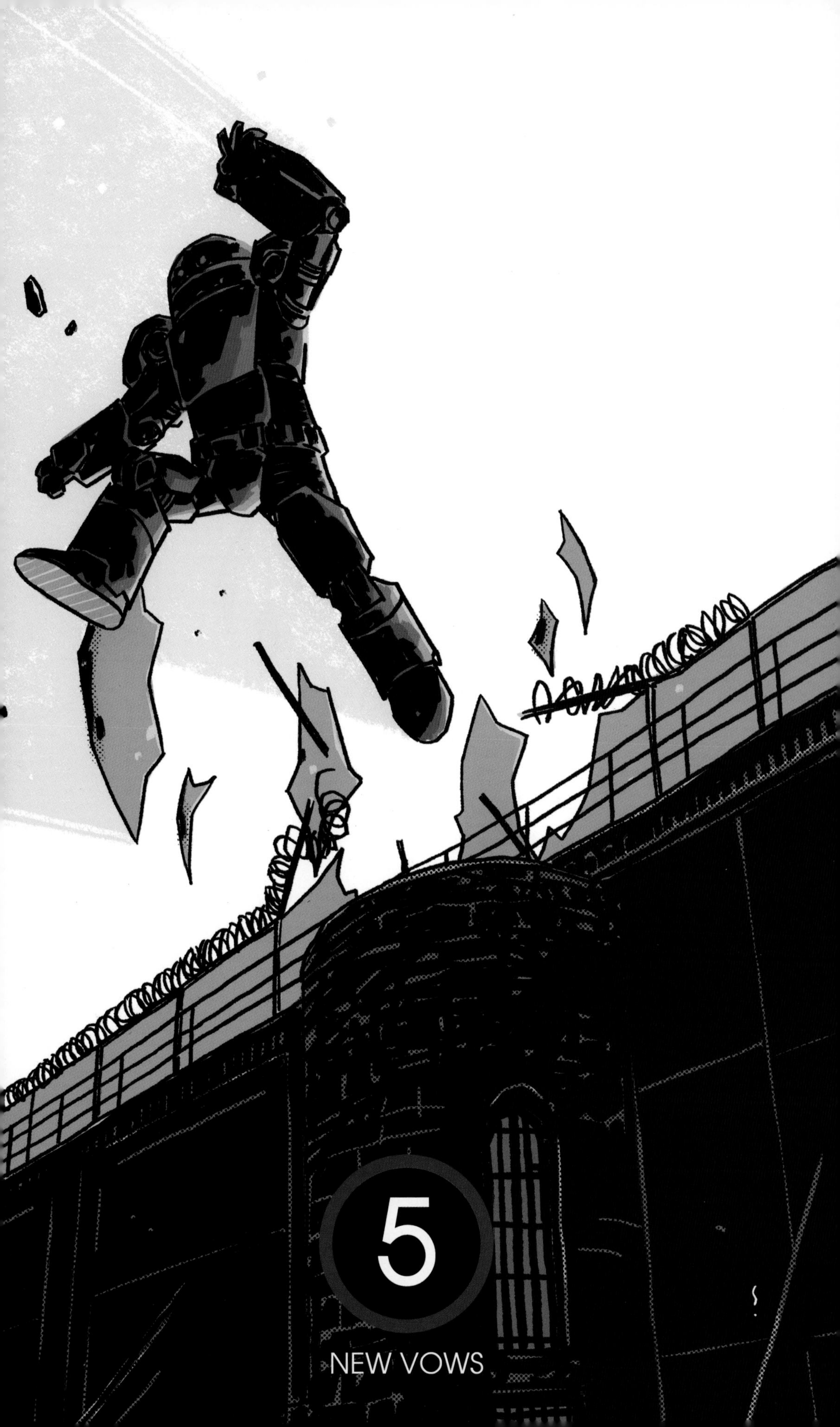

5
NEW VOWS

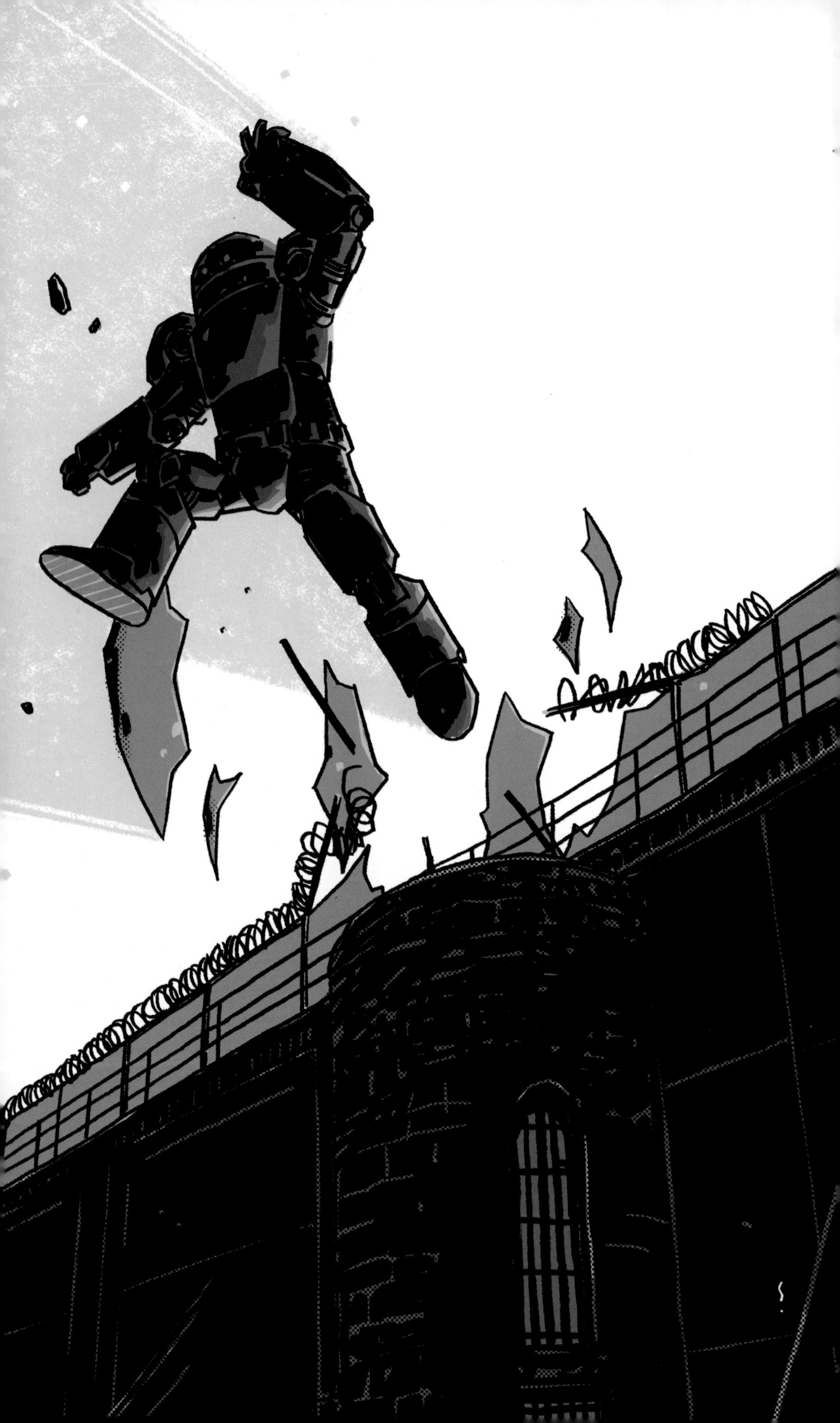

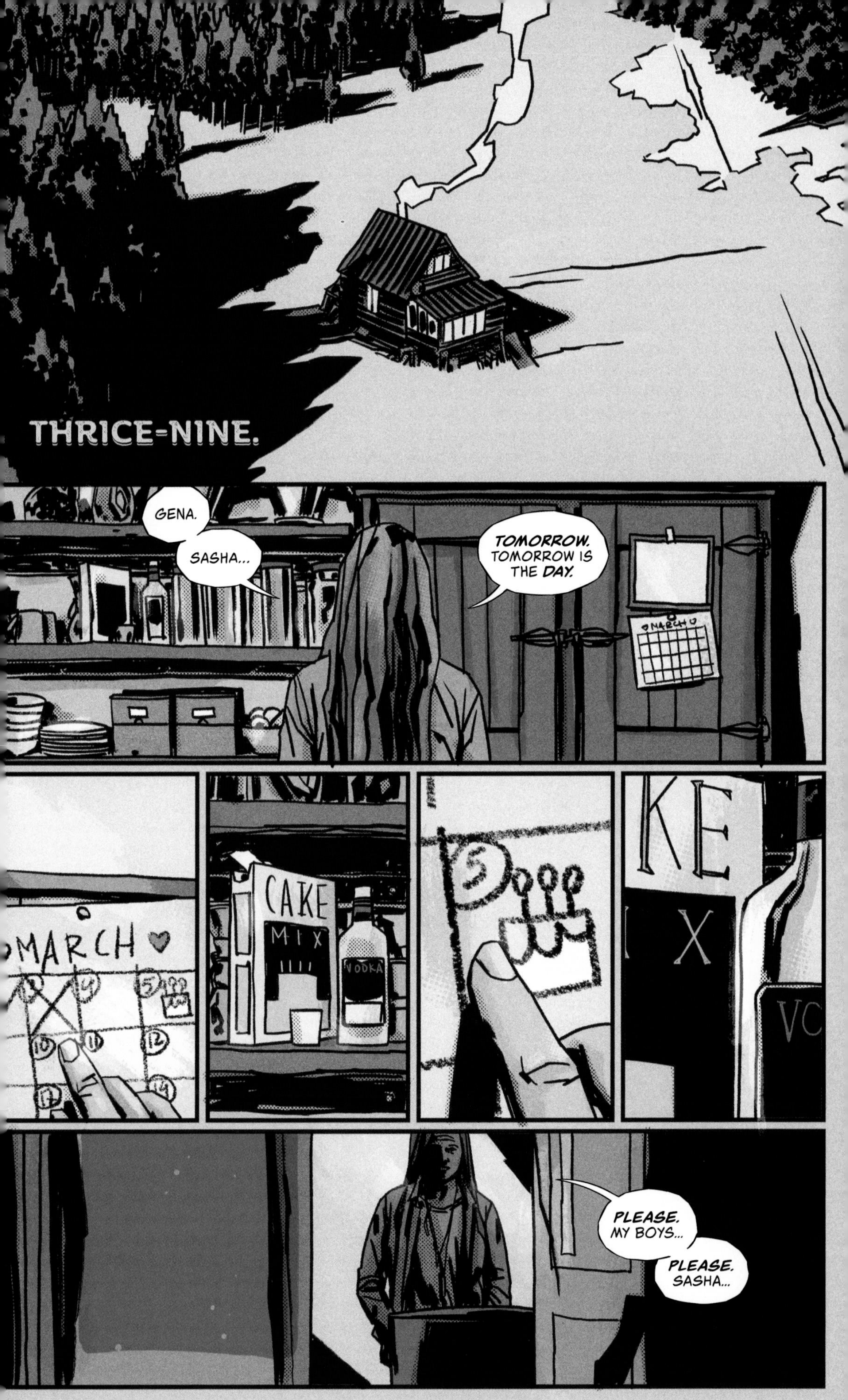
THRICE-NINE.
GENA.
SASHA...
TOMORROW. TOMORROW IS THE DAY.
MARCH
MARCH
CAKE MIX
VODKA
PLEASE. MY BOYS...
PLEASE. SASHA...

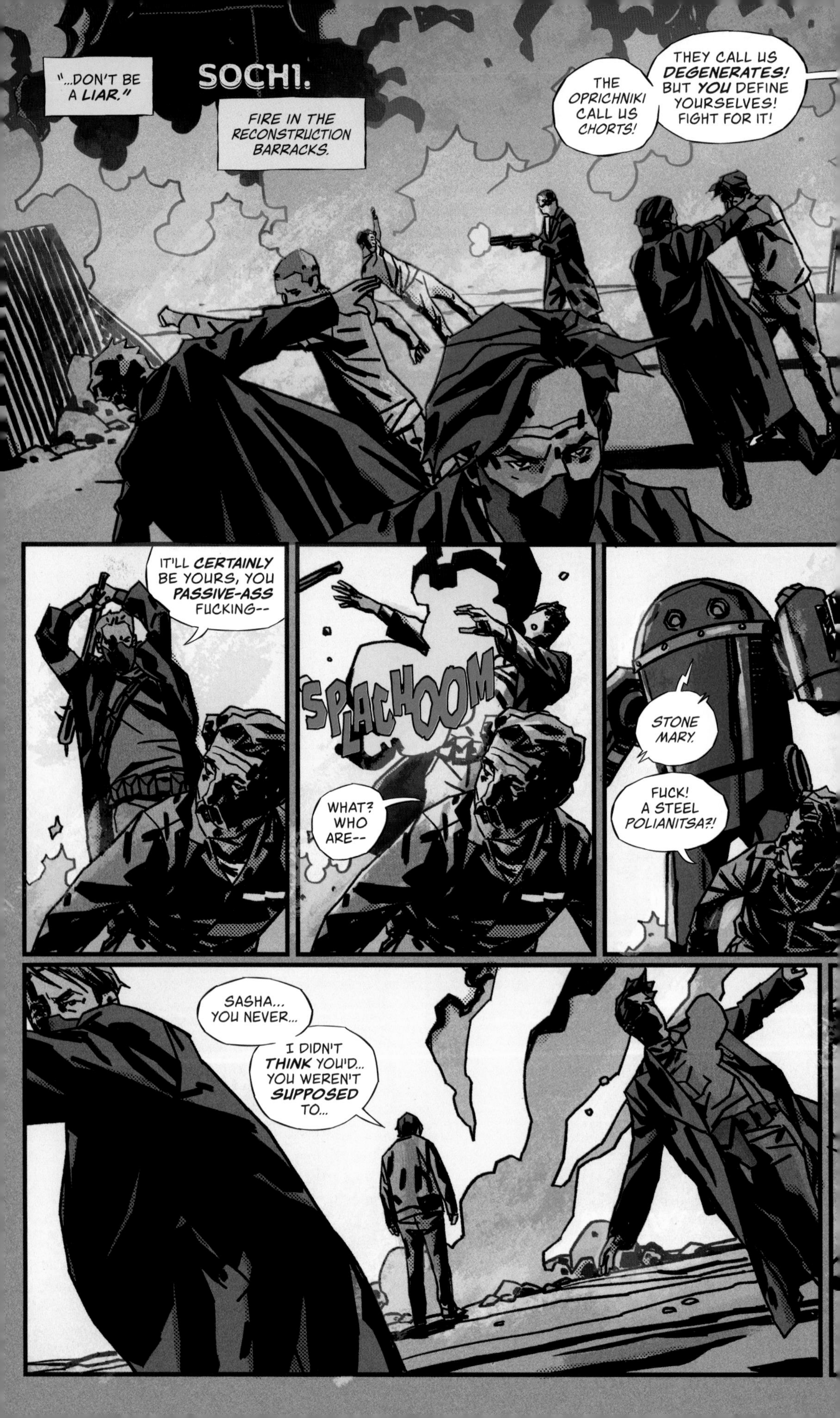
"...DON'T BE A LIAR."
SOCHI.
FIRE IN THE RECONSTRUCTION BARRACKS.
THE OPRICHNIKI CALL US CHORTS!
THEY CALL US DEGENERATES! BUT YOU DEFINE YOURSELVES! FIGHT FOR IT!
IT'LL CERTAINLY BE YOURS, YOU PASSIVE-ASS FUCKING--
SPLACHOOM
WHAT? WHO ARE--
STONE MARY.
FUCK! A STEEL POLIANITSA?!
SASHA... YOU NEVER...
I DIDN'T THINK YOU'D... YOU WEREN'T SUPPOSED TO...

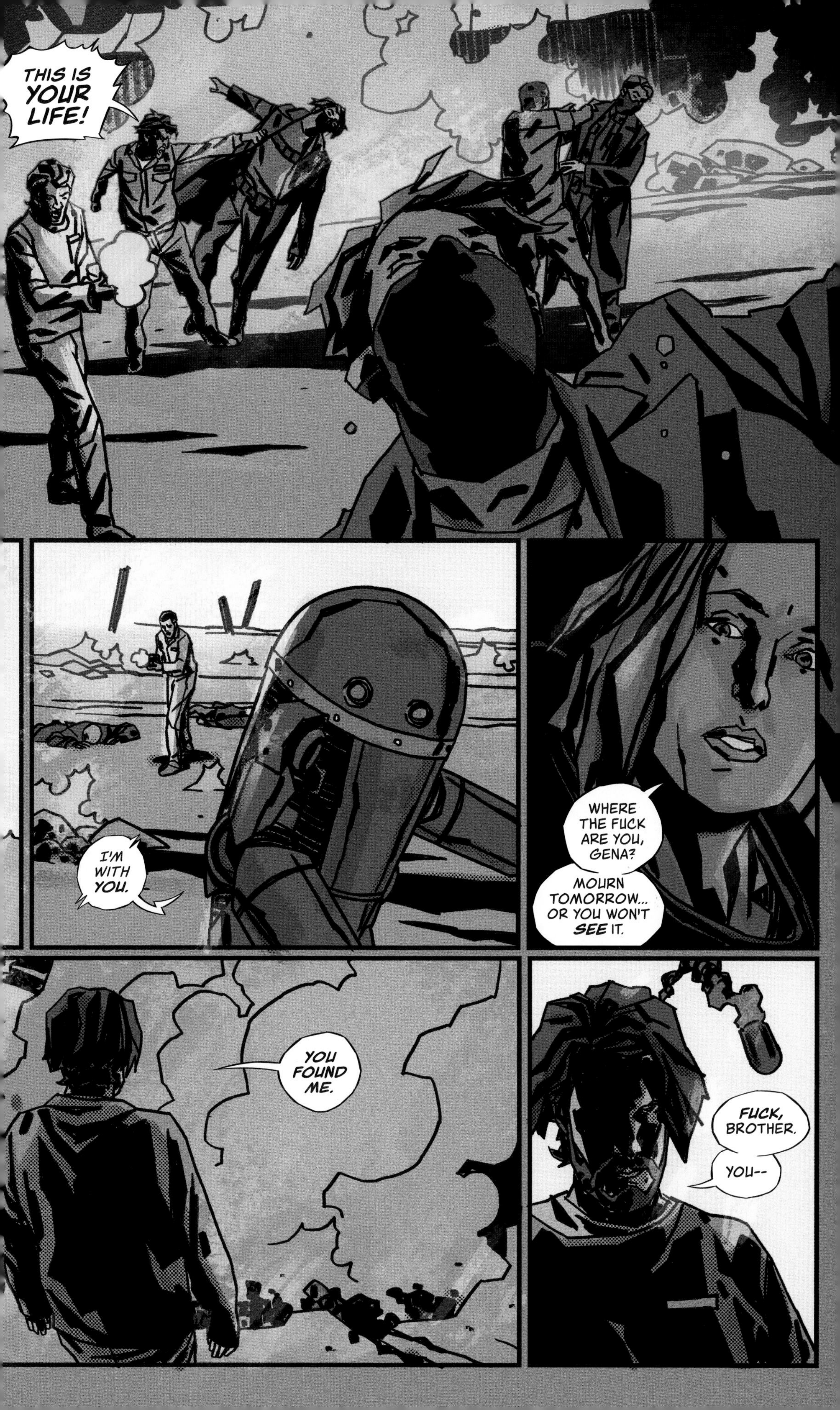
THIS IS YOUR LIFE!
I'M WITH YOU.
WHERE THE FUCK ARE YOU, GENA?
MOURN TOMORROW... OR YOU WON'T SEE IT.
YOU FOUND ME.
FUCK, BROTHER.
YOU--

GET FUCKING DOWN!

FUCK! GET THE FUCK OFF ME! YOU'RE NOT A FUCKING OPRICHNIK!

SO WHO AND WHAT THE FUCK ARE YOU?!

MARIA KAMENAYA. I KNEW YOUR BROTHER...

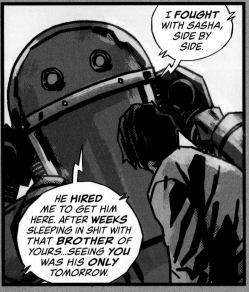

I FOUGHT WITH SASHA, SIDE BY SIDE.

HE HIRED ME TO GET HIM HERE. AFTER WEEKS SLEEPING IN SHIT WITH THAT BROTHER OF YOURS...SEEING YOU WAS HIS ONLY TOMORROW.

FEEL IT WHEN YOU'RE FREE. MISS HIM THEN.

HE WOULDN'T WANT YOU TO DIE HERE. IT CONSUMED HIM.

HE FOUGHT FOR YOU, GENA.

LET'S GO.

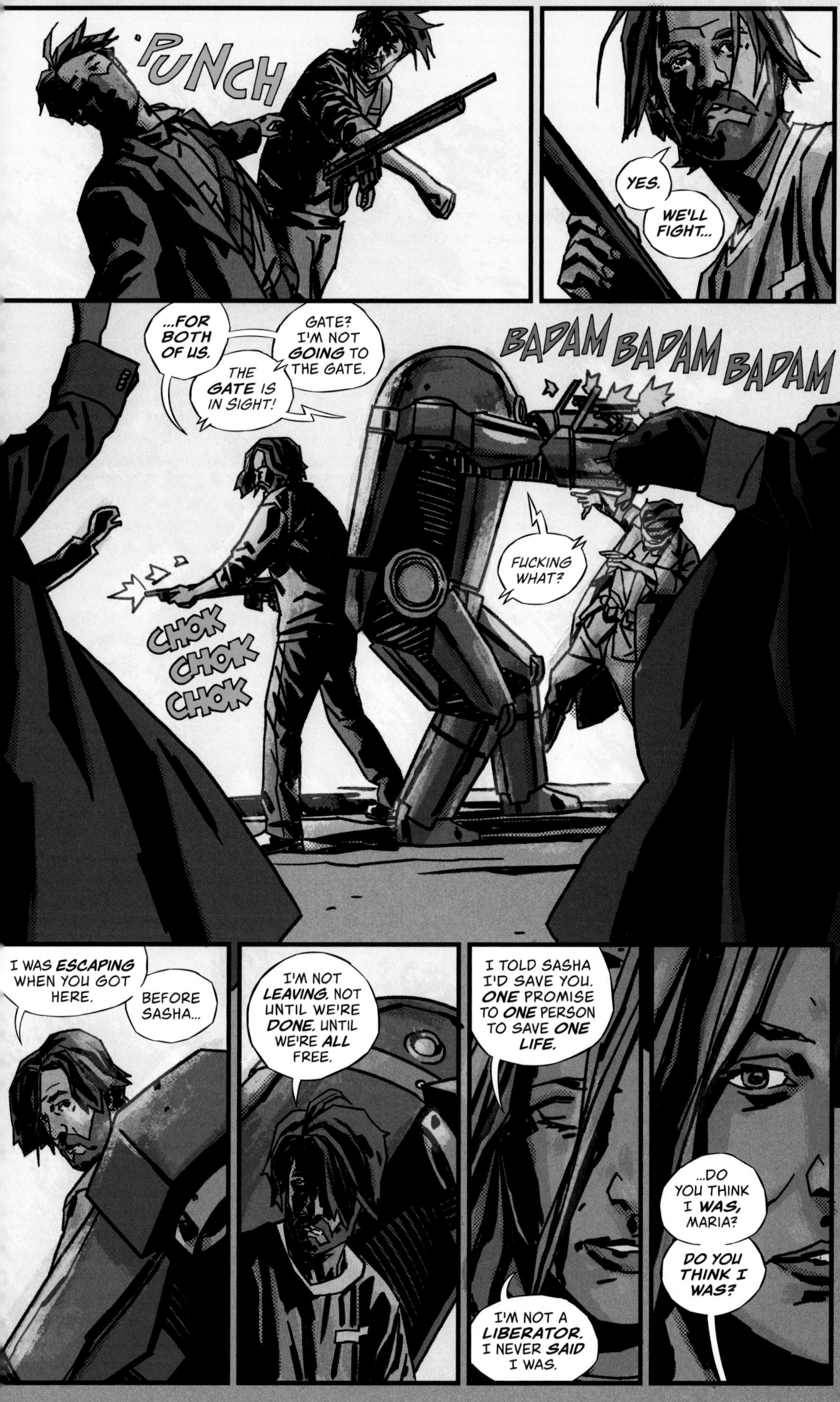
PUNCH
YES.
WE'LL FIGHT...
...FOR BOTH OF US.
GATE? I'M NOT GOING TO THE GATE.
THE GATE IS IN SIGHT!
BADAM BADAM BADAM
FUCKING WHAT?
CHOK CHOK CHOK
I WAS ESCAPING WHEN YOU GOT HERE.
BEFORE SASHA...
I'M NOT LEAVING. NOT UNTIL WE'RE DONE. UNTIL WE'RE ALL FREE.
I TOLD SASHA I'D SAVE YOU. ONE PROMISE TO ONE PERSON TO SAVE ONE LIFE.
I'M NOT A LIBERATOR. I NEVER SAID I WAS.
...DO YOU THINK I WAS, MARIA?
DO YOU THINK I WAS?

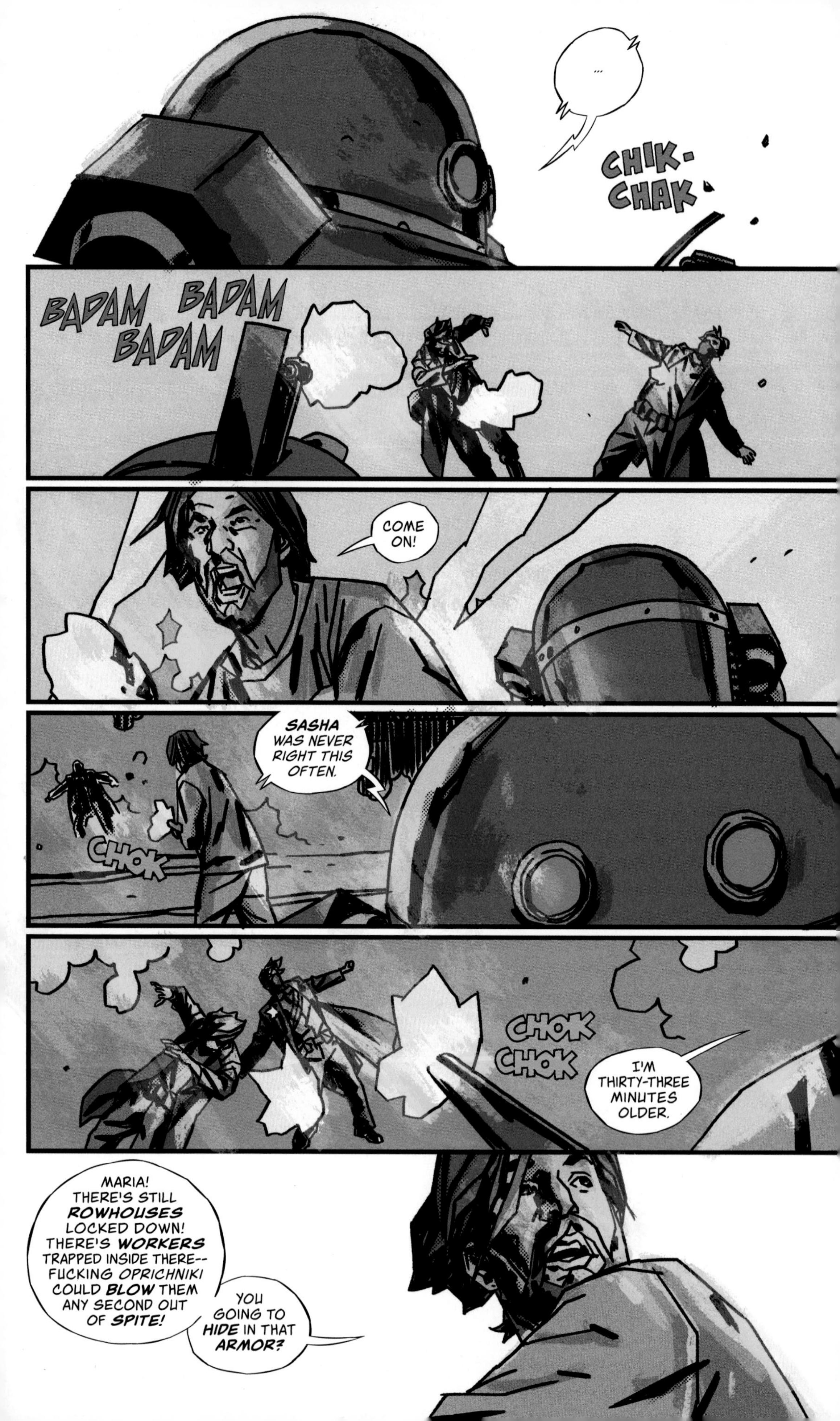
...
CHIK-CHAK
BADAM BADAM BADAM
COME ON!
SASHA WAS NEVER RIGHT THIS OFTEN.
CHOK
CHOK CHOK
I'M THIRTY-THREE MINUTES OLDER.
MARIA! THERE'S STILL ROWHOUSES LOCKED DOWN! THERE'S WORKERS TRAPPED INSIDE THERE-- FUCKING OPRICHNIKI COULD BLOW THEM ANY SECOND OUT OF SPITE!
YOU GOING TO HIDE IN THAT ARMOR?

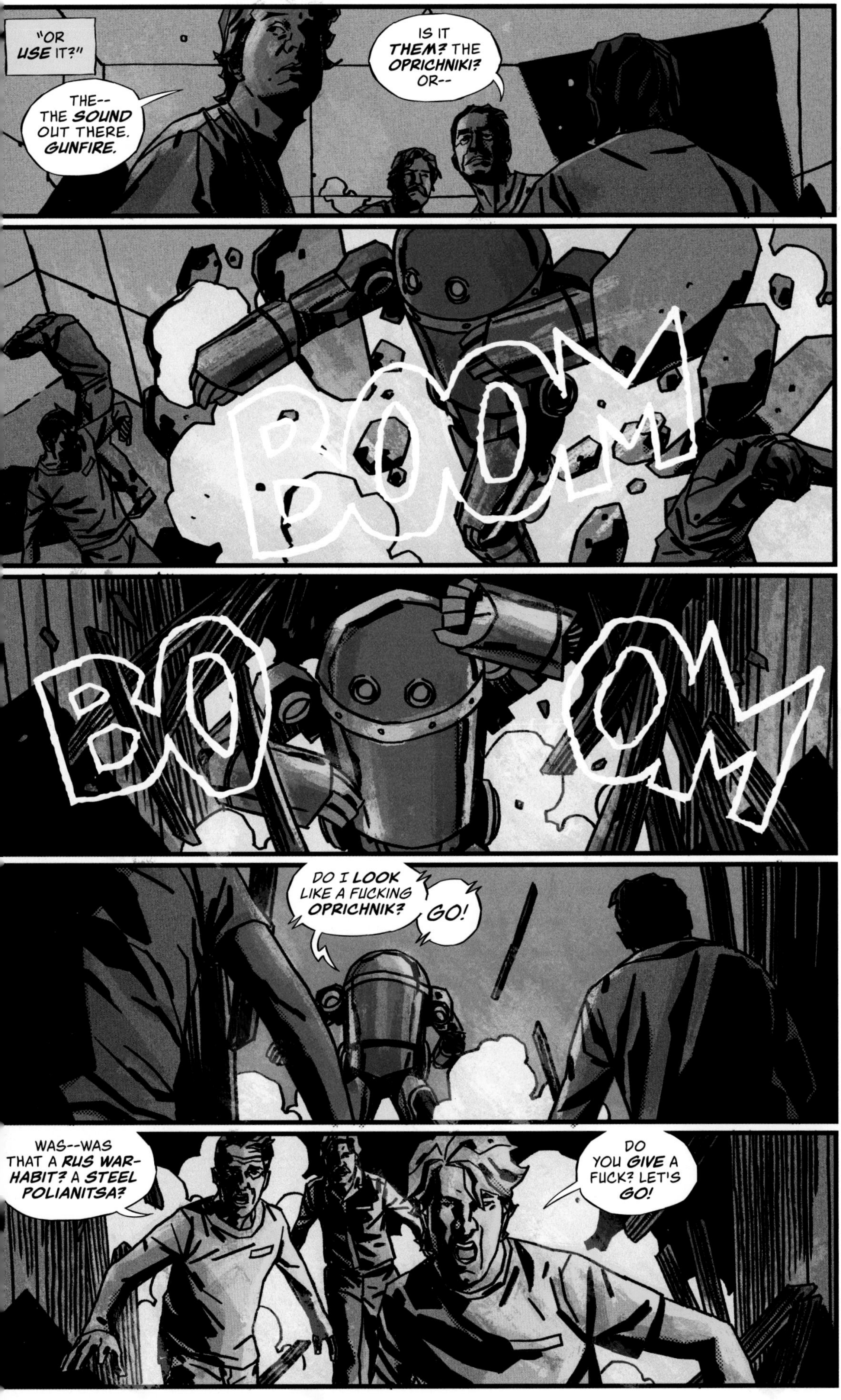
"OR USE IT?"
THE-- THE SOUND OUT THERE. GUNFIRE.
IS IT THEM? THE OPRICHNIKI? OR--
BOOM
BOOM
DO I LOOK LIKE A FUCKING OPRICHNIK?
GO!
WAS--WAS THAT A RUS WAR-HABIT? A STEEL POLIANITSA?
DO YOU GIVE A FUCK? LET'S GO!

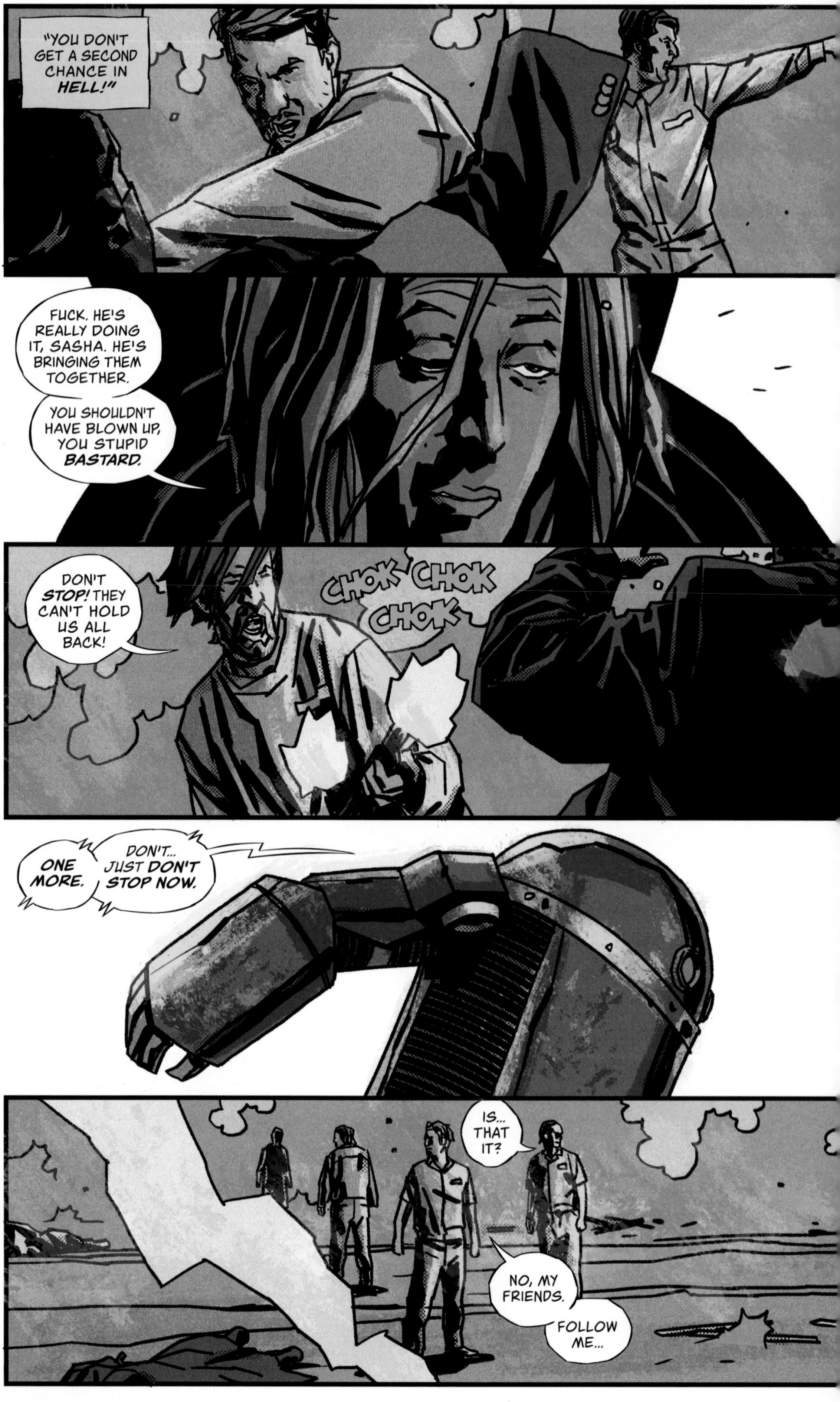
"YOU DON'T GET A SECOND CHANCE IN HELL!"
FUCK. HE'S REALLY DOING IT, SASHA. HE'S BRINGING THEM TOGETHER.
YOU SHOULDN'T HAVE BLOWN UP, YOU STUPID BASTARD.
DON'T STOP! THEY CAN'T HOLD US ALL BACK!
CHOK CHOK CHOK
ONE MORE.
DON'T... JUST DON'T STOP NOW.
IS... THAT IT?
NO, MY FRIENDS.
FOLLOW ME...

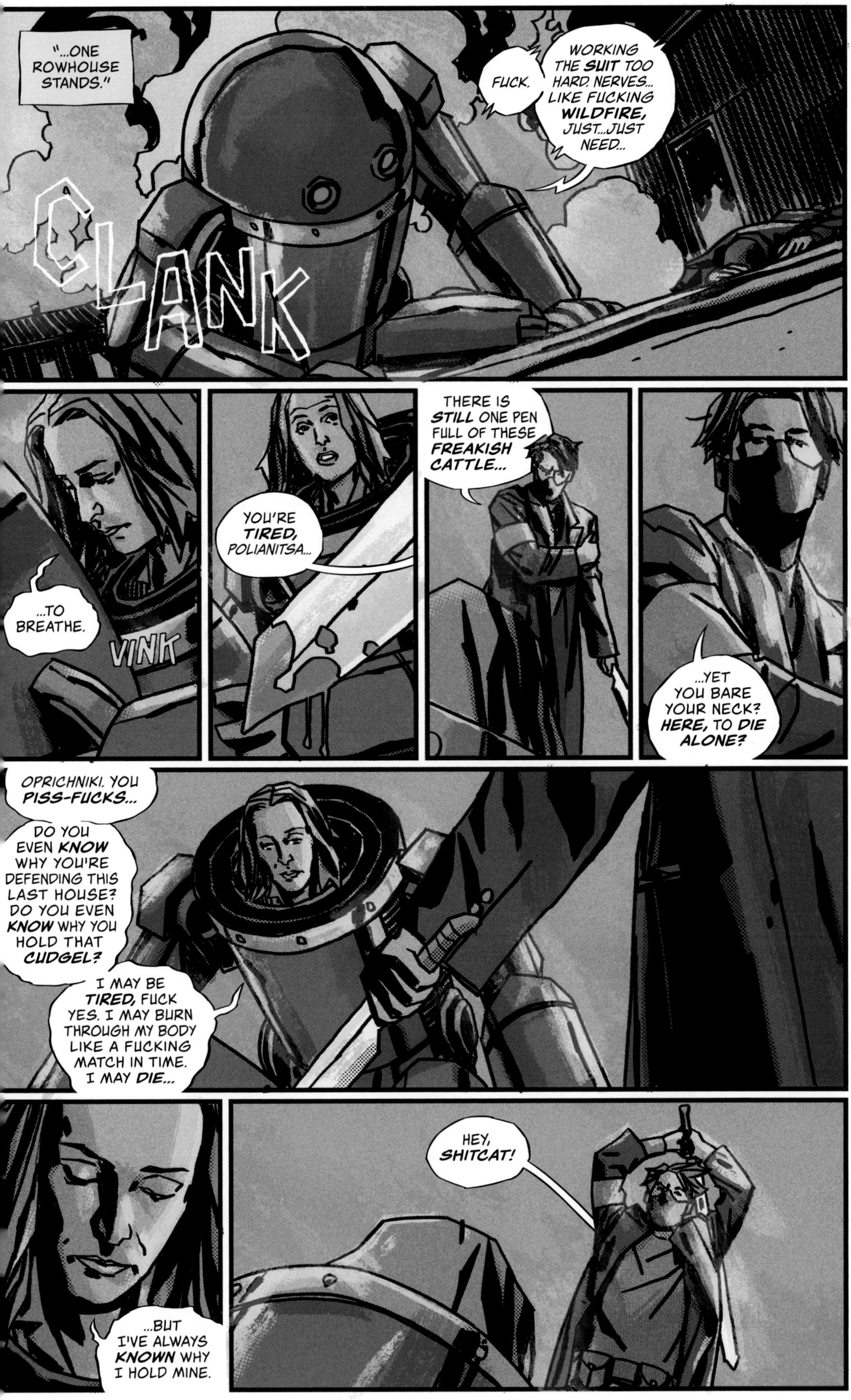
"...ONE ROWHOUSE STANDS."
FUCK.
WORKING THE SUIT TOO HARD. NERVES... LIKE FUCKING WILDFIRE, JUST...JUST NEED...
CLANK
...TO BREATHE.
VINK
YOU'RE TIRED, POLIANITSA...
THERE IS STILL ONE PEN FULL OF THESE FREAKISH CATTLE...
...YET YOU BARE YOUR NECK? HERE, TO DIE ALONE?
OPRICHNIKI. YOU PISS-FUCKS...
DO YOU EVEN KNOW WHY YOU'RE DEFENDING THIS LAST HOUSE? DO YOU EVEN KNOW WHY YOU HOLD THAT CUDGEL?
I MAY BE TIRED, FUCK YES. I MAY BURN THROUGH MY BODY LIKE A FUCKING MATCH IN TIME. I MAY DIE...
...BUT I'VE ALWAYS KNOWN WHY I HOLD MINE.
HEY, SHITCAT!

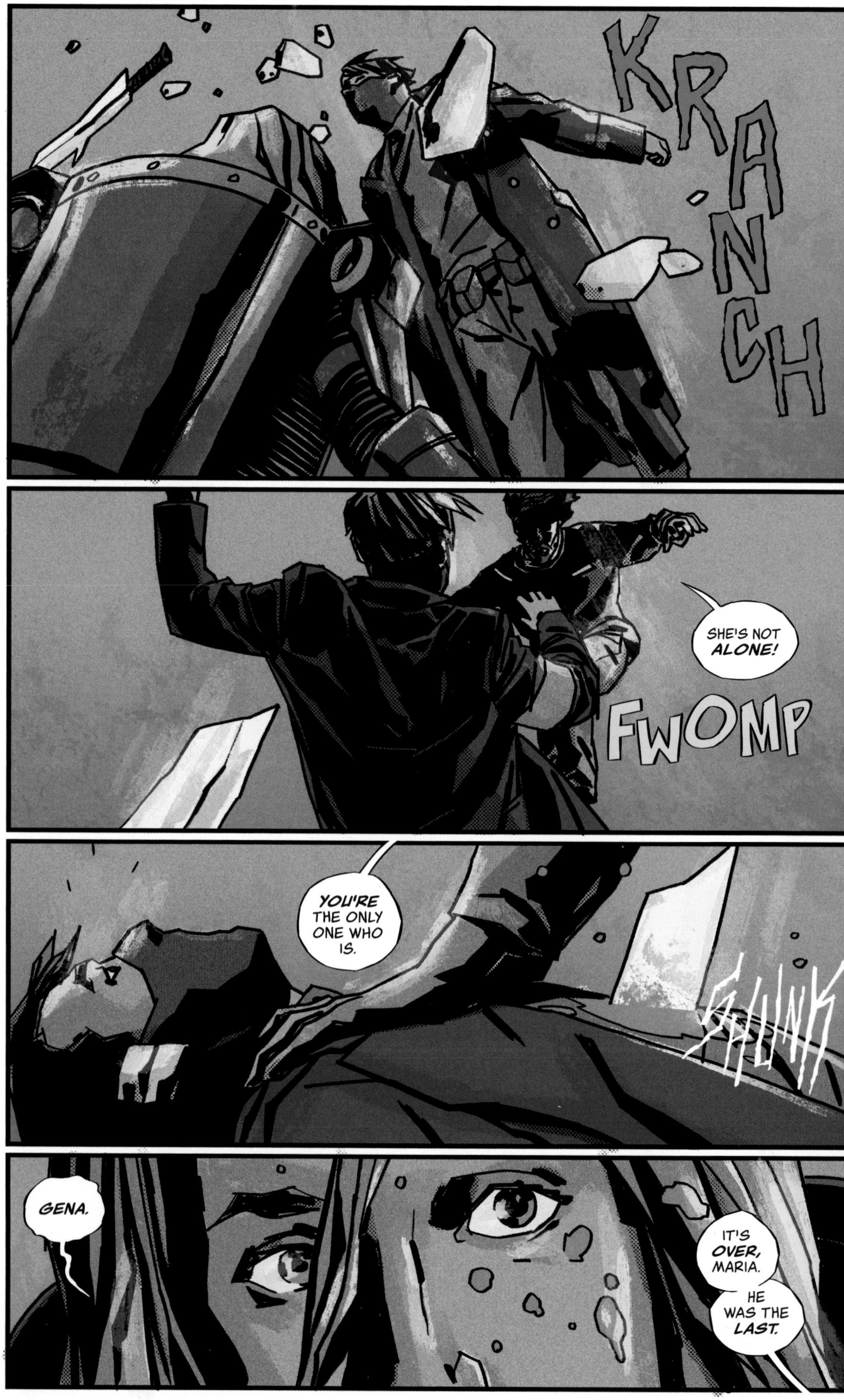
KRANCH
SHE'S NOT ALONE!
FWOMP
YOU'RE THE ONLY ONE WHO IS.
SHUNK
GENA.
IT'S OVER, MARIA.
HE WAS THE LAST.

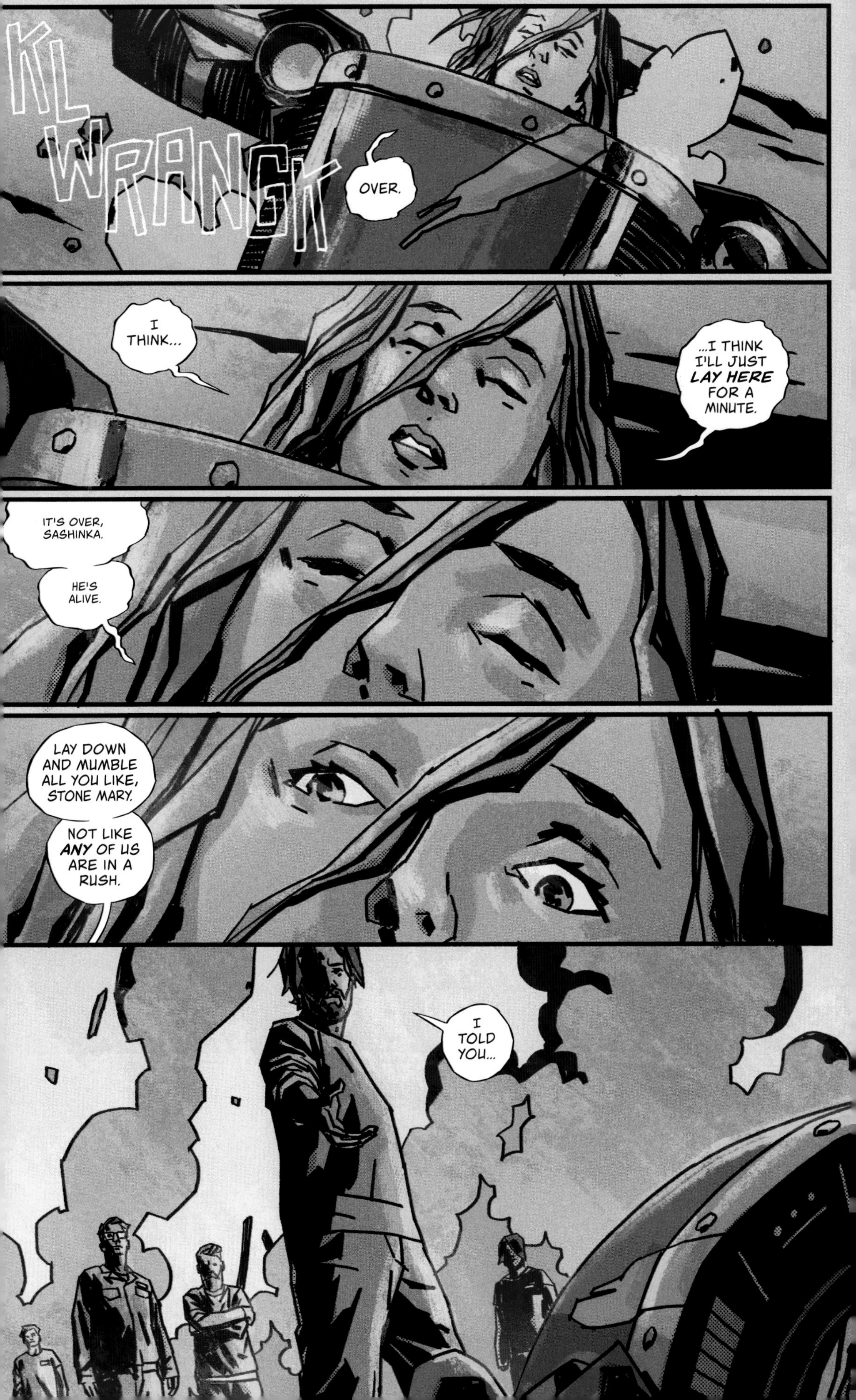
KL WRANGK
OVER.
I THINK...
...I THINK I'LL JUST LAY HERE FOR A MINUTE.
IT'S OVER, SASHINKA.
HE'S ALIVE.
LAY DOWN AND MUMBLE ALL YOU LIKE, STONE MARY.
NOT LIKE ANY OF US ARE IN A RUSH.
I TOLD YOU...

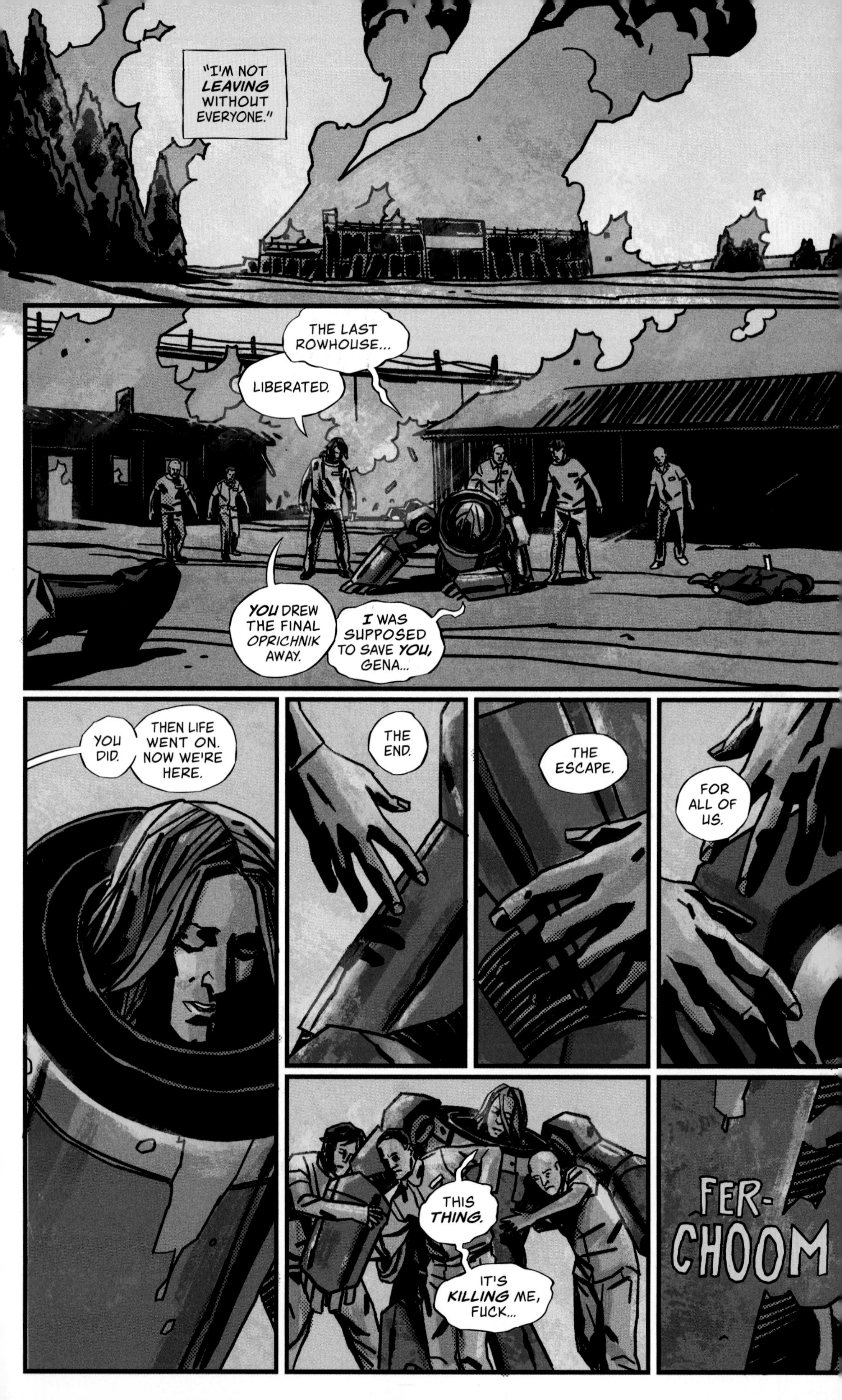
"I'M NOT LEAVING WITHOUT EVERYONE."
THE LAST ROWHOUSE...
LIBERATED.
YOU DREW THE FINAL OPRICHNIK AWAY.
I WAS SUPPOSED TO SAVE YOU, GENA...
YOU DID.
THEN LIFE WENT ON. NOW WE'RE HERE.
THE END.
THE ESCAPE.
FOR ALL OF US.
THIS THING.
IT'S KILLING ME, FUCK...
FER-CHOOM

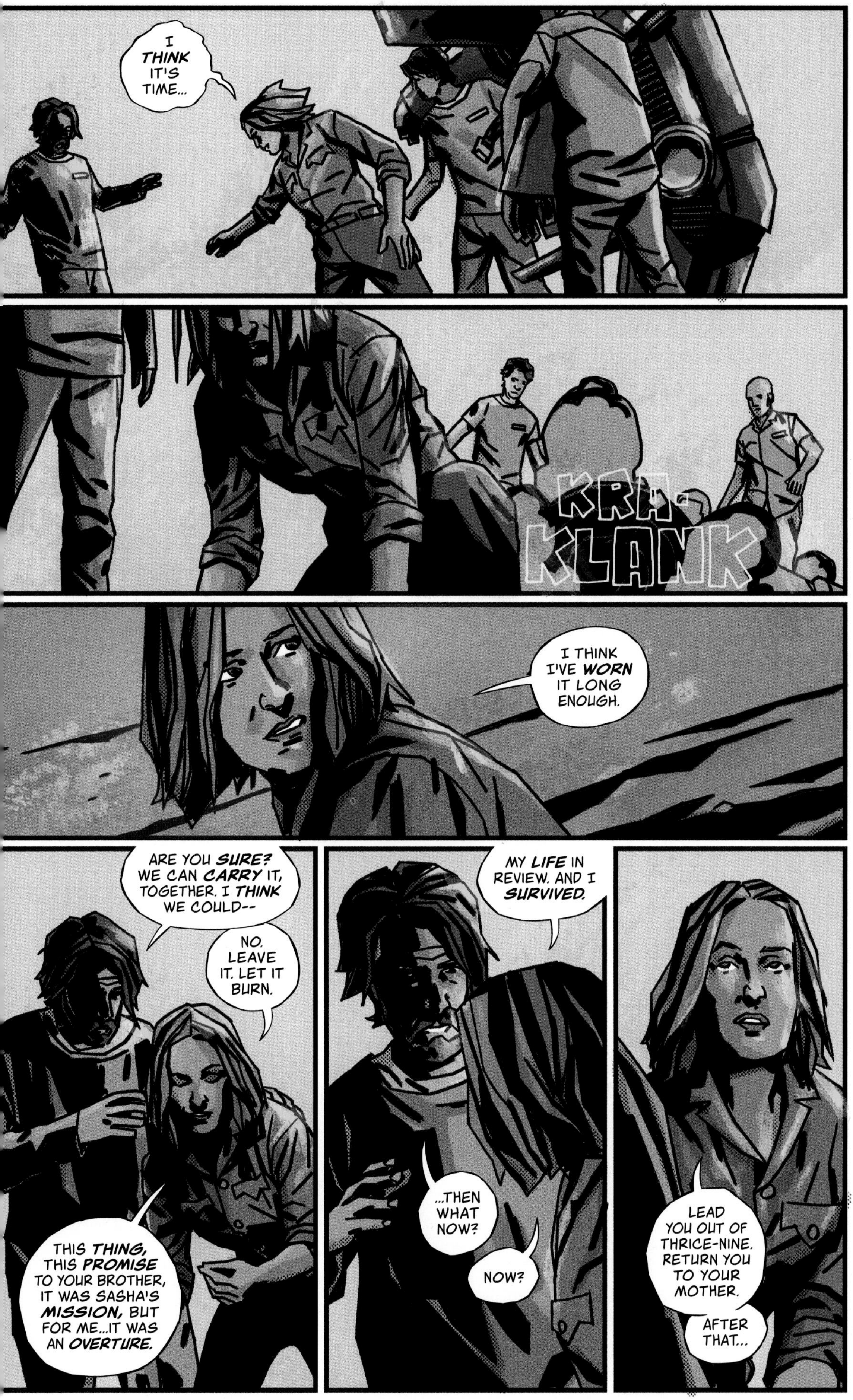
I THINK IT'S TIME...
KRA-KLANK
I THINK I'VE WORN IT LONG ENOUGH.
ARE YOU SURE? WE CAN CARRY IT, TOGETHER. I THINK WE COULD--
NO. LEAVE IT. LET IT BURN.
THIS THING, THIS PROMISE TO YOUR BROTHER, IT WAS SASHA'S MISSION, BUT FOR ME...IT WAS AN OVERTURE.
MY LIFE IN REVIEW. AND I SURVIVED.
...THEN WHAT NOW?
NOW?
LEAD YOU OUT OF THRICE-NINE. RETURN YOU TO YOUR MOTHER.
AFTER THAT...

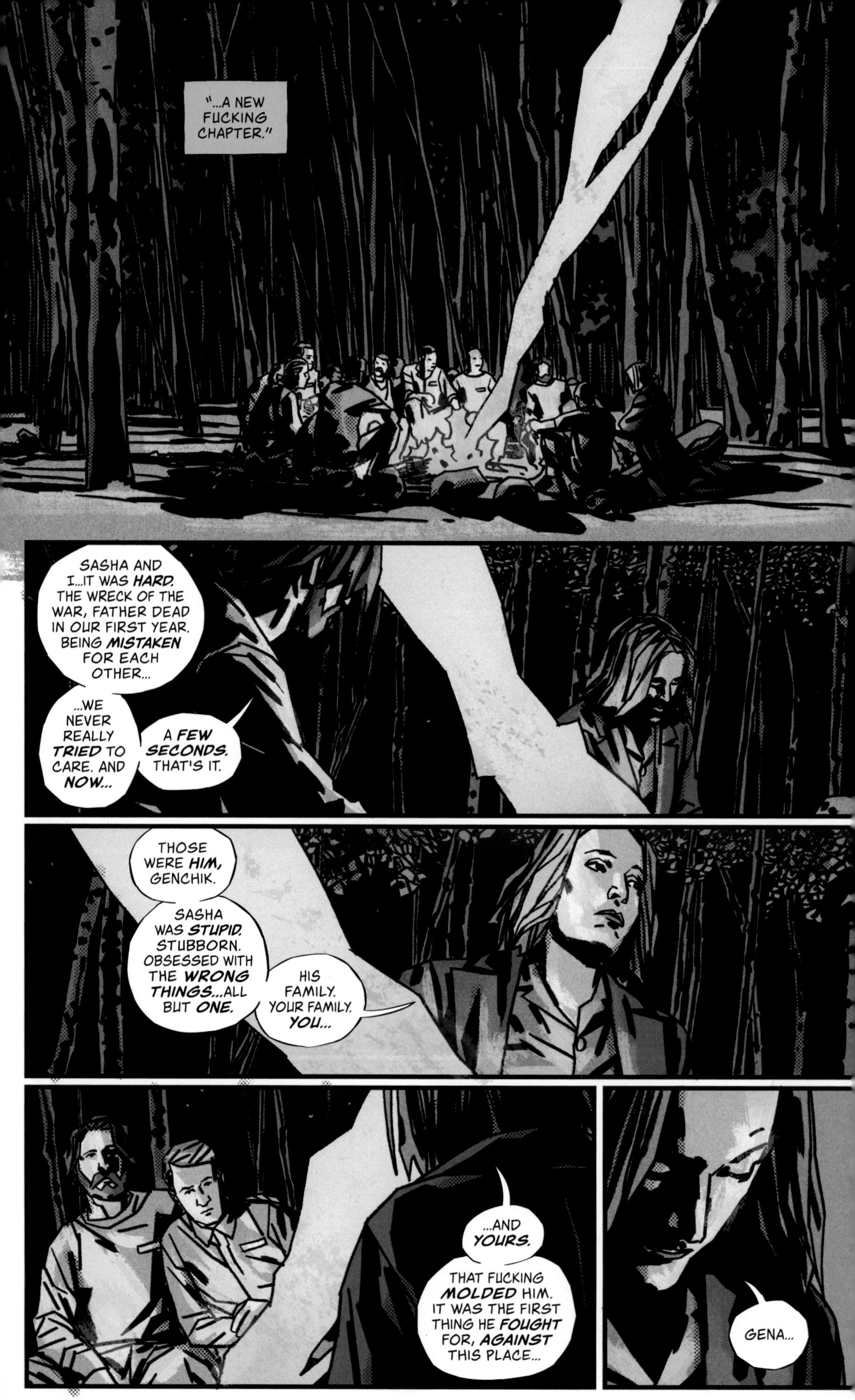
"...A NEW FUCKING CHAPTER."
SASHA AND I...IT WAS HARD. THE WRECK OF THE WAR, FATHER DEAD IN OUR FIRST YEAR. BEING MISTAKEN FOR EACH OTHER...
...WE NEVER REALLY TRIED TO CARE. AND NOW...
A FEW SECONDS. THAT'S IT.
THOSE WERE HIM, GENCHIK.
SASHA WAS STUPID. STUBBORN. OBSESSED WITH THE WRONG THINGS...ALL BUT ONE.
HIS FAMILY. YOUR FAMILY. YOU...
...AND YOURS.
THAT FUCKING MOLDED HIM. IT WAS THE FIRST THING HE FOUGHT FOR, AGAINST THIS PLACE...
GENA...

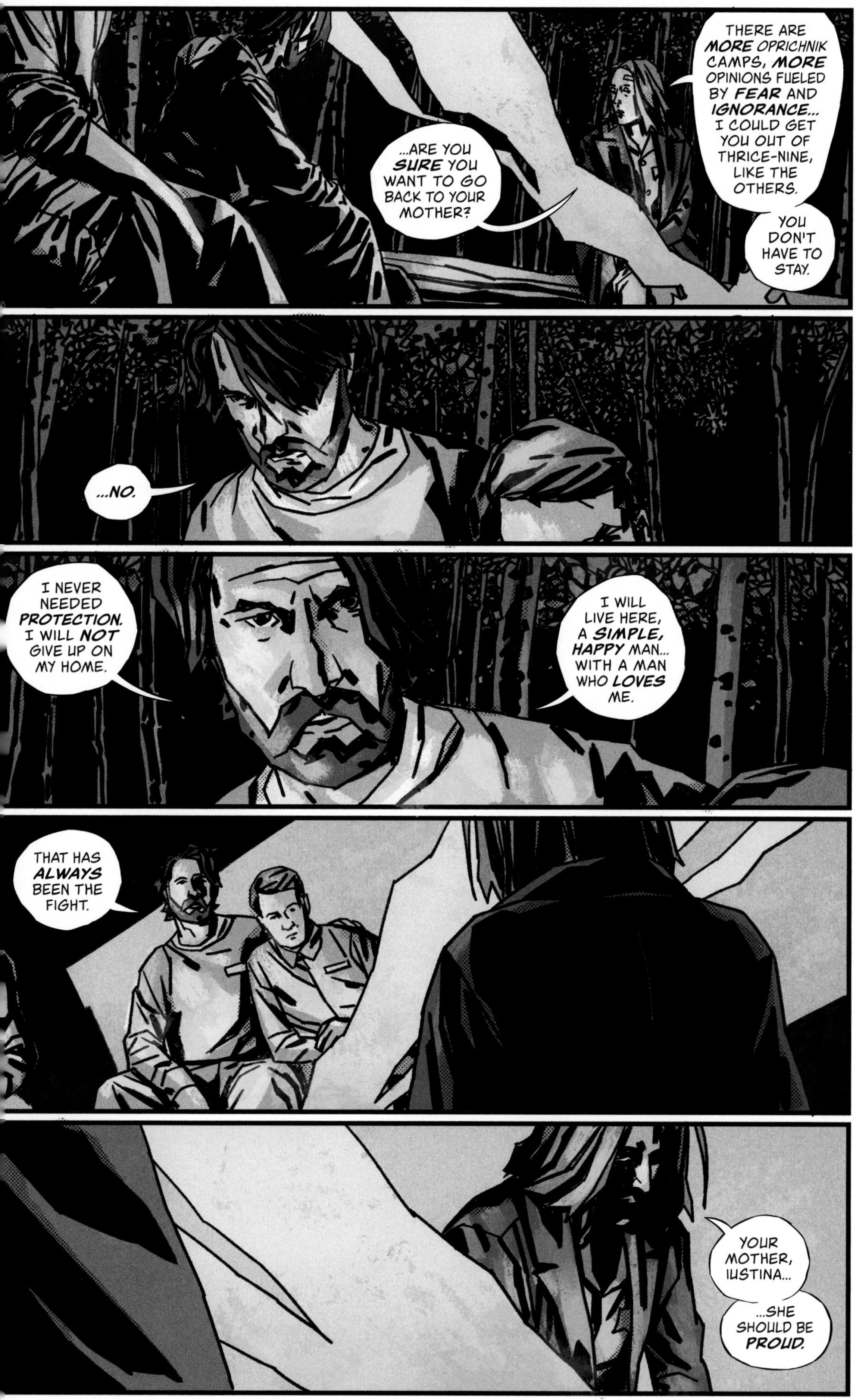
THERE ARE MORE OPRICHNIK CAMPS, MORE OPINIONS FUELED BY FEAR AND IGNORANCE... I COULD GET YOU OUT OF THRICE-NINE, LIKE THE OTHERS.
...ARE YOU SURE YOU WANT TO GO BACK TO YOUR MOTHER?
YOU DON'T HAVE TO STAY.
...NO.
I NEVER NEEDED PROTECTION. I WILL NOT GIVE UP ON MY HOME.
I WILL LIVE HERE, A SIMPLE, HAPPY MAN... WITH A MAN WHO LOVES ME.
THAT HAS ALWAYS BEEN THE FIGHT.
YOUR MOTHER, IUSTINA...
...SHE SHOULD BE PROUD.

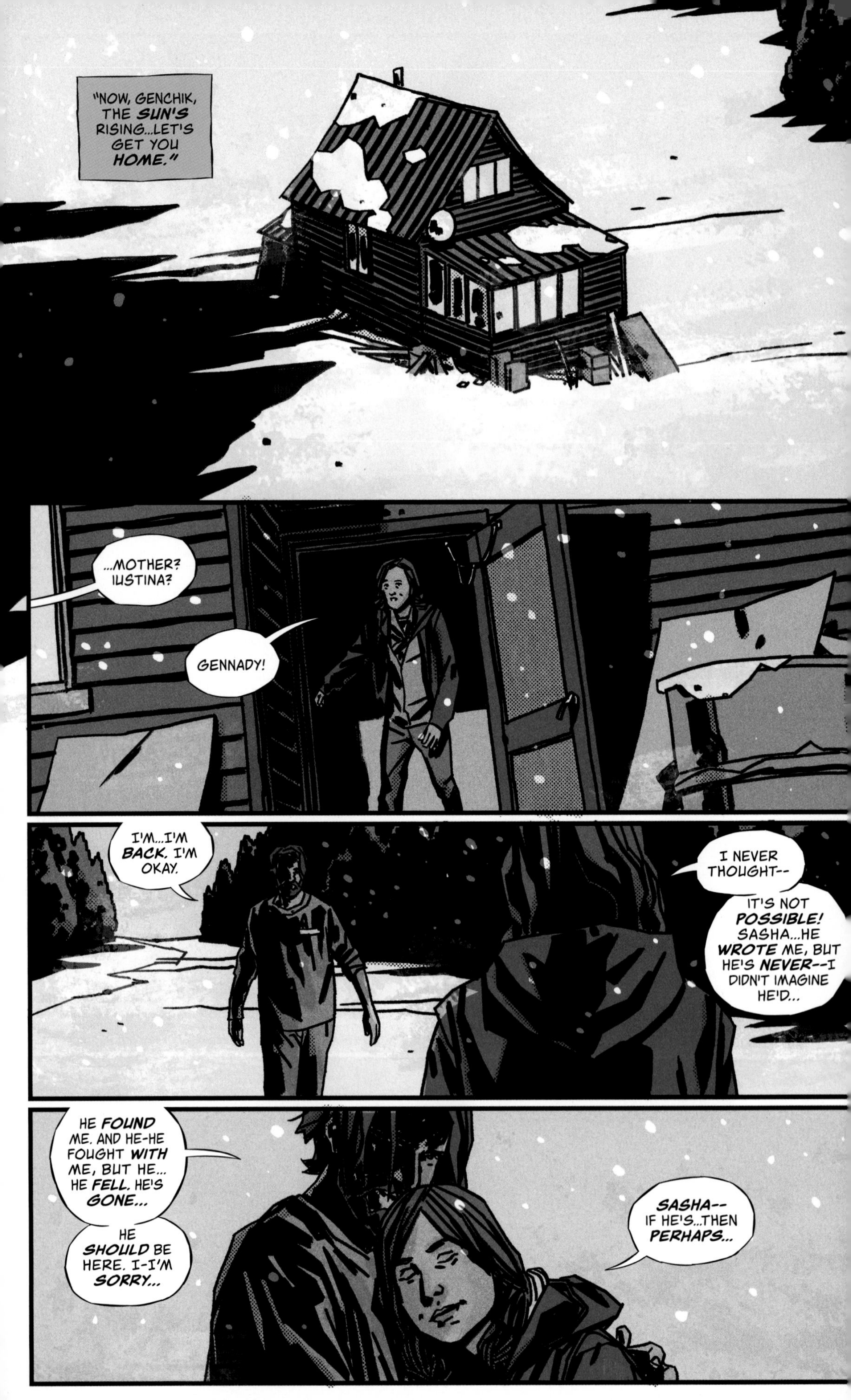
"NOW, GENCHIK, THE SUN'S RISING...LET'S GET YOU HOME."
...MOTHER? IUSTINA?
GENNADY!
I'M...I'M BACK. I'M OKAY.
I NEVER THOUGHT--
IT'S NOT POSSIBLE! SASHA...HE WROTE ME, BUT HE'S NEVER--I DIDN'T IMAGINE HE'D...
HE FOUND ME. AND HE-HE FOUGHT WITH ME, BUT HE... HE FELL. HE'S GONE...
HE SHOULD BE HERE. I-I'M SORRY...
SASHA-- IF HE'S...THEN PERHAPS...

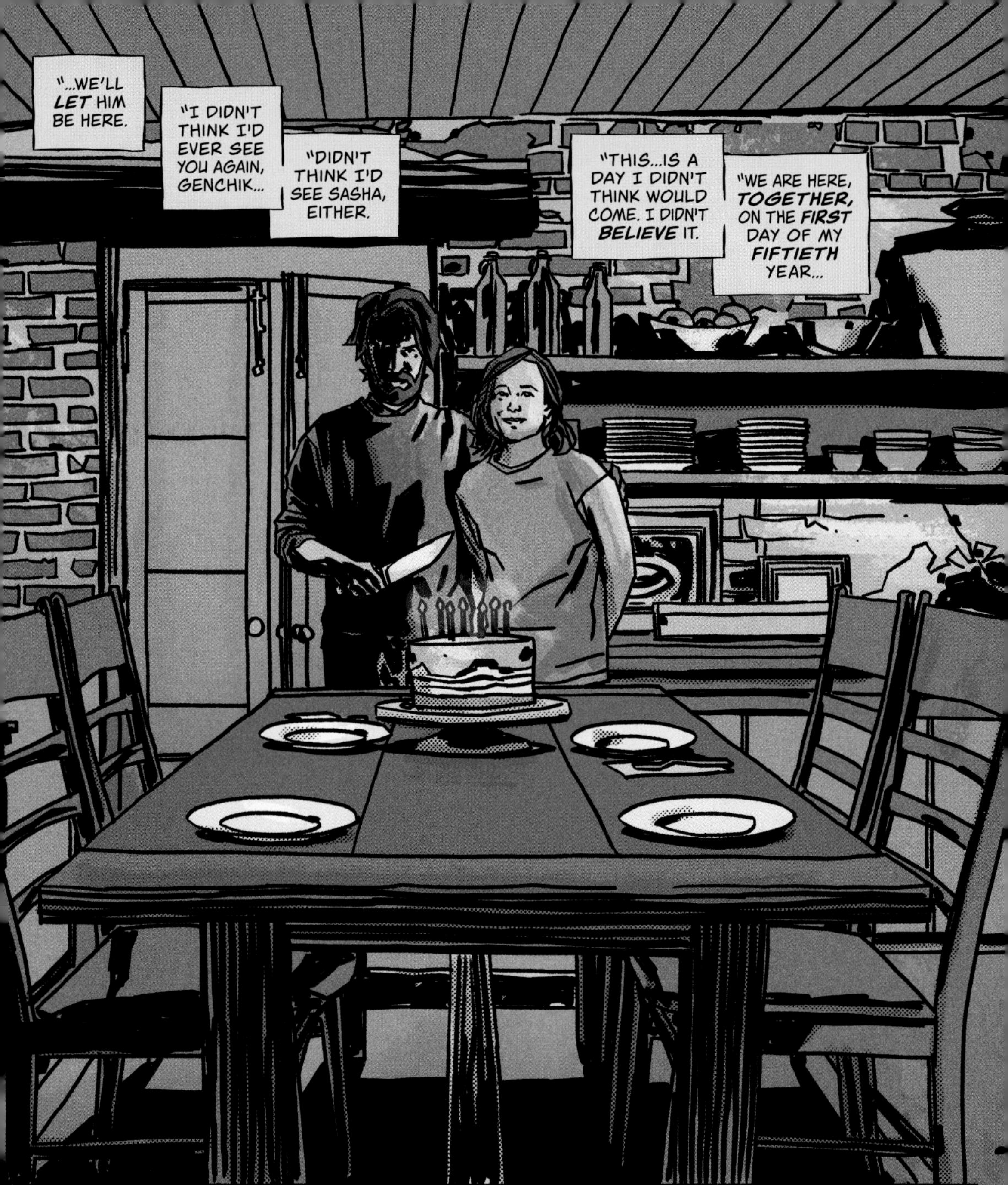
"...WE'LL LET HIM BE HERE.
"I DIDN'T THINK I'D EVER SEE YOU AGAIN, GENCHIK...
"DIDN'T THINK I'D SEE SASHA, EITHER.
"THIS...IS A DAY I DIDN'T THINK WOULD COME. I DIDN'T BELIEVE IT.
"WE ARE HERE, TOGETHER, ON THE FIRST DAY OF MY FIFTIETH YEAR...

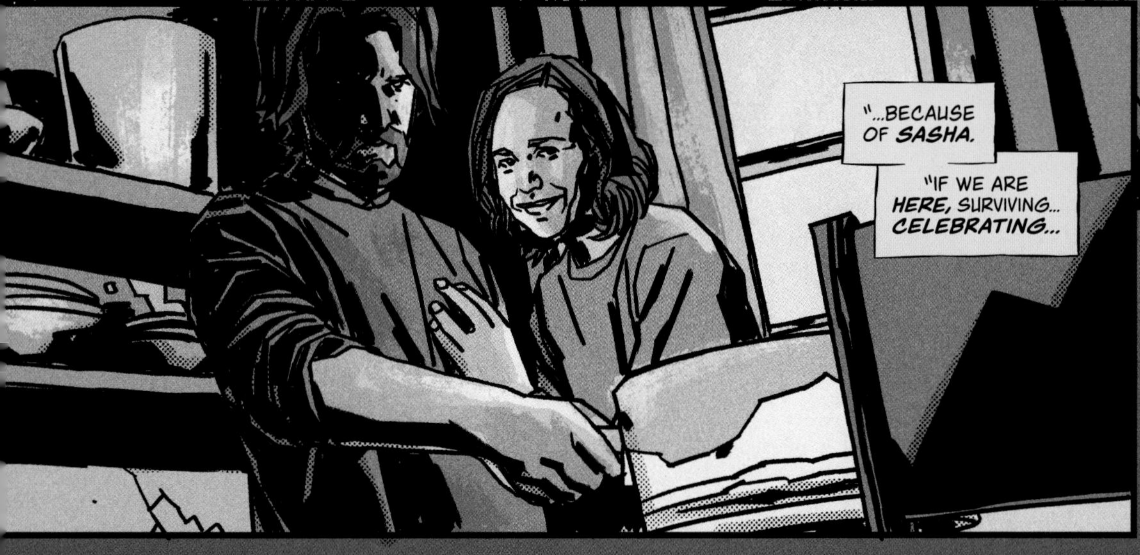
"...BECAUSE OF SASHA.
"IF WE ARE HERE, SURVIVING... CELEBRATING...

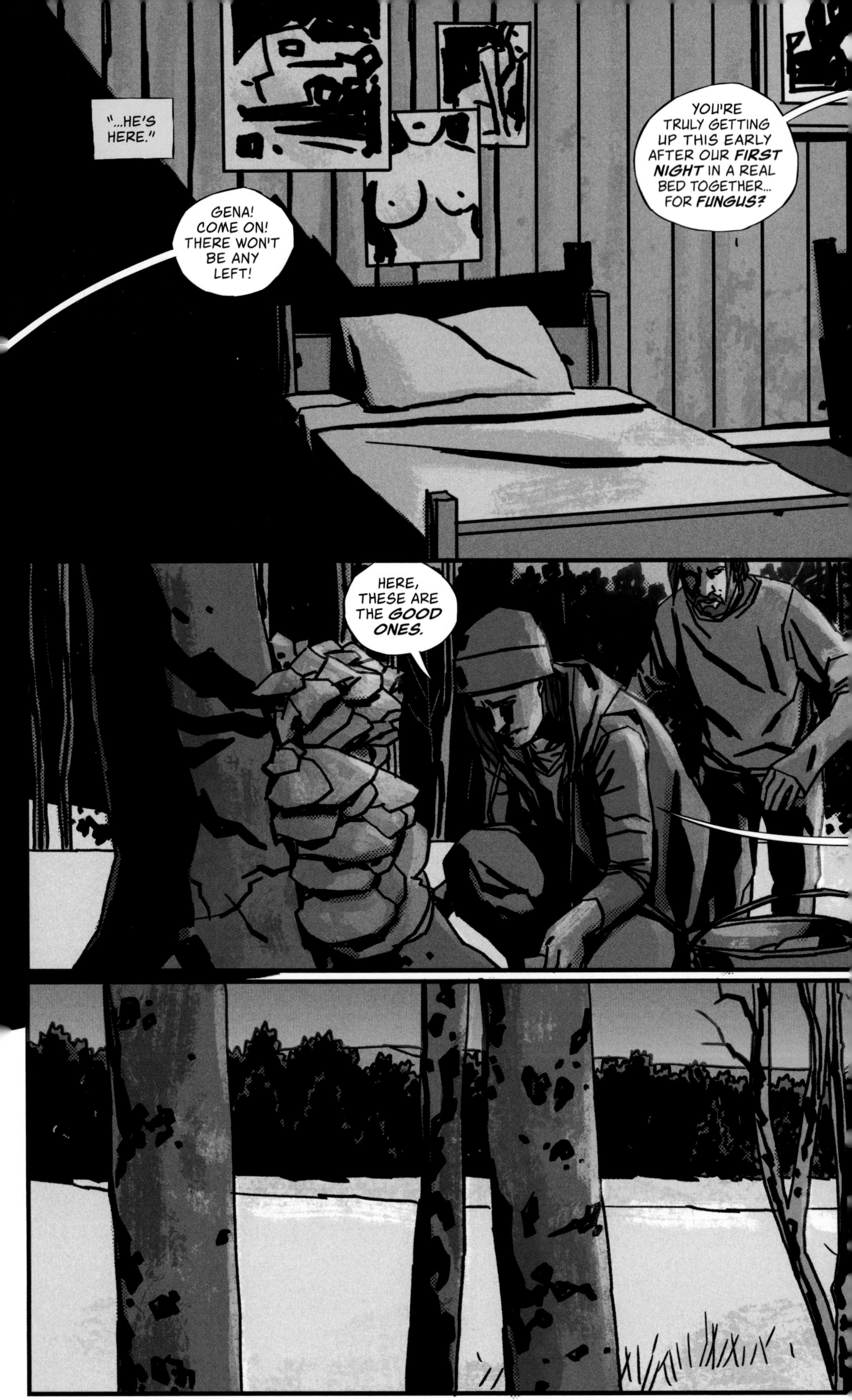
"...HE'S HERE."
GENA! COME ON! THERE WON'T BE ANY LEFT!
YOU'RE TRULY GETTING UP THIS EARLY AFTER OUR FIRST NIGHT IN A REAL BED TOGETHER... FOR FUNGUS?
HERE, THESE ARE THE GOOD ONES.

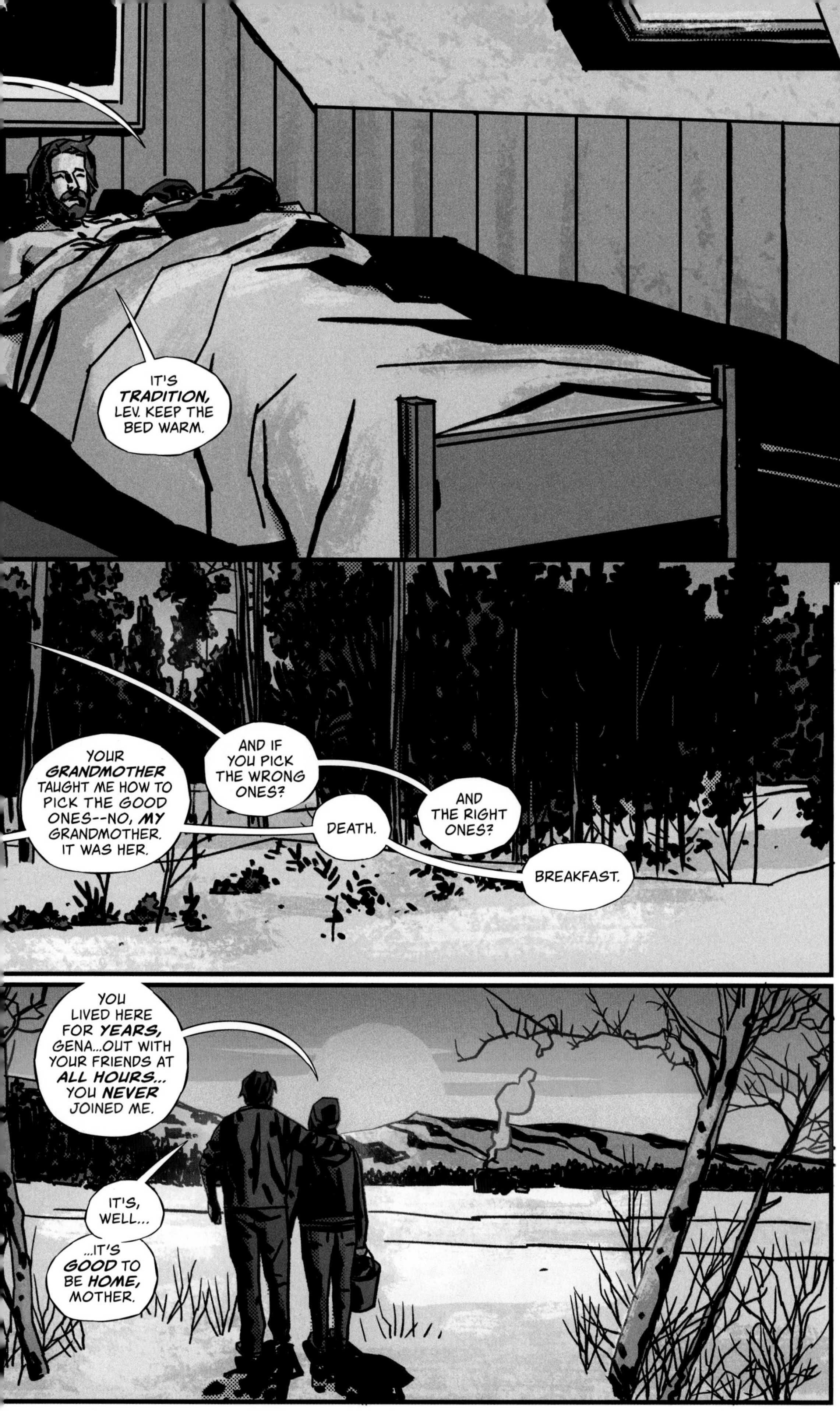
IT'S TRADITION, LEV. KEEP THE BED WARM.
YOUR GRANDMOTHER TAUGHT ME HOW TO PICK THE GOOD ONES--NO, MY GRANDMOTHER. IT WAS HER.
AND IF YOU PICK THE WRONG ONES?
DEATH.
AND THE RIGHT ONES?
BREAKFAST.
YOU LIVED HERE FOR YEARS, GENA...OUT WITH YOUR FRIENDS AT ALL HOURS... YOU NEVER JOINED ME.
IT'S, WELL...
...IT'S GOOD TO BE HOME, MOTHER.

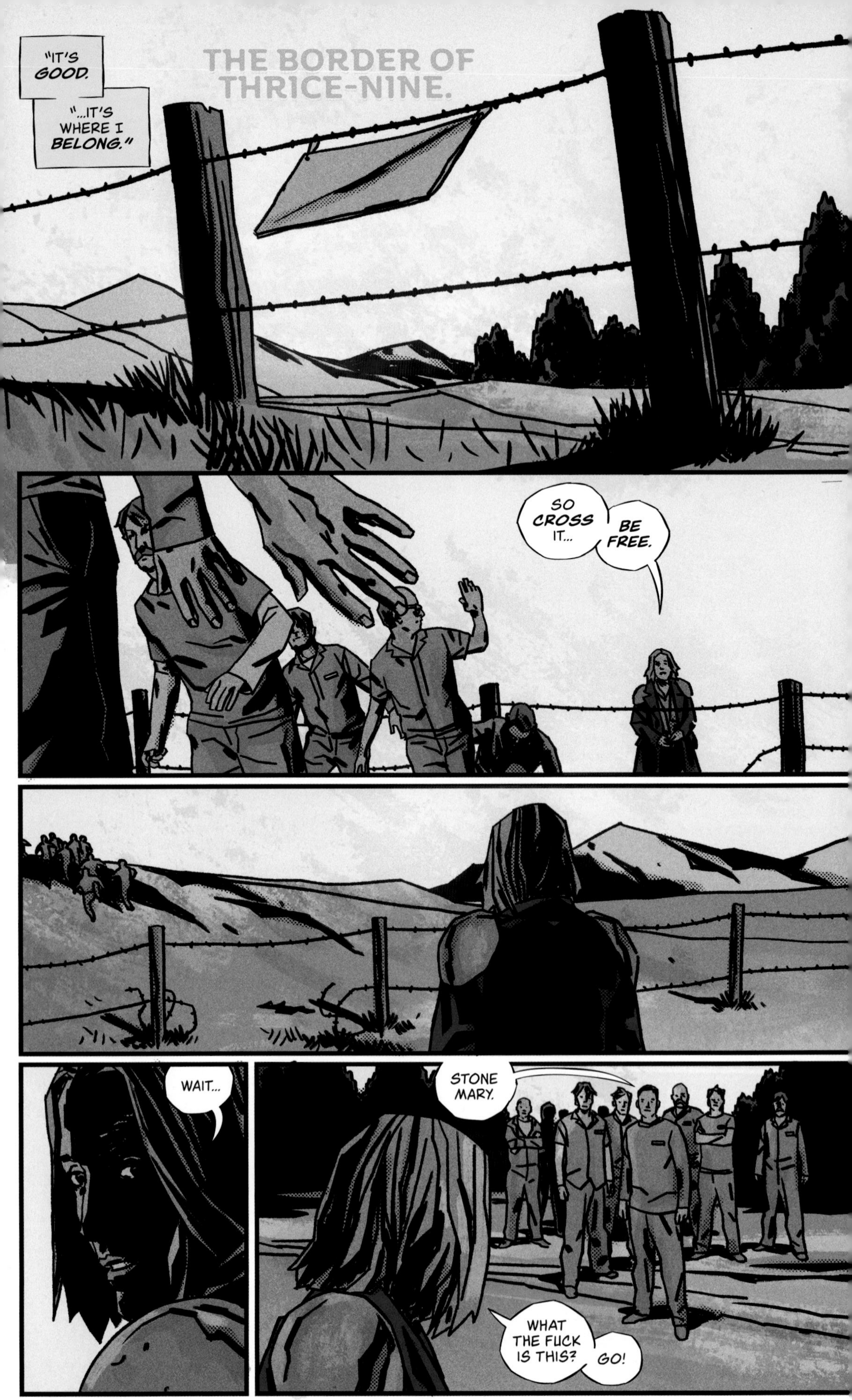
"IT'S GOOD.
"...IT'S WHERE I BELONG."
THE BORDER OF THRICE-NINE.
SO CROSS IT...
BE FREE.
WAIT...
STONE MARY.
WHAT THE FUCK IS THIS?
GO!

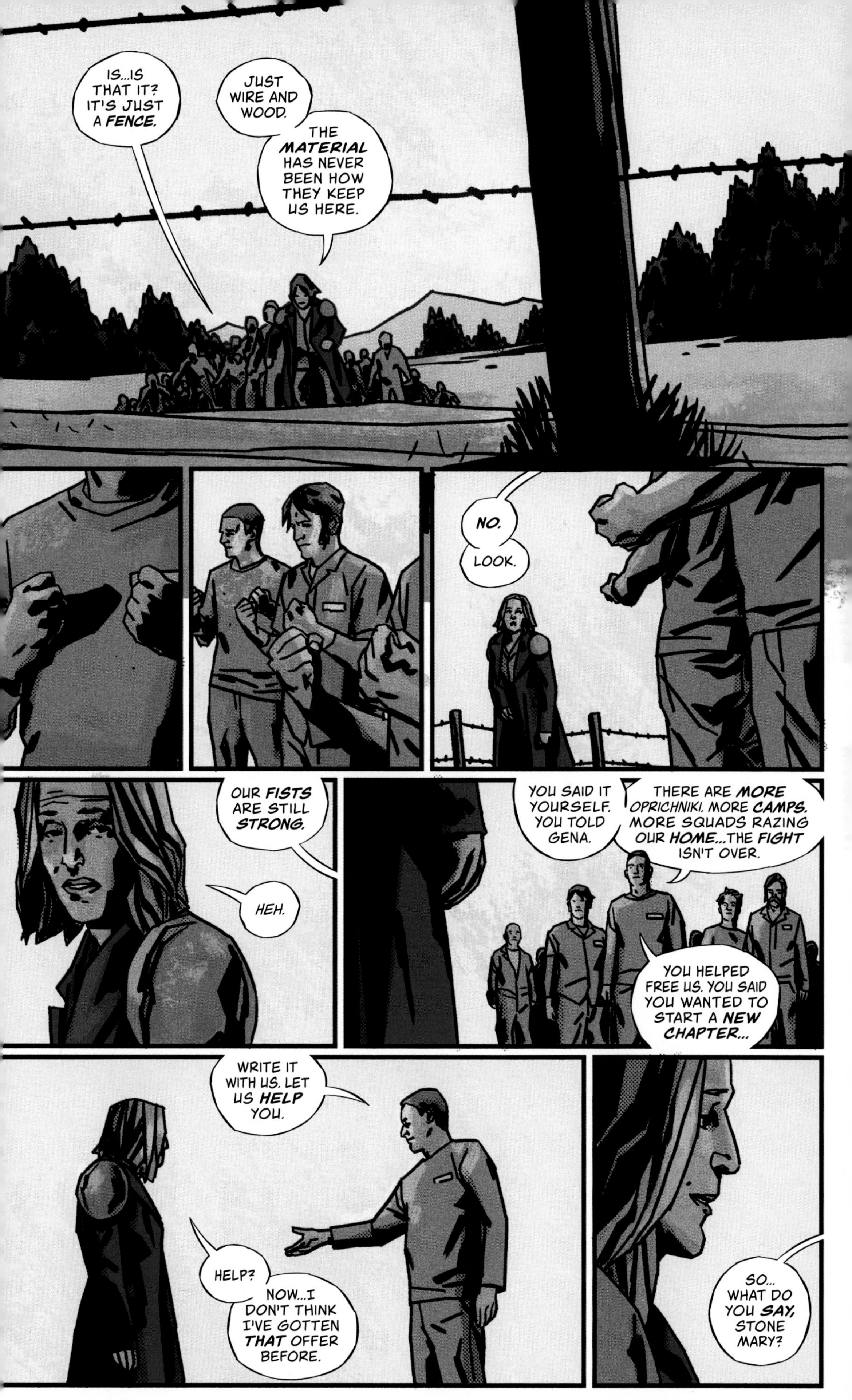
IS...IS THAT IT? IT'S JUST A *FENCE.*
JUST WIRE AND WOOD.
THE *MATERIAL* HAS NEVER BEEN HOW THEY KEEP US HERE.
NO.
LOOK.
OUR *FISTS* ARE STILL *STRONG.*
HEH.
YOU SAID IT YOURSELF. YOU TOLD GENA.
THERE ARE *MORE* OPRICHNIKI. MORE *CAMPS.* MORE SQUADS RAZING OUR *HOME*...THE *FIGHT* ISN'T OVER.
YOU HELPED FREE US. YOU SAID YOU WANTED TO START A *NEW CHAPTER...*
WRITE IT WITH US. LET US *HELP* YOU.
HELP?
NOW...I DON'T THINK I'VE GOTTEN *THAT* OFFER BEFORE.
SO... WHAT DO YOU *SAY,* STONE MARY?

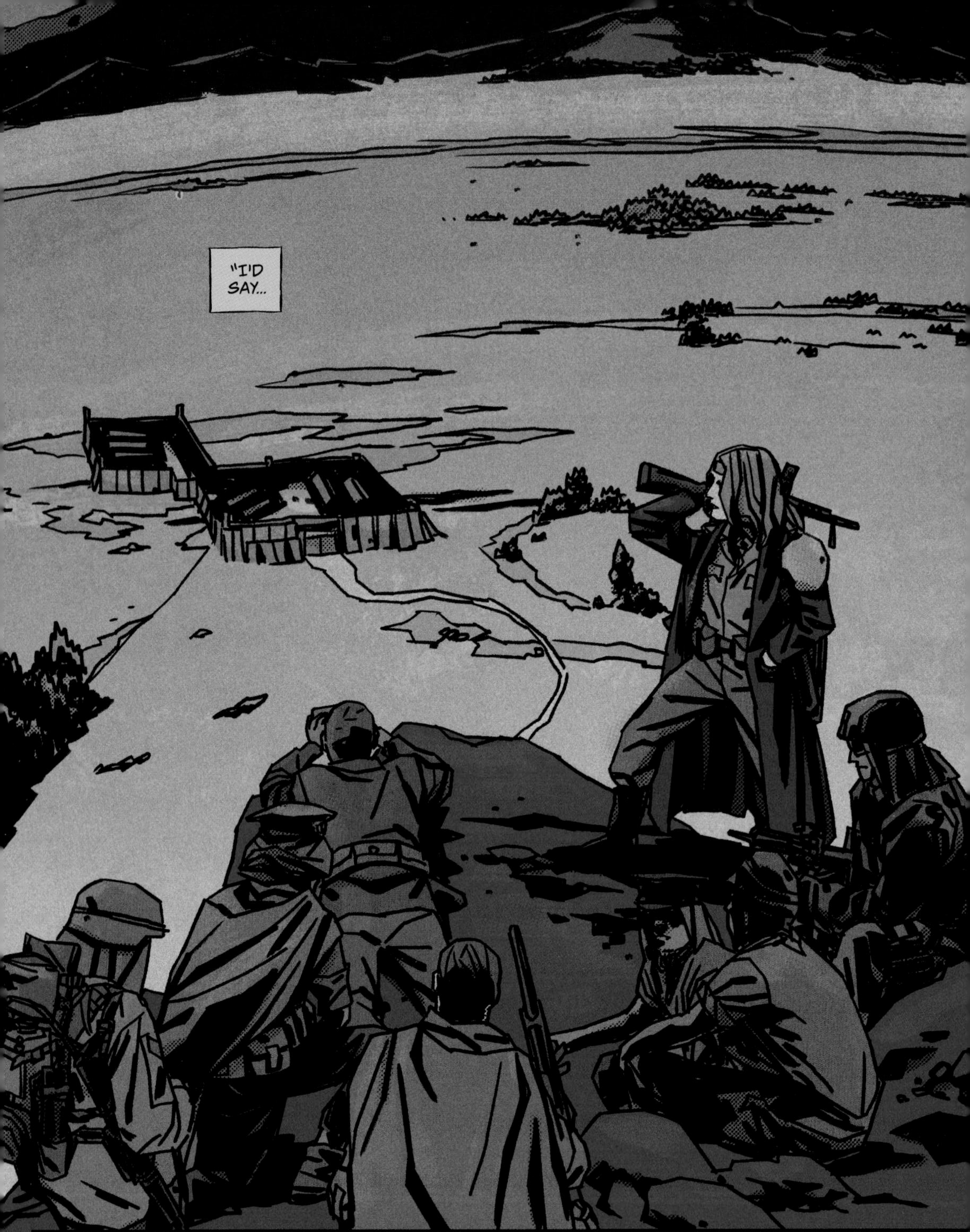
"I'D SAY...

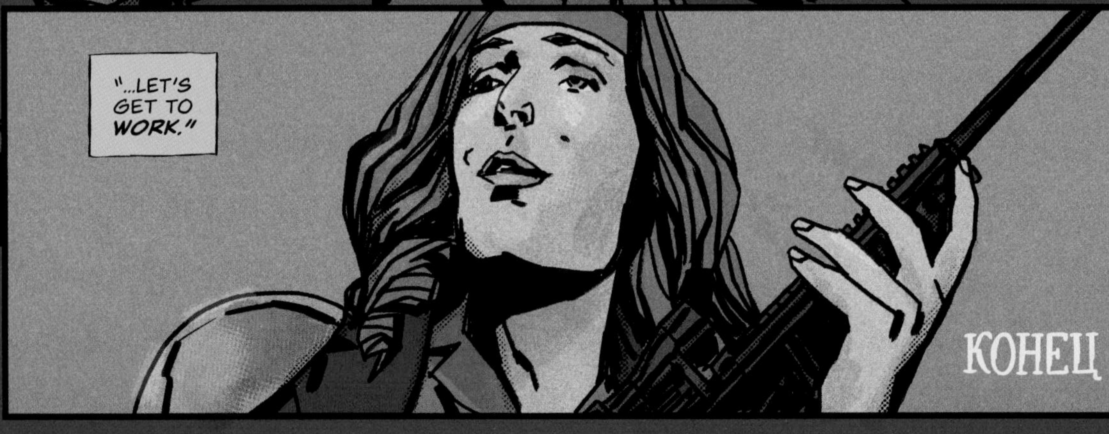
"...LET'S GET TO WORK."
КОНЕЦ

Issue 1
RUSS BRAUN w/ **JOSE VILLARRUBIA**
Dragon's Lair exclusive cover

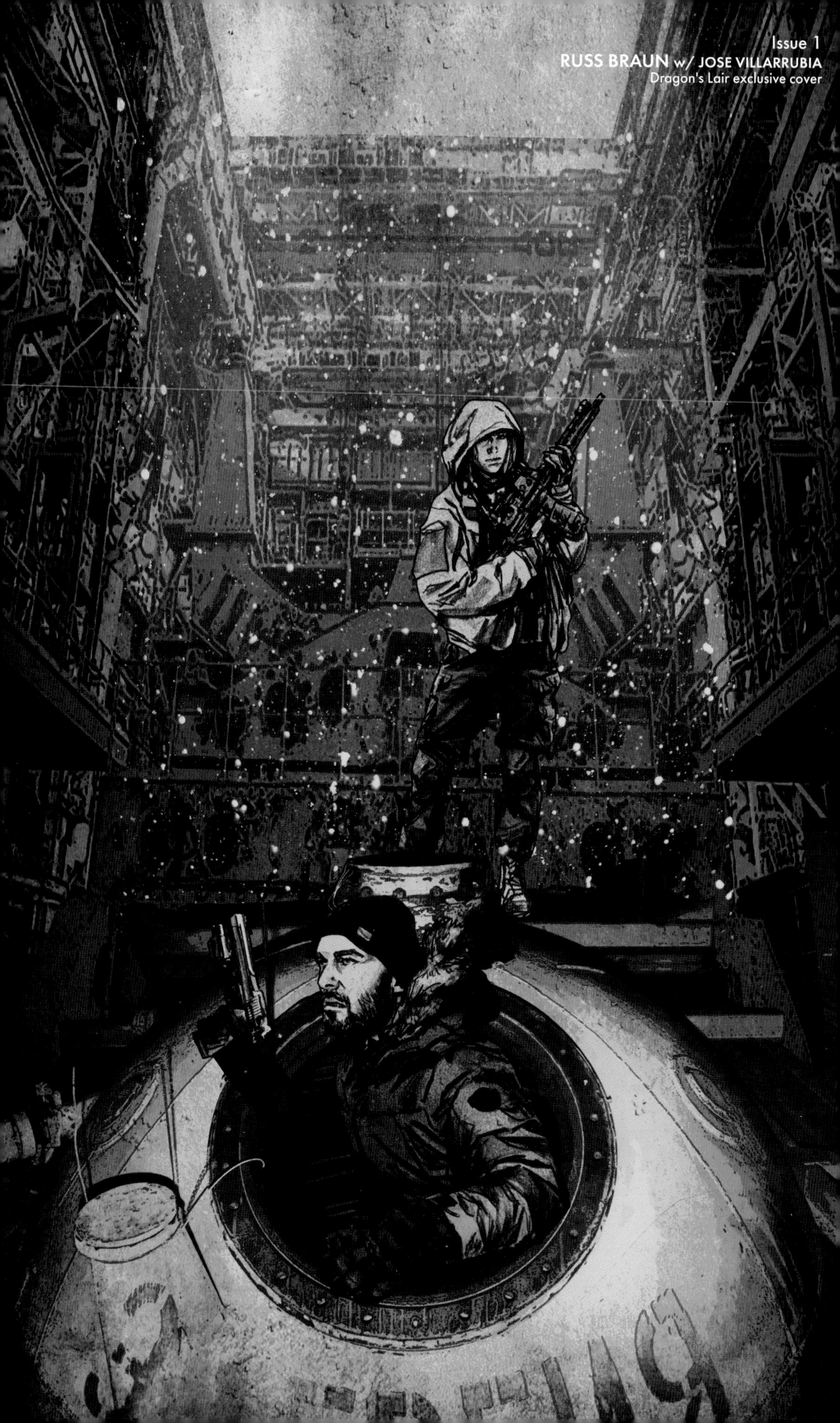

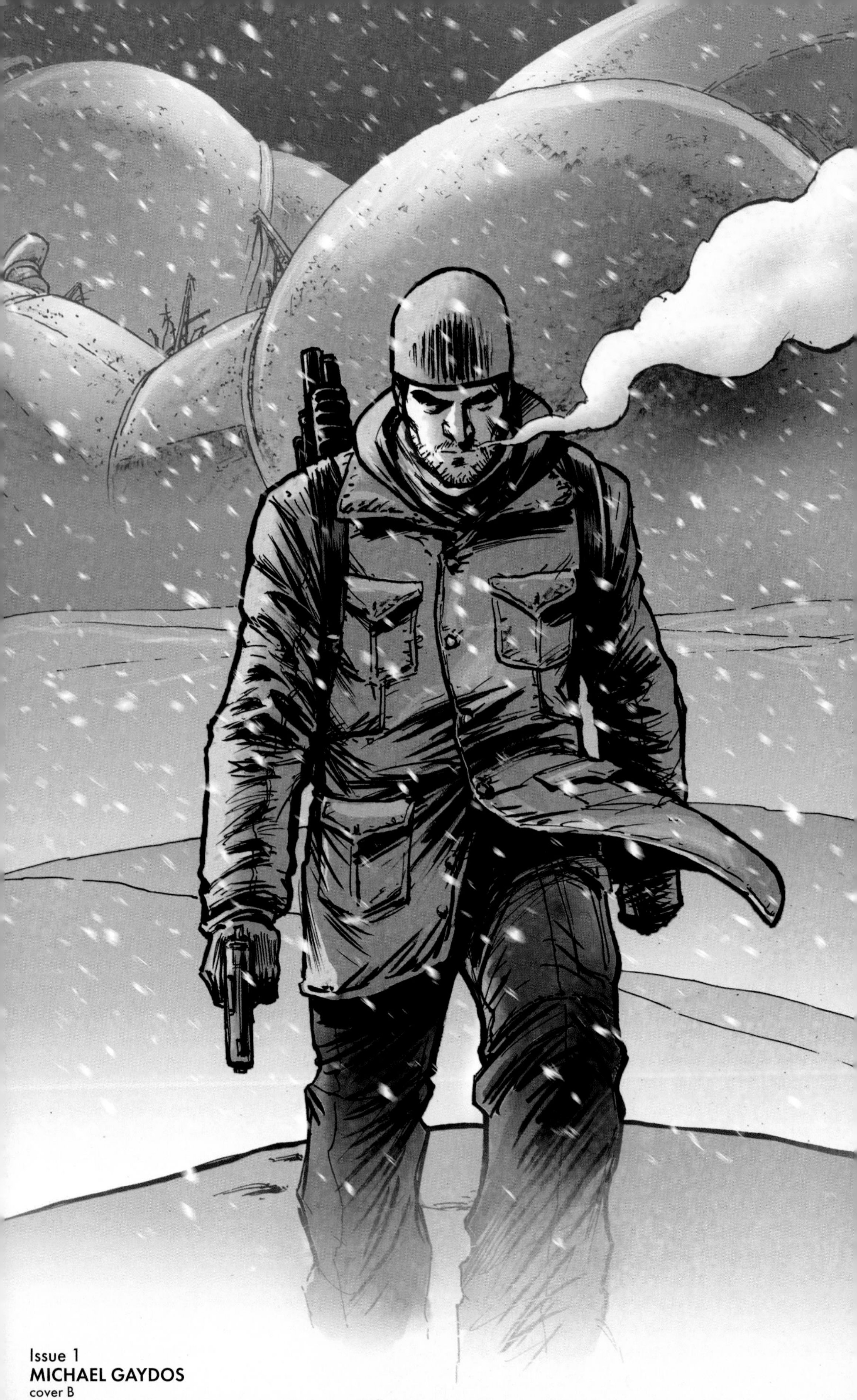

Issue 1
MICHAEL GAYDOS
cover B

DEAD KINGS™

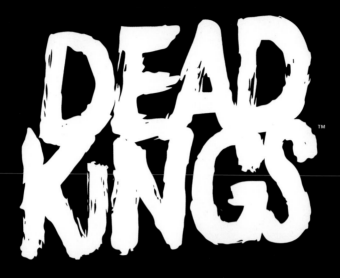

BEHIND THE SCENES

DEAD KINGS™

KINGS

#1

story by
STEVE ORLANDO

PAGE 4 - 5

Again setting the tone and offering a study in stark contrast, this is another DOUBLE PAGE SPLASH, the last of them but the most important as an endpoint in showing the reader where we've come from in the story. This is THE PRESENT.

And it's the THRICE-NINE, the wreckage of the Empire of Rus, and the waste of the war we just saw at its height twenty years ago. This is where we get that Simon Stahlenhag feel, Matt. The war ended, and the architecture of war, buildings, turrets, massive monoliths, signal towers, war machines, it all was just left where it lay to rust and be overtaken by the dust and snow and moss.

A post-military-industrial-complex life began to form, almost rural, almost quaint, but lonely and foreboding, built within the skeletons of this Great Iron War now decades deceased.

Small cities are begin to regenerate within the corpses of larger ones that were destroyed, like fish colonies in the body of a fallen dead whale, dotting the tundra with their communication lights and couriers. Within this setting, think UTICA, NY. Every city and every community is just barely past being on life support.

Liberty? What's that? There IS a government in Thrice-Nine, but it has failed its people to such an extent that it can only maintain its position by becoming a loose police state the size of a continent, headed by gangs of the Oprichniki, secret police born out of the remnants of the last Imperial Military. They ride oily mechanical horses but wear real dog's heads around their neck as their symbol, and carry shotguns hidden within ornamental brooms.

"The kings are all dead...leaving their mad court to rule."

Massive war machines stand like mountains in the background as we have a desolate shot of SUZDAL, one of the cities in the former GOLDEN RING, a ring of cities once meant to preserve the memory of the most important and significant events in Russian history as "Open-Air Museums." They were converted into HISTORIC BARRICADES to protect that same history during the Great Iron War, and fell anyway, letting die Russia's history. This is desolate. It's tough. It's hopeless. It's The Volga Boatmen in feel. Perhaps we see some people scurrying around, perhaps not. It's not snowing right now, but there's dirty tan snow everywhere.

This is what the world has wrought in the twenty years since Gena and Sasha were born. I see this as a daytime shot, but the weather and sky is so bleak, how could you tell?

inks by
MATTHEW DOW SMITH

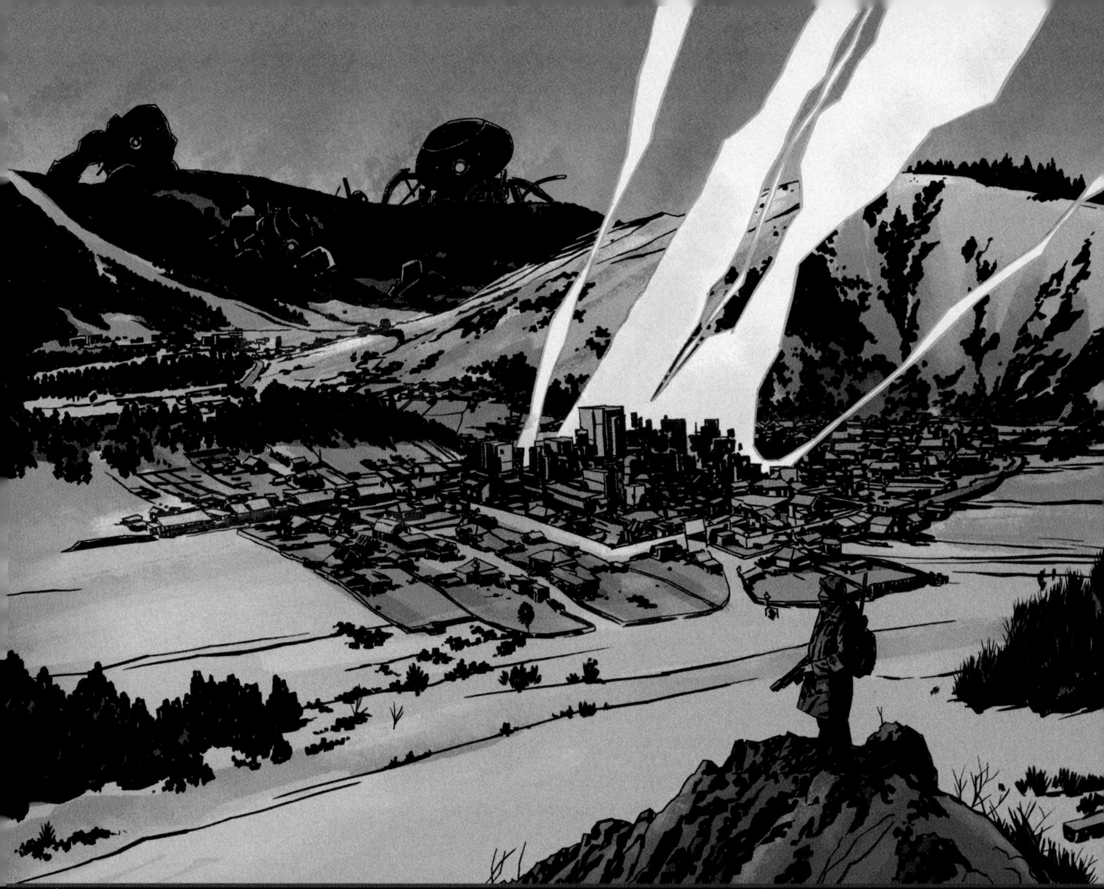

colors by
LAUREN AFFE

PAGES 4&5 PROCESS

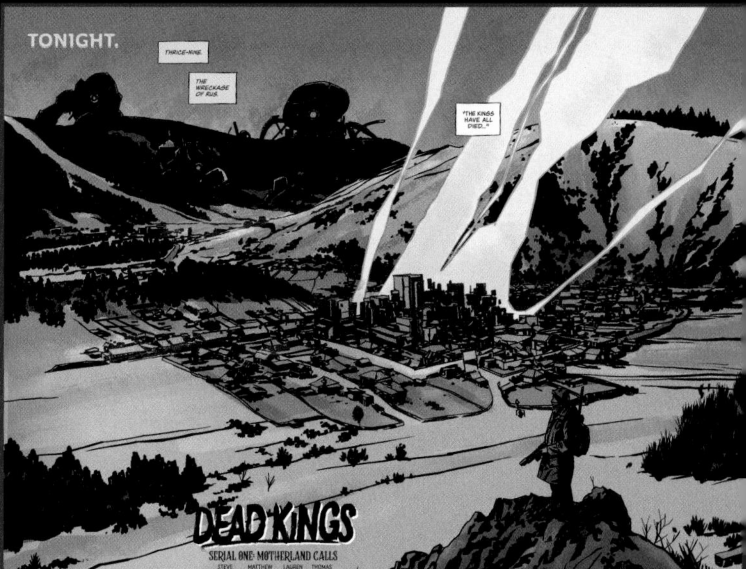

TONIGHT.
THRICE-NINE.
THE WRECKAGE OF RUS.
"THE KINGS HAVE ALL DIED..."
DEAD KINGS
SERIAL ONE: MOTHERLAND CALLS
STEVE ORLANDO
MATTHEW DOW SMITH
LAUREN AFFE
THOMAS MAUER

lettering by
THOMAS MAUER

DEAD KINGS ™

#2

PAGES 6 - 7:

This is a DOUBLE PAGE SPREAD that opens with a BIG WIDESCREEN
FLASHBACK PANEL (we'll have TWO of these before cutting the
present, maybe this spread is three equal widescreeen panels
in all?) of MARIA IN HER GLORY, in FULL BATTLE ARMOR during
the GREAT IRON WAR we also showed last issue.

The FIRST shot is in the middle of the Iron War as massive
IRON MECHS loom in the background, but we're on the ground as
Maria, in her BATTLE ARMOR, leads some OPRICHNIKI in a raid on
a SMALL FARM TOWN. The Oprichniki BURN and MASSACRE the folk
in the background as Maria, conflicted, RIPS THE ROOF off a
small house in the focus, SHOCKED and HEARTBROKEN to discover
only DOGS AND CHILDREN and no parents. Her face is CONTORTED
with shame and grief.

Our SECOND shot shows Maria's FACE as we sell even more her
HEARTBREAK, every bad thing she's done is catching up with her
in this moment as her moral void has just become faulty. We're
tight on her face, this is the split second war and moral
compromise breaks her soul.

Then we cut back to the PRESENT. LATER AT NIGHT. An ASH SNOW
blows. SASHA and MARIA sit around a CAMPFIRE built in the
torn-off hood of an ARMORED LIMOUSINE. They sit next to each
other on the windshield, warming themselves. Maybe there
are parts of the MECHANICAL HORSES in the fire, broken up so
their oil can leak out and burn. We're TIGHT on them here,
Maria closer to us, with her thousand yard stare as she looks
over the horizon of her past. We can even hold off on the
full reveal until the next page if you want. Maria notes her
betrayal by the Oprichniki after she refuses to break the
rules of engagement. She says she was raised in Khridoli,
still believed in honor, and when that became a burden the
people that created her traded her in for someone with less
conflicts. She would not be like the Oprichniki as the war
turned, so she had no use. She was a puppet. A toy her masters
cast in the trash after years of being a true believer. There
is real, raw betrayal and weight on her face here, and Sasha
can see that as he peers at her.

story by
STEVE ORLANDO

inks b
MATTHEW DOW SMIT

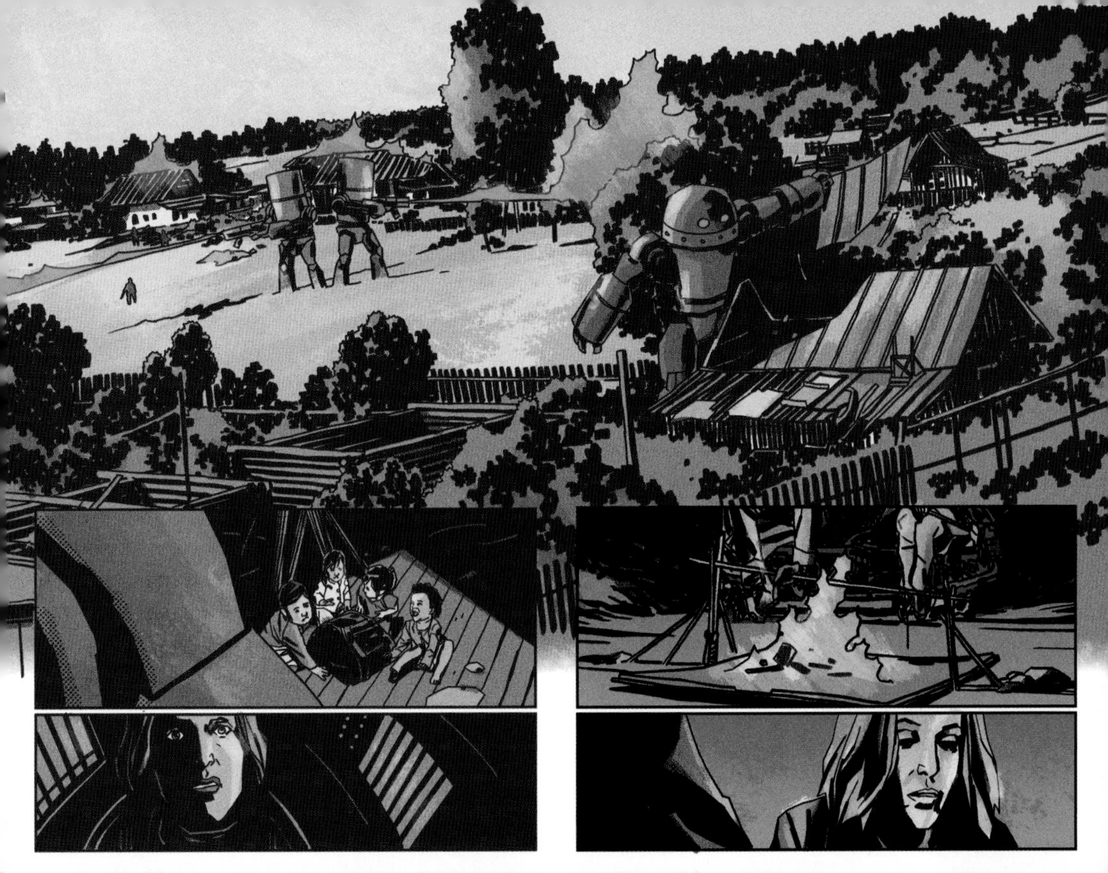

colors by

LAUREN AFF

PAGES 6&7 PROCESS

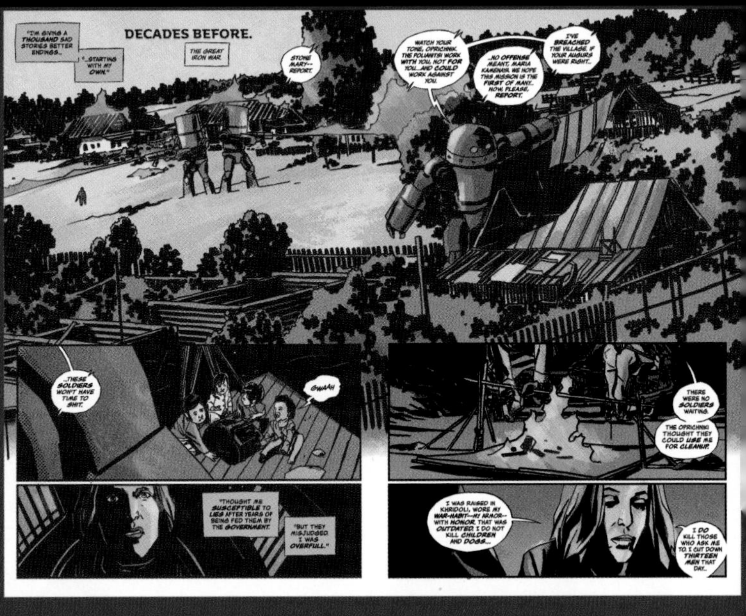

"I'M GIVING A THOUSAND SAD STORIES BETTER ENDINGS...
"...STARTING WITH MY OWN."
DECADES BEFORE.
THE GREAT IRON WAR.
STONE MARY-- REPORT.
WATCH YOUR TONE, OPRICHNIK. THE POLIANITSI WORK WITH YOU, NOT FOR YOU...AND COULD WORK AGAINST YOU.
...NO OFFENSE MEANT, MARIA KAMENAYA. WE HOPE THIS MISSION IS THE FIRST OF MANY... NOW, PLEASE, REPORT.
I'VE BREACHED THE VILLAGE. IF YOUR AUGURS WERE RIGHT...
...THESE SOLDIERS WON'T HAVE TIME TO SHIT.
GWAAH
THERE WERE NO SOLDIERS WAITING.
THE OPRICHNIKI THOUGHT THEY COULD USE ME FOR CLEANUP.
"THOUGHT ME SUSCEPTIBLE TO LIES AFTER YEARS OF BEING FED THEM BY THE GOVERNMENT.
"BUT THEY MISJUDGED. I WAS OVERFULL."
I WAS RAISED IN KHRIDOLI, WORE MY WAR-HABIT--MY ARMOR--WITH HONOR. THAT WAS OUTDATED. I DO NOT KILL CHILDREN AND DOGS...
I DO KILL THOSE WHO ASK ME TO. I CUT DOWN THIRTEEN MEN THAT DAY...

lettering by

THOMAS MAUER

DEAD KINGS™

#4

story by
STEVE ORLANDO

PAGES 4 - 5:

In a SPLASH or a NEAR SPLASH, Maria is rescued by SASHA who BURSTS WILDLY BACK INTO THE TRAIN, which has stopped teleporting due to the damage to its hull. Sasha IS BARELY in control here, basically he's a wrecking ball in human, armored form. His arrival pastes a few of the Oprichniki as he bursts into the train. Maria HURLS herself away and just barely avoids being splattered herself.

In the stunned pause of shock caused by Sasha's arrival, he has a quick back and forth with Maria who musters enough wit to chide him about what part of the suit to use to kill the remaining Oprichniki, and how to control the suit. Sasha is confused, then figures out the control Maria mentioned.

He turns to MURDER the remaining and attacking Oprichniki using a RIVET LAUNCHER in the chest of the armor, pulverizing them with the types of rivets you'd used in steelwork.

Sasha grabs and wounded but rallying Maria, who tells the dying Oprichniki to fuck off as they leave, to watch her go...

inks by
MATTHEW DOW SMITH

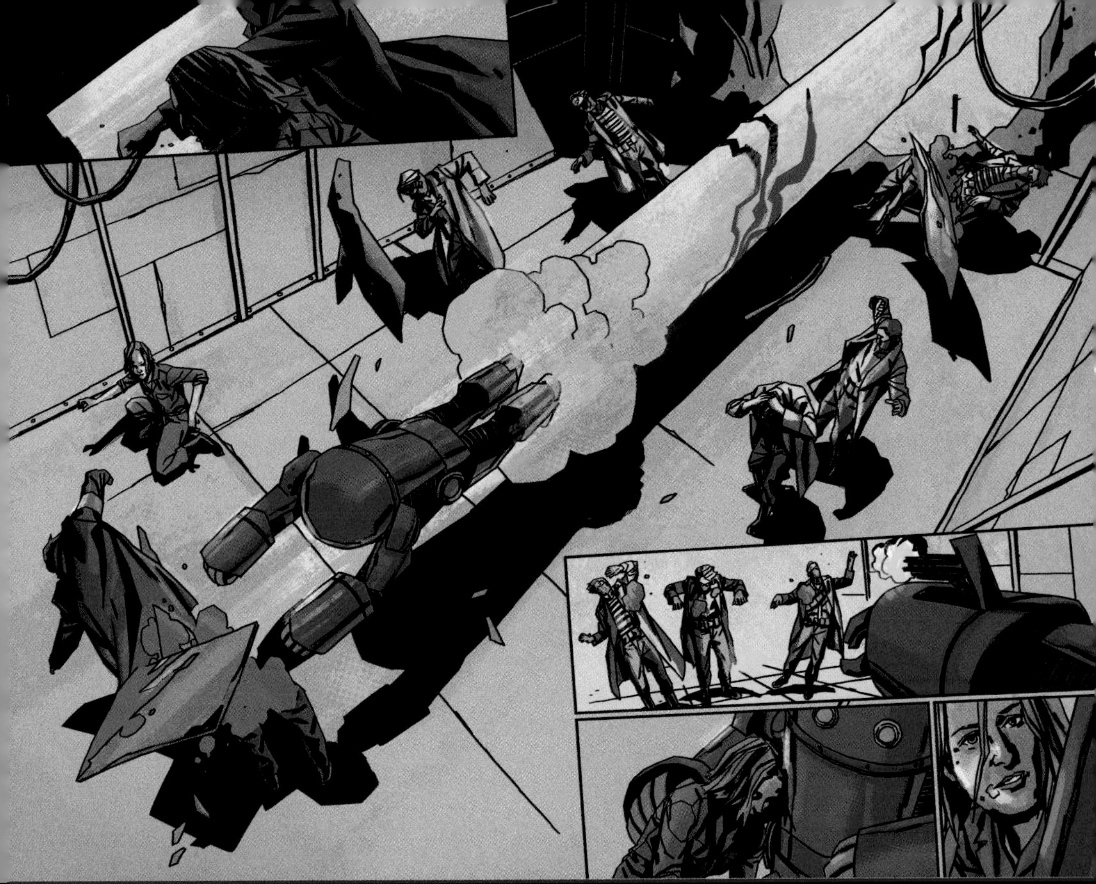

colors b
LAUREN AFF

PAGES 4&5 PROCESS

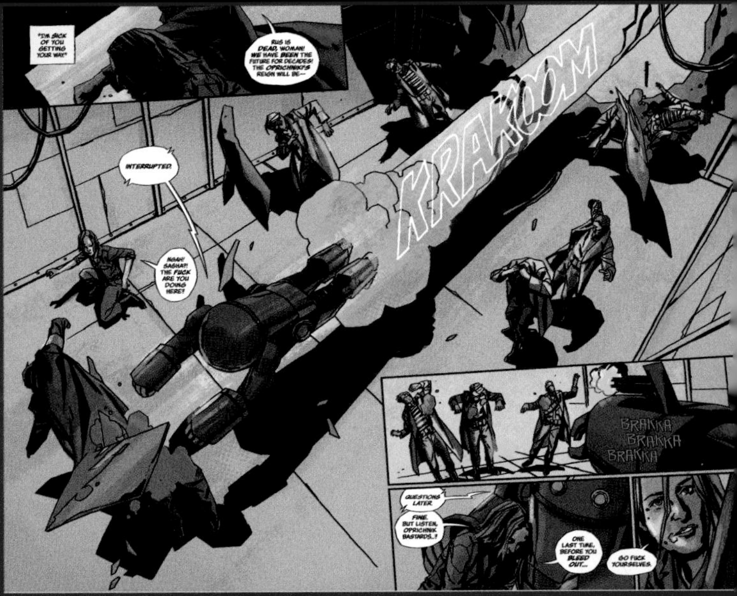

"I'M SICK OF YOU GETTING YOUR WAY."
RUS IS DEAD, WOMAN! WE HAVE BEEN THE FUTURE FOR DECADES! THE OPRICHNIKI'S REIGN WILL BE—
KRAKOOM
INTERRUPTED.
NGAH! SASHA?! THE FUCK ARE YOU DOING HERE?
BRAKKA BRAKKA BRAKKA
QUESTIONS LATER.
FINE. BUT LISTEN, OPRICHNIK BASTARDS...!
ONE LAST TIME, BEFORE YOU BLEED OUT...
GO FUCK YOURSELVES.

lettering by
THOMAS MAUER

DEAD KINGS

Issue Five of a Five-Issue Miniseries

from Steve Orlando for Matthew Dow Smith, Mike
Marts, Christina Harrington

and Aftershock Comics.

PAGE 1:

Hey Matt! Hey Lauren! Hey Thomas! Here it is,
our big finale! Let's bring this wild ride home
as only this team can, folks!

We open in THRICE-NINE. This is NOT a flashback,
it's RIGHT NOW. We see GENA AND SASHA'S MOTHER,
IUSTINA. She's at THE WINDOW OF HER HOUSE, the
same one we've seen before. It's RAINING. We
get a BIG HEARTBREAKING SHOT to open up.

Then the turns to the house interior, revealing
its shabby beauty. Tacked to the wall is a
CALENDAR. A few days away is HER BIRTHDAY, with
a little drawing of a CAKE on it, CIRCLED. She
traces her finger across the map to show it's
the DAY BEFORE her birthday, tapping the day
before, then the day itself.

We end with her turning to her KITCHEN SHELF
where she's got CAKE INGREDIENTS and a BOTTLE
OF VODKA. Which is she going to use when the
day comes? Will her sons be there to celebrate
her 50th birthday with her?

DEAD KINGS

Issue Five of a Five-Issue Miniseries

from Steve Orlando for Matthew Dow Smith, Mike Marts, Christina Harrington

and Aftershock Comics.

PAGE 1:

PANEL 1:

1 CAPTION:
Thrice-Nine.

PANEL 2:

2 IUSTINA:
Gena.

3 IUSTINA:
Sasha…

4 IUSTINA:
Tomorrow. Tomorrow is the day.

PANEL 3:

PANEL 4:

PANEL 5:

PANEL 6:

PANEL 7:

5 IUSTINA:
Please. My boys...

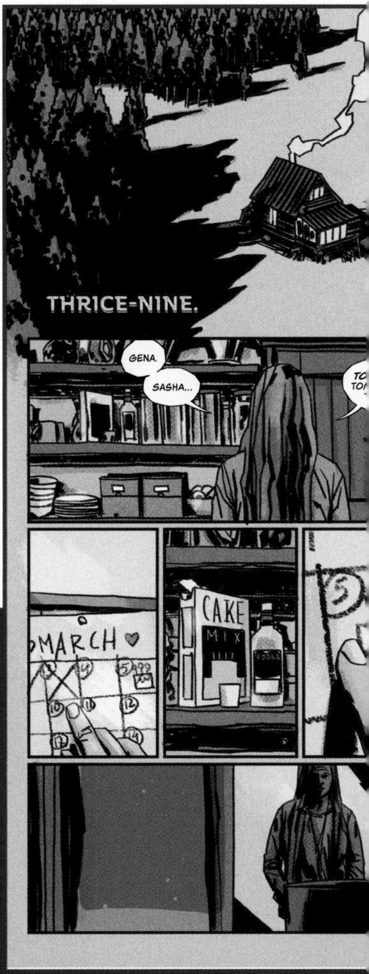
THRICE-NINE.
GENA.
SASHA...
MARCH
CAKE
MIX

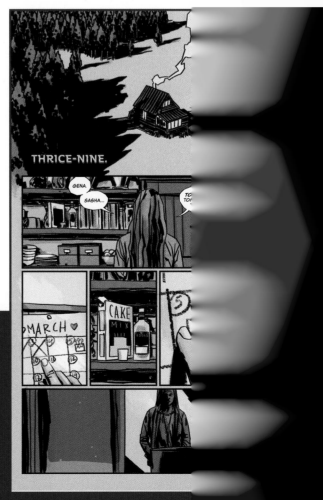

script by
TEVE ORLANDO

lettering by
THOMAS MAUER

ABOUT THE CREATORS OF

DEAD KINGS™

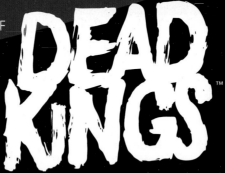

STEVE ORLANDO

writer

@thesteveorlando

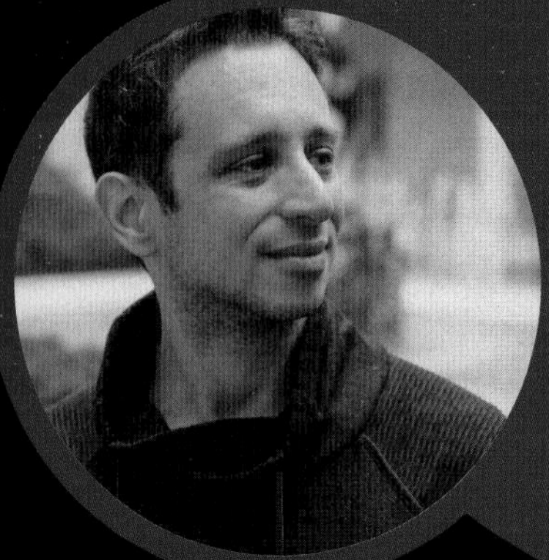

Orlando writes and produces comics, including *Virgil* (IGN's best Graphic Novel of 2015), *Undertow* and stories in the Eisner Award Nominated *Outlaw Territory* for Image Comics. He launched 2015's *Midnighter* and 2016's *Midnighter and Apollo*, both nominated for GLAAD awards, and took part in *Justice League: Gods and Men, Batman and Robin Eternal* and most recently *Wonder Woman, Supergirl, Batman/The Shadow, Justice League of America* and *The Unexpected* for DC Entertainment, as well as *Crude* for Skybound Entertainment and DEAD KINGS for AfterShock Comics.

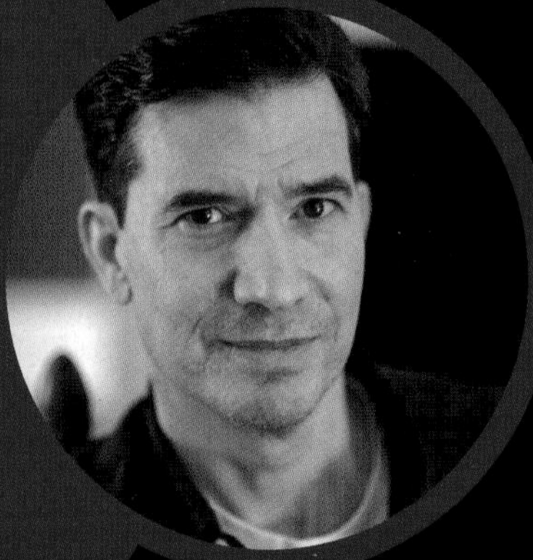

MATTHEW DOW SMITH

artist

@matthewdowsmith

Matthew Dow Smith is a writer and comic book artist who has worked for nearly every major American comic book publisher. His art has appeared in DC's *Suicide Squad: Hell to Pay*, Mike Mignola's *Hellboy*, and Marvel's *Uncanny X-Men*. He was the long-time artist on IDW's *X-Files* comic, as well as the writer of their middle grade *X-Files* comic book series, *X-Files: Origins*. He is the writer/artist of the upcoming *The October Girl* graphic novel series, which is currently in development as a television series, and wrote the final book of Archaia Publishing's *Dark Crystal* prequel graphic novel series, *Dark Crystal: Creation Myths*, and recently wrote his first story for DC.

LAUREN AFFE colorist

@laurenaffe

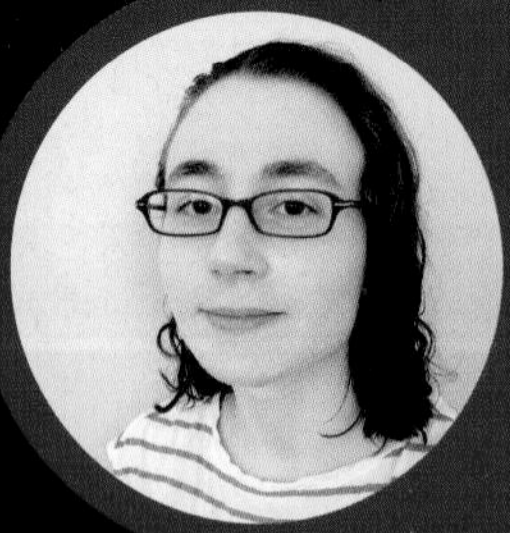

Lauren has been working in comics since graduating from SCAD in 2010. She has operated as color artist on many creator owned titles from Dark Horse Comics (*Buzzkill, The Ghost Fleet, The Paybacks*) and Image Comics (*Five Ghosts*). This has led to work on Dynamite Entertainment's *Turok: Dinosaur Hunter* relaunch as well as projects for Marvel Comics. In addition to THE REVISIONIST and DEAD KINGS for AfterShock she is currently working on new projects for Stela, Random House and Image Comics.

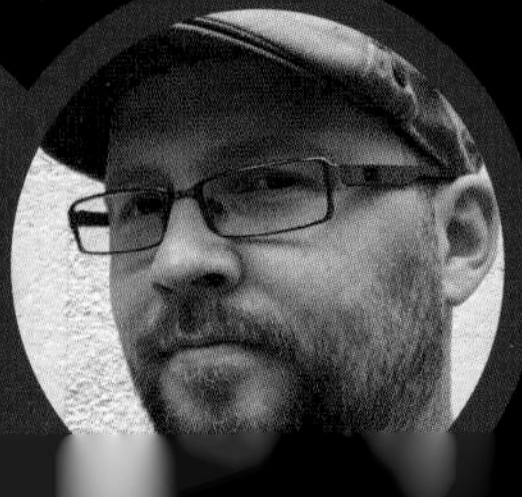

THOMAS MAUER letterer

@thomasmauer

Thomas Mauer has lent his lettering and design talent to Harvey and Eisner Award nominated and winning titles including Image's *Popgun* anthologies and Dark Horse Comics' *The Guns of Shadow Valley*. Among his recent work are Black Mask Studios' *4 Kids Walk Into a Bank*, Image Comics' *Crude, Elsewhere, The Beauty and The Realm*, *Lark's Killer* from Devil's Due, and IDW's *Antar: The*